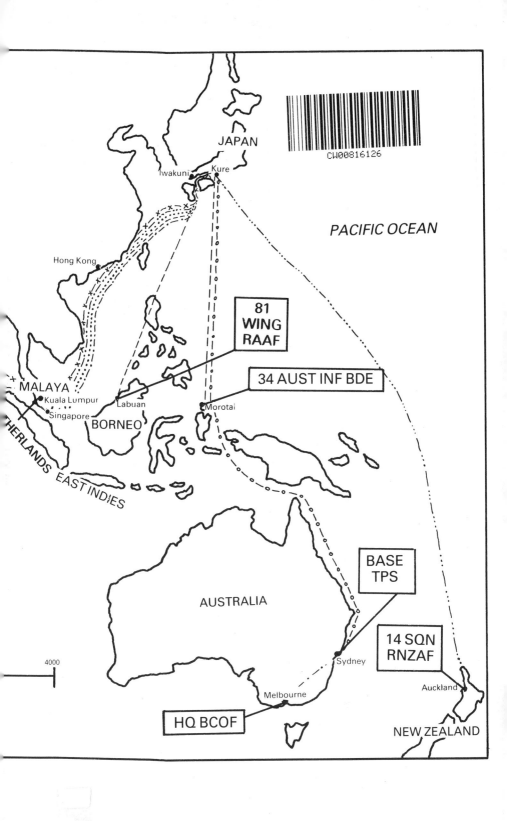

JAPAN

Iwakuni · Kure

PACIFIC OCEAN

Hong Kong

81
WING
RAAF

34 AUST INF BDE

MALAYA
Kuala Lumpur
Singapore
BORNEO
Labuan
Morotai

NETHERLANDS EAST INDIES

BASE
TPS

AUSTRALIA

14 SQN
RNZAF

4000

Sydney

Auckland

Melbourne

HQ BCOF

NEW ZEALAND

Japan

and the

British Commonwealth Occupation Force 1946–52

Japan

and the

British Commonwealth Occupation Force 1946–52

PETER BATES

BRASSEY'S (UK)
LONDON • NEW YORK

First English edition 1993

UK editorial offices: Brassey's, 165 Great Dover Street, London SE1 4YA
orders: Marston Book Services, PO Box 87, Oxford OX2 0DT

USA orders: Macmillan Publishing Company, Front and Brown Streets Riverside, NJ
08075

Distributed in North America to booksellers and wholesalers by the Macmillan Publishing Company, NY 10022

Peter Bates has asserted his moral right to
be identified as author of this work

Library of Congress Cataloging in Publication Data
available

British Library Cataloguing in Publication Data
A catalogue record for this book is available from the British Library

ISBN 1-85753 000 4

Typeset by M Rules
Printed in Great Britain by BPCC Wheatons Ltd, Exeter

Contents

Foreword

by
Field Marshal The Lord Bramall
KG GCB OBE MC JP

Having myself been a member of the British Commonwealth Occupation Force in Japan (BCOF), I am delighted to write a Foreword to this very well researched and excellently written book on the subject by Peter Bates.

It was high time that more was heard of the contribution of the British, Indian, Australian and New Zealand contingents, all under Commonwealth command, to this important and successful occupation, and also that their considerable efforts were put into a proper prospective.

Although the Force had no direct responsibility for the military government of Japan in the early days, and later on for the putting in place of the democratic institutions which were to benefit Japan so much, its mere presence and the way it carried out its task made a significant contribution to the Japanese attitude to the occupation generally.

Nor was its task – our task – all that easy. When we started to arrive from India, Australia and New Zealand, and I, being on the advance party, was able to appreciate some of the problems more than most, we had no idea about what sort of reception we were going to receive, particularly after the atomic bombing of Hiroshima, which was in our designated area, and of Nagasaki. Conditions for the reception of such a force, in a Japan which was still very backward in many respects, were often primitive and amenities few and far between; and many of the men in the contingents, particularly the British, had been away at war for a long time and were thinking more about going home than they were about further service so far away. Only the Australians and New Zealanders raised special volunteer contingents for the occasion.

However, as a result of herculean efforts by the staff, the contingent soon settled down and, thanks to good leadership and very high professional standards all round, the whole force soon greatly impressed the Japanese with its bearing and behaviour towards civilians. This helped to produce an excellent cooperative atmosphere throughout BCOF's area and greatly supported General MacArthur in his formidable task, brilliantly carried out, of governing the country and converting it to democracy.

The Force was lucky enough to have some most distinguished commanders at the helm, particularly Northcote and Robertson from Australia, Cowan from Britain and Thimayya from India, all of whom had made their mark in World War II and some of whom were to go on to higher things; and we all responded to their impressive leadership.

For those of us who were there it was an unforgettable experience – from the stark, charred wilderness of what was once Hiroshima to the little rural villages where the women still carried their babies on their backs, which had hardly changed since the days of Pinkerton and Madame Butterfly!

So this book will bring back many nostalgic memories to those who served in BCOF of the conditions we lived in and the problems we had to face and solve. But for the historian, too, the book will provide a most interesting insight into this peripheral but at the same time quite unique episode in Britain's vast post-war military activity and deployment.

I wish the author well in his most commendable endeavour.

Introduction

This book came to be written because of an American lady called Carmen Johnson. Carmen was a member of the US military government team on the island of Shikoku in Japan between 1946 and 1948. In the course of her duties she had a number of contacts with British Commonwealth personnel and made lasting friendships with some of them, including my brother Paul. She resented the determination of her fellow Americans to ignore the British presence in the occupation which persisted even in academic circles, and suggested to Paul that a history of the British Commonwealth Occupation Force (BCOF) should be written while there were veterans of it still alive and able to make a contribution.

I have as a former member of BCOF myself taken up Carmen's suggestion with excitement but also with some foreboding. An amateur historian walks the paths of research and analysis with apprehension: and one can be easily seduced by the richness and unfamiliarity of the records available into fascinating but entirely irrelevant directions. (I remember a particularly enticing set of documents in a Foreign Office file dealing with the supply of a wooden leg to a Chinese general during the war). But I have been encouraged by the support and cooperation of the real scholars and the record-keepers, and by the scores of old comrades who have responded with enthusiasm to my enquiries: and I have listed my acknowledgements to them all separately.

It has been suggested elsewhere that military failures do not attract much attention from historians, and that it is because BCOF fell into this category that the historical bookshelf is so bare. But to the 80,000 or more men and women who served in the Force, it was not a failure, but an unforgettable experience. Of course it was something of a sideshow in the vast pattern of British post-war military activity and commitment but, as I hope to show, it had many unique aspects.

The BCOF story falls into three distinct phases: first, the truly integrated and fully representative period from 1946 to 1948 when the four national contingents served together in prosecuting the objectives of the occupation; then the period of slow decline from 1948 to 1950 when Australia continued to carry out the task single-handed; and finally the period of revival from 1950 to 1952 in response to the pressures of the Korean war. This account tends to concentrate on the varied and colourful initial period and its preliminaries, but endeavours not to neglect the subsequent phases.

Acknowledgements

My first task must be to acknowledge the initial help and encouragement of Professor Ian Nish, himself a veteran of the occupation. He introduced me to some of the existing material relating to the British Commonwealth participation in the occupation of Japan, and was good enough to arrange for me to attend the two most recent symposia in the series he organised on the subject at the Suntory-Toyota International Centre of the London School of Economics. I must also thank Sir Hugh Cortazzi and Professor T B Millar for allowing me to quote from their contributions to the July 1991 symposium.

I am grateful to the Controller of HM Stationery Office for permission to quote from Crown Copyright records; and for permission to quote from their respective records to the Regional Director of the Australian Archives and the Director of the Australian War Memorial in Canberra; the Director of the MacArthur Memorial in Norfolk, Virginia; and the Trustees of the Broadlands Archives. Their staffs, and those of the Imperial War Museum and the National Army Museum in London, have been very helpful. I am most grateful to the *Sydney Morning Herald*, whose coverage of the occupation period was particularly comprehensive and whose records were a most valuable source of information; and I must thank *The Times* of London for permission to quote from the issues of 1 January and 5 February 1947, and the *Penrith Press* of Penrith, NSW, for cuttings about Frank Loyal Weaver. I would like to thank Arthur W John for permission to quote from *Uneasy lies the head that wears a crown*, the only history previously written about the British Commonwealth Occupation Force in Japan; John Slim for permission to quote from his father's great book *Defeat into Victory*; the Naval Historical Society of Australia for permission to quote from their Monograph No.13 *The British Pacific Fleet 1945*; and Sir Fitzroy Maclean and the Editor of *The Scotsman* for permission to quote from the former's 1946 article on the British Commonwealth Force.

I owe a special vote of thanks to all those friends and colleagues, both old and new, who served in Japan and whom I have been able to run to earth. They have responded enthusiastically to my request to search their memories for recollections of that period so long ago, and I think have enjoyed doing so: but I am still very grateful to them. I was particularly lucky to be able to consult quantities of letters sent home from Japan by Peter Arthur of the Mahrattas, and by Jean-Pierre Boillot of the French Navy. I have listed everybody by name in the *Sources* at the end of the book, and have used them frequently as references, as the *Notes* will show.

The veterans' associations in the United Kingdom, Australia and New Zealand have also been most supportive and I have been impressed by their vigour and dedication. They have provided me with a great deal of helpful information, and I would like to thank the following in particular:

Bob Bell, BCOF Association of Australia (NSW Branch)
Jim Wallace, BCOF Veterans Association of NSW
Arthur Williams, BCOF Veterans Association, UK Branch
Charlie Smyth, BCAIR Japan Association
Eric Goldsack, New Zealand J Force and BCOF Veterans
    Association

Finally, I should thank my publishers, and in particular Jenny Shaw, for their encouragement and helpful suggestions: and my wife for immense patience and tolerance for the way in which I have had to concentrate on writing to the exclusion of most other activities. At least she has had the consolation of travelling with me on two extended trips to Australia and New Zealand, and the pleasure of meeting some of my ex-service friends there.

Abbreviations

ACJ	Allied Council for Japan
AIF	Australian Imperial Force
AMF	Australian Military Forces
ARA	Australian Regular Army
BCAIR	British Commonwealth Air Component or Group
BCOF	British Commonwealth Occupation Force
BRICOSAT	British Commonwealth Sub Area Tokyo
BRINDIV	British and Indian Division
BRINDJAP	British and Indian Troops, Japan
BRITCOM BASE	British Commonwealth Base, Kure
CIGS	Chief of the Imperial General Staff
CMF	Citizen Military Forces
FANY	First Aid Nursing Yeomanry
FEC	Far Eastern Commission
INA	Indian National Army
J FORCE	New Zealand Brigade for Japan, later 2 NZEF (2nd New Zealand Expeditionary Force)
JCOSA	Joint Chiefs of Staff, Australia
PMF	Permanent Military Forces
SCAP	Supreme Commander for the Allied Powers
SEAC	South East Asia Command
SWNCC	State/War/Navy Coordinating Committee
UKLIM	United Kingdom Liaison Mission, Japan

List of Illustrations

MAPS AND FIGURES

Front End Paper   The Mobilisation of BCOF 1945-46
Map I   SCAP's Major Occupation Areas 1946
Back End Paper   Dispositions of BCOF on or about 30 June 1946
Fig. 6.1   SCAP Organisation 1946
Fig. 6.2   Organisation of BCOF 1946
Fig. 18.1   BCOF Strengths 1946-49

PHOTOGRAPHS

Most of the photographs are Crown copyright and are reproduced by the courtesy of the Trustees of the Imperial War Museum. The exceptions are Nos. 4 and 13, which are reproduced from the BCAIR Japan Association's collection; No. 2 which has been supplied by Mr Eric Saxon; and Nos. 9, 10, and 12, which are from the author's collection.

1   An Australian sailor nails up the British Landing Force sign, Yokosuka, 30 August 1945
2   Kure, BCOF's principal base
3   Hiroshima, February 1946
4   Lieutenant General Northcott and Air Vice Marshal Bouchier at Kuala Lumpur, to inspect 11 and 17 Squadrons RAF before departure for Japan
5   The Commander-in-Chief BCOF with his formation commanders

Prologue

On 30 August 1945, following the unconditional surrender of the
Japanese nation, a party of 536 sailors and marines from the British
Commonwealth under the command of Captain H J Buchanan of
the Royal Australian Navy landed in Japan as part of the initial
forces of occupation. They were drawn from the British battleship
King George V, the British cruiser *Newfoundland*, the New Zealand
cruiser *Gambia*, and the Australian destroyers *Nizam* and *Napier*.
These ships were part of the British Pacific Fleet lying in Tokyo Bay
with the rest of the vast Allied armada which had been bombarding
the Japanese homeland in preparation for invasion and was now in
attendance on the surrender.

The party had been allocated the responsibility of taking over
and disarming the Japanese naval establishments on three small
island fortresses at the entrance to Tokyo Bay guarding the great
naval base of Yokosuka, and a sector of the base itself, and the men
carried out their task wi th excitement and alacrity. 'There was a fine
spice of danger to keep every man on the alert for some unautho-
rised act of treachery'.[1] They were conscious of their special role
and raised a roughly-lettered sign outside the small building in
Yokosuka requisitioned for their use reading 'HEADQUARTERS
B L F' for 'British Landing Force'. Later a party of 20 Royal Marines
from HMS *Swiftsure* took up guard over the British Embassy in
Tokyo itself, where the unaccustomed splendour of their full-dress
uniforms drew awed comments from the American troops already
there.

All the British personnel were withdrawn within a few weeks.

They had been the forerunners of a British Commonwealth
Occupation Force 37,000 strong – a self-contained Army Corps
drawn from four Commonwealth countries, with its own artillery
and armour, and supported by its own Navy and Air Force - which
would after many fits and starts take up its share of the occupation
of Japan in early 1946, and would be represented there until the
peace treaty with Japan in 1952.

1
The End of the War

By the beginning of 1945 the situation of Japan had become desperate. The growing tide of military reverses was bringing the Americans closer and closer to the Japanese homeland; heavy merchant shipping losses had reduced to a trickle the flow of essential food, oil and raw materials from the occupied territories in the south; and the American strategic bombing offensive was devastating Japanese cities and morale. From March onwards, as the intensive bombing continued with awesome fire raids on Tokyo and other major cities, and the naval blockade was intensified with close mining of Japanese waters, Japan's ability to continue the struggle was in steep decline.

The American Joint Chiefs of Staff nevertheless believed that a successful invasion of Japan would be necessary to achieve her unconditional surrender. Their intention was to launch an invasion of the southern island of Kyushu in November 1945, to capture sea and air bases for the main invasion of Honshu in March 1946, in the knowledge that, following the German defeat in Europe, forces redeployed from the European theatre would be available to assist in these operations. In preparation for them, General MacArthur was appointed to command all army forces in the Pacific theatre, with Admiral Nimitz in command of all naval forces: and arrangements were set in train to transfer the South West Pacific area out of MacArthur's responsibility, partly to South East Asia Command and partly to Australian command, in order to allow him to concentrate on the main task in hand.

On 25 May 1945, MacArthur and Nimitz were formally directed

to plan for the invasion of Kyushu (Operation OLYMPIC) to take place on 1 November 1945 and of Honshu (Operation CORONET) on 1 March 1946. Following intensification of the blockade and air bombardment of Japan, OLYMPIC was to be carried out by the veteran US 6th Army under General Krueger, which was already available in the theatre, while CORONET would be undertaken subsequently by the US 8th and 1st Armies, the latter on redeployment from Europe.

However, the Joint Chiefs of Staff and their political leaders remained intensely concerned to find an alternative way of bringing about a Japanese surrender without the need for an invasion. The ferocious resistance by Japanese forces to the landings at Iwojima and Okinawa again emphasised the likelihood of heavy losses, the fear of which had always been a major consideration. MacArthur himself had previously said that an invasion might cost a million casualties, although in June his staff responded to Washington's enquiries with considerably reduced estimates of likely losses. Even these caused concern to President Truman, and to allay these fears and secure presidential backing, MacArthur provided an optimistic statement suggesting that actual losses would be much lower, especially if the Russians attacked from Siberia beforehand (as Stalin had undertaken to do), and pressing 'most earnestly' for no change in OLYMPIC.[1] The President accordingly endorsed the plan for the operation on 19 June, but it was felt essential to examine every possibility of obtaining a Japanese surrender before the date fixed for the Kyushu invasion.

At the Potsdam Conference in July between the Allied leaders and their political and military staffs, therefore, this was high on the agenda, and led to the issue of the so-called Potsdam Declaration by the United States, Britain and China, urging the Japanese government to surrender unconditionally, subject to certain ill-defined assurances for the future. The alternative was forecast as prompt and utter destruction (the atomic bomb was nearing the point of operational availability). On the premise that the defeat of the enemy's armed forces in the Japanese homeland was still likely to be a prerequisite to unconditional surrender, and that such a defeat would establish the optimum prospect of capitulation by Japanese 'forces outside the main Japanese islands' in the words of the Joint Chiefs of Staff, the Combined Chiefs of Staff also discussed at Potsdam a larger British participation in the operations against

Japan.[2] Up to that time the British contribution to the main attack on Japan had been limited to the continued activities of the British Pacific Fleet serving as part of the US 3rd Fleet; but, following a request from the Joint Chiefs of Staff in June, plans were in train for the establishment of a British force of heavy bomber aircraft (TIGER Force) to be redeployed from Europe and to be based on Okinawa for very long-range bombing of Japan. This force was to consist of 10 squadrons, totalling 220 aircraft, with 23,000 RAF operational and construction personnel, supported by 12,390 Army construction and administrative personnel – a substantial force of nearly 36,000 men. The intention was to start operations with the first five squadrons on 1 December 1945, but the force had to be self-supporting, and shortages of construction personnel were hampering the progress of the venture.

Meanwhile, the Joint Chiefs of Staff were planning on the invasion being a grandiose and entirely American effort, which would eventually involve nearly three million men, with a fleet and air force larger than in OVERLORD (the Normandy landings), which they were determined to surpass. This would absorb almost all available US strength, and they thought that in this situation the British could help best by pursuing operations in the outer zone of the South West Pacific. However, the British Chiefs of Staff and Churchill had other ideas. They were equally determined that Britain should play a part in the land assault, which they considered would be feasible as a result of the decline of Japanese opposition in South East Asia and the prospect of the capture of Singapore and the opening of the Malacca Strait. On the basis of their proposals, it was agreed in principle between Truman and Churchill that a British Commonwealth land force of from three to five divisions, together with the British Pacific Fleet and, if possible, a small tactical air force, would take part in the operations in the spring of 1946. Units of the British East Indies Fleet would probably also take part. At that time the Combined Chiefs decided that the planning date for the end of organised resistance by Japan should be 15 November 1946. They thought it could still be a long war.

The British Cabinet endorsed the Churchill-Truman agreement in order to ensure, for largely political reasons, that Britain would be properly represented in the final defeat of Japan. An important motive was the desire to re-establish British prestige and interests in the Far East after the calamities of Singapore and Hong Kong.

Churchill had already contacted Dominion Governments on the concept of a joint Commonwealth force which he considered would be a striking demonstration of Commonwealth solidarity: it was important, he thought, that 'we share with the Americans the burden of the assault on Japan.'[3]

The Supreme Allied Commander South East Asia, Lord Mountbatten, was advised of the decision in a directive of 20 July.[4] It informed him that he would be required to provide a proportion of this force, together with the assault lift for two divisions, and that this requirement would have priority over all his other tasks – the liberation of Malaya and Singapore (for which Operation ZIPPER was planned to take place in September 1945) and offensive operations into Thailand, Java and Sumatra.

Further informal discussions with MacArthur on the nature of the Commonwealth participation in the assault on Japan suggested a much more restrictive American attitude.[5] He did not want the British to take part as a separate force in the assault. The landing areas would be heavily defended and would call for the closest cooperation between the Services and within the ground forces themselves. Accepting the British in the assault phase, with their different organisation, composition, equipment, training procedures and doctrines would, he believed, excessively complicate the command arrangements, the operation and the logistic support. His provisional proposals were for a corps of three divisions, which would be re-equipped with US equipment and supported from the US: they would be used as an integral corps within the US Army, although the divisions might be used separately within American corps if the situation demanded it. The corps would be used as an assault fighting reserve, which meant that it would not take part in the actual assault unless some unforeseen situation required it, but it would be put ashore very soon after D-day. What MacArthur wanted was to treat the British force as if it were an American constituent part of his own Army.

This was not at all palatable to the British Chiefs of Staff, but in a paper to the Cabinet Defence Committee on 7 August they reluctantly recommended that it be accepted as a basis for detailed discussion, on the stipulation that British uniform was retained and the corps only split up in case of emergency.[6] They suggested that the corps should be made up of a British division from the UK or North West Europe, to be shipped across the Atlantic in October, to train

and equip alongside the Canadian volunteer division already training there for use under US command in the main operations, and
that these two divisions would be ultimately mounted from the west
coast of the USA. The third division would be an Australian division
to be mounted either in Borneo or Morotai in the Netherlands East
Indies. Although the US saw difficulty in integrating a small tactical
air force, it was still hoped to include a British Commonwealth air
component, mainly of RAF and RAAF squadrons. No allowance
was being made for a British/Indian division, or for contingents
from New Zealand or South Africa. MacArthur was known to be
anxious to avoid the logistic and linguistic complications which
using a British/Indian division would involve. As for New Zealand,
the Government there had already volunteered the inclusion of two
brigades from its division in Italy, and it was hoped that MacArthur
would agree to use a New Zealand contingent in the later build-up.
No South African land force was being suggested, but it might be
possible to use one or two air force squadrons from South East Asia.
But the Chiefs were quite clear on one count: they wanted the land
force commander to be a British officer.

The Foreign Office were alarmed by this heavily modified proposal for Commonwealth participation. 'Our original offer of up to
five divisions was made very largely with a political object, that is,
to remove any idea in the United States that we were not pulling our
weight in the Far East and to re-establish our position in the eyes of
the Far Eastern peoples', said the Foreign Secretary. 'The magnitude of our effort in South East Asia has never been realised in the
United States or elsewhere . . . It is questionable whether our participation on the limited scale and under the restrictive conditions
proposed by General MacArthur will achieve our political objects
or result in any credit.'[7] These prophetic words might later be said
to be equally relevant to the occupation itself. However, the time factor made argument undesirable, and it was appreciated that the
first British proposal to participate in the main assault on Japan had
come so late that 'this is the best they can do for us'. The Foreign
Office therefore agreed in principle but pressed for maximum individuality and maximum publicity for the Commonwealth effort,
publicising if necessary the fact that the UK had offered more than
had been accepted. From the safety of Whitehall they also pressed
for the force's participation in the initial assault, rather than just
being used as a reserve.

Following his defeat in the General Election, Churchill had been replaced by Attlee at the end of July, and it was under Attlee's chairmanship that the Cabinet accepted the Chiefs of Staff's proposals on 8 August, although with some misgivings, and authorised the Chiefs to pursue the arrangements with MacArthur and Nimitz for shipment of the British forces to the United States for training and re-equipment there. The Cabinet also instructed the Foreign Office to pursue the matter of increasing the publicity for British forces in Japanese war.[8]

Immediately following this, on the recommendation of the Chiefs of Staff, Attlee proposed to the Dominion Prime Ministers that General Sir Charles Keightley should be appointed commander of the land forces, and Admiral Tennant commander of the naval component, both British. (Keightley had a distinguished record as a divisional commander in the Middle East and Italy, and had commanded 5 Corps in Italy since 1944). It was also proposed that the air force commander should be an Australian if air force participation was achieved. The New Zealand Government agreed to these appointments, but there was an ominous silence from Australia.

Meanwhile, confused reactions in Tokyo combined with continuing hopes that the Russians, whom the Japanese had asked to mediate, would help to find a peaceful solution, led to what was interpreted as a formal dismissal by the Japanese government of the Potsdam Declaration. In proof that the alternative for Japan was indeed 'prompt and utter destruction', the first atomic bomb was dropped on Hiroshima on 6 August, and was followed by a broadcast early on the next day by Truman which forecast the dropping of similar bombs elsewhere in Japan if the surrender terms were not accepted. The damage caused, although severe, was less than that caused by previous American B29 raids, but the significance of this new weapon was immediately appreciated in Tokyo, and urgent discussions in the Japanese Supreme War Council and with the Emperor now focussed on the exact conditions for the acceptance of the terms of the surrender which they now believed to be unavoidable.

In the early hours of 9 August news was received in Tokyo of the declaration of war on Japan by Russia, which it had been agreed between the Allies at Yalta would take place two to three months after the German surrender. Russian forces immediately invaded Manchuria and south Sakhalin in considerable strength. While the

debate in Tokyo became more agitated under the pressure of this
new blow, the second atomic bomb was dropped on Nagasaki. This
final combination of crises led directly to the Emperor's decision to
cut through the continuing disagreements between the peace party
and the war party in the Japanese government, and an offer of surrender was made from Tokyo on 10 August, on the understanding
that the terms did not 'comprise any demand which prejudices the
prerogative' of the Emperor as a sovereign ruler.

The US response on 11 August on behalf of the major Allies
made it clear that 'from the moment of surrender the authority of
the Emperor and the Japanese Government to rule the state shall be
subject to the Supreme Commander of the Allied Powers, who will
take such steps as he deems proper to effectuate the surrender
terms'. But this at least confirmed the Allies' intention to allow the
Emperor to remain on the throne and the governmental authority to
remain in place. Although there was further frenzied argument from
the military dissenters in the Japanese Cabinet, on 14 August the
Emperor once more took the overriding decision to accept the
Potsdam terms in full and end the war, and issued the famous
Imperial Rescript which he broadcast the following day.

The surrender came as a welcome surprise to the British
Commonwealth forces in the Pacific and South East Asia. When on
leave in the UK in July, General Slim had been told in great secrecy
about the atomic bomb, its devastating power, and the intention to
drop it on Japan, and after Hiroshima and Nagasaki 'I was not
altogether surprised when my wife and I, flying back to my command (HQ Allied Land Forces South East Asia), heard in Rome
that Japan had surrendered unconditionally.'[9] But the
Commonwealth forces in the field were distant from the mounting
onslaught on Japan itself and indeed the publicity surrounding it.
The only British involvement had been through the British Pacific
Fleet which, following earlier operations against Sakishima Gunto,
had been involved since July as part of the US 3rd Fleet in direct air
strikes and naval bombardment on mainland Japan.
Commonwealth land forces, however, were still engaged in attacking
the Japanese empire at the more remote fringes of its occupied territories.

In the South East Asian theatre, the British 12th Army was
mopping up the remnants of the Japanese forces in Burma after the
recapture of Rangoon in May. The 14th Army was preparing itself at

bases in South India and Rangoon to embark for assaults on the west coast of Malaya (Operation ZIPPER) and subsequently on the island of Singapore itself (Operation MAILFIST). ZIPPER had been authorised in May and was originally scheduled for August 1945, but this had been delayed until September by shortages of landing craft and the need to reinforce many British units which had been severely weakened by the repatriation of personnel with long overseas service.

In the South Pacific, Australian forces had, as requested by MacArthur in late 1944, taken over responsibility for dealing with the Japanese forces in their Mandated Territories (the Solomons, New Britain and the eastern half of New Guinea) which had been by-passed by the American advances. The 1st Australian Army was engaged in continuing offensives against the Japanese in all these areas up to the time of the surrender. Many thought these operations unnecessary and wasteful in casualties, but the Australian high command believed that morale would suffer if a purely static role was adopted, and the troops responded well to the demands on them.[10] Meanwhile, between May and July 1945 the 1st Australian Corps had carried out successful landings in Borneo, capturing Tarakan, Brunei and Balikpapan, and were driving the remaining Japanese back into the hills.

The news of the surrender took some while to reach all those still engaged in arduous battle, especially in the South West Pacific. Some organised groups of Japanese in Borneo, Brunei and Sarawak continued to fight until the end of October, when the last 400 surrendered to Australian Z Force-led guerrillas. In the mountains of New Guinea men were still fighting and dying many days after the surrender. One Australian platoon commander remembered being woken in the night before yet another operation by an excited soldier – 'the war's over – they've dropped a big bomb on Japan – we don't have to attack in the morning' – and regretted that he had personally shot and killed a Japanese soldier the previous day.[11] It now suddenly seemed so unnecessary.

But when it finally got through, the news was naturally received with immense relief. The Australians, the British and the Indians had fought exhausting campaigns against a persistent and relentless enemy, and they knew how high the cost of victory could be. As Slim had noted, many armies talked about fighting to the last man and the last round, but the Japanese were the only ones who actually did it. In spite of a sure optimism on the eventual outcome, there had been everywhere a mood of sombre resignation to the awful nature of the battles still to come. The celebration of surrender was enormous and sustained. 'We realised were going to live', said a British infantry officer with 14th Army.[12] Throughout the monsoon-flooded tented camps in Rangoon where 5th Indian Division was preparing for the assault on Malaya, there was a sustained 'feu de joie' which itself sounded like a pitched battle and lasted most of the night. On Bougainville, where the Australian army were fighting hard to reduce the large Japanese garrison left behind there, every man fired rifles, pistols and machine guns into the air for what a RNZAF pilot described as 'an extremely dangerous couple of hours'.[13]

Even then there were suspicions and doubts. On the day of the surrender the Imperial Japanese Forces totalled 6,983,000, of whom 2,576,000 were in Japan. In spite of the losses already incurred in the field (estimated at 1,270,000), it was a vast army still, with its commanders and government still in being and its Emperor still on his throne. There were 630,000 armed Japanese troops facing the British Commonwealth forces in South East Asia and the South West Pacific alone. Would the local Japanese commanders overseas, ignorant of the devastation of their homeland, reject the surrender call and fight on to the death, as they so often had before? Slim noted that 'opinions differed widely as to whether . . . Japanese fanaticism would hold in desperate resistance to the brink of mass national suicide in Japan itself and elsewhere . . .'[14]. A US State Department paper in June had suggested that even after unconditional surrender and the collapse of organised resistance, some army units might continue sporadic and isolated resistance, probably in the mountainous interior, and that some of them might even escape to the Asiatic mainland to continue fighting together with Japanese armies there, where it was probable that a considerable body of troops might refuse to surrender.[15]

We know now of the continuing split in the cabinet in Tokyo; how small groups of officers did refuse to accept the decision; how rebel Guards officers occupied part of the Imperial Palace and tried to stop the Emperor's message of submission being broadcast; how others, more senior, showed their rejection of defeat and failure by committing suicide. It was a reasonable assumption that enforcing the surrender throughout the Japanese dominion would not be easy and could be bloody. Terauchi, Commander-in-Chief of the Japanese Southern Army based in Saigon, was reported to have issued instructions in May that all subordinate commanders were to commit suicide in the traditional manner to avoid falling into Allied hands, and that in the event of an Allied attack, all Allied prisoners in Java, civilian and military, were to be slaughtered.[16] It was this doubt as to Japanese reactions which led to Mountbatten's decision to carry out the Malayan landings as planned. It was therefore an immense relief to find that, once the initial difficulties of communication had been overcome, the Japanese military adhered precisely to the surrender and disarmament arrangements.

The Japanese homeland had been preparing to mount the fiercest resistance in history to the anticipated invasion. Conscription had been extended to all males aged between 15 and 60 and all females aged between 17 and 45, and a vast militia had been mobilised to supplement the 2½ million regular troops of the garrison. Enormous networks of underground caves had been stocked with thousands of tons of food and ammunition. Every available weapon had been made ready for use, from modern firearms to muzzle-loading muskets and bamboo spears. Small children had even been trained to strap explosives round their waists in order to roll under tank treads and blow themselves up. The whole population had expected the Imperial Rescript to be a command to fight to the death, and every man, woman and child would have obeyed it.[17] Their obedience to the command to make peace instead was equally complete and unquestioning.

2

The Occupation Proposals

By the middle of August the speed of events had accelerated so much that plans for the invasion of Japan were being rapidly converted into plans for the occupation of a defeated enemy's territory. On 10 August the Chief of the Imperial General Staff in London was able to give the Cabinet advance notice that the US plan for the Japanese homeland provided in principle for the inclusion of a British contingent, and that this would in the first instance have to be found from South East Asia Command (SEAC), although arrangements would be made for the inclusion of troops from Australia, New Zealand and Canada.[1]

On 13 August, two days before the actual surrender, the British Chiefs of Staff had stated their view to the Cabinet Defence Committee that, while recognising that the Americans would naturally play the dominant part, it was essential that British Commonwealth forces should participate in the occupation of Japan, even though it was not necessary for them to arrive in the first flight.[2] They considered that the force should be composed of British, Indian, Australian, New Zealand and possibly Canadian contingents, each of approximately brigade group strength, together with an air component. The British and Indian land forces would come from SEAC. It was recognised that, since agreement to this proposal would have to be secured from the Americans, the Dominions and the Indian Government, there would be some delay and, although the forces should be earmarked and a force commander appointed, shipping should not yet be allocated. The Cabinet Defence Committee endorsed the proposal in the belief

11

that participation was an essential step towards safeguarding British economic interests in the future in and with Japan: and Attlee cabled the Dominion Prime Ministers to ensure their support.[3]

The Chiefs of Staff accordingly issued a new directive to Mountbatten on the same day stating that, in addition to the reoccupation of key areas of occupied territories and the disarmament of Japanese forces and release of British and Allied POWs and internees, a main task would be participation in the occupation of Japan.[4] Mountbatten was required to earmark at once a force of one brigade group from the British/Indian troops under his command, to form part of the British Commonwealth occupational force in due course.

The Chiefs added that arrangements for these dispositions still had to be made with the Australian, New Zealand and Canadian governments, but clearly assumed that they would be merely formal confirmation of the proposals. They were encouraged by the US Chiefs of Staff's confirmation on 17 August of their acceptance in principle of the participation of British ground forces in the occupation, subject to determination of their size and composition at a later date.

However, when the proposals for participation in the occupation were put forward by the British Cabinet and the Chiefs of Staff to Commonwealth governments, they provoked some unexpected responses. The Canadian Government's reaction was immediately unfavourable. Canada's wartime concerns had been almost entirely directed towards Europe, where the Canadian Army had assumed an important role in the defence of Britain and subsequently in the invasion of the European continent, and where Canadian interests and ethnic connections were largely based.

The war against Japan had initially involved Canada in the unhappy and useless defence of Hong Kong, where two battalions of Canadian troops sent there in late 1941 had suffered heavy casualties, with the survivors thrown into a painful captivity. There was no enthusiasm for further participation in the Pacific campaigns. Canadian forces were fully extended in Europe and on coastal defence on both Atlantic and Pacific coasts, and there was no possibility of raising additional troops for the war in the Pacific while the European war continued without introducing conscription, which the Canadian Government considered to be politically impossible.

After victory in Europe, arrangements were in fact made to raise a volunteer force of divisional strength to serve under United States command in the final assault on Japan (known as the Canadian Army Pacific Force – CAPF for short). This formation was in the course of being trained and re-equipped with American equipment in the United States at the time of the surrender. But the end of the war made this unnecessary, and a number of mutinies in the summer of 1945 among Canadian servicemen, who had all volunteered for the duration of hostilities only, emphasised to their government the overriding need for rapid demobilisation.

The Canadian response to the Attlee message of 13 August, therefore, was negative.[5] Canada was not prepared to furnish a brigade group for occupation or other operational duties in the Pacific theatre as suggested. 'We now have considerable occupation forces in Europe and we are not ready to undertake any further commitment of this nature involving either Army or Air Force units.' Because of the previous Hong Kong connection, Canada agreed to the inclusion of a Canadian warship in the British Pacific Fleet sent to accept the surrender of Hong Kong, but that was the limit of their involvement. Japan and the Far East remained of little interest in those days: Canadian eyes looked east and not west.

It was a sign of their greater sensivity to the US relationship that the Canadians also complained that the US Chiefs of Staff had been informed, by copy of Attlee's message of 13 August to them, of the possible participation of Canada before the Canadian views had been received. Attlee was forced to express his regret at this error, with the excuse that the urgency of the situation had left no alternative.

New Zealand, although it recognised its Pacific interests, was more heavily dependent economically on the UK and more closely linked emotionally with it, and was predictably supportive of the British proposal. In announcing this, the New Zealand Prime Minister stressed the importance his government attached to the desirability of proving their unity and solidarity with 'the mother country'.[6] But the New Zealand units in Italy were the only possible source of operational troops and there were to be problems in finding enough volunteers from them to go to Japan.

The Australian response, on the other hand, took a strongly independent line which was to inflame relations considerably with Britain at the political level and give rise to a long and bruising

argument on the arrangements for British Commonwealth participation in the occupation. The Australian Government was
determined that its position should be recognised as a principal
Pacific power, and that its long ordeal in bearing 'the heat and burden' of the struggle against Japan should be acknowledged by an
independent role for Australian forces in the occupation.

The lead in this was taken by the Australian Minister for
External Affairs, Dr HV Evatt, who had long been a protagonist of
Australia's independence as a nation and of the development of a
new concept in British Commonwealth relations which reconciled
full Dominion autonomy with full British cooperation. Evatt had
been shocked and stung by the lack of consultation with Australia
on the decisions which had been taken at Potsdam on the Japanese
surrender terms, and had since mobilised a diplomatic and public
campaign to press for full Australian involvement as a principal
party in the Japanese peace settlement. He believed strongly that
this would be reinforced by Australia's separate participation in the
occupation. (There were curious echoes throughout this activity of
the successful efforts of Prime Minister Billy Hughes to obtain for
Australia a voice in the Versailles peace negotiation at the end of the
First World War.)

The Australian Government accordingly told the British
Government on 17 August that it wanted all Australian troops on
occupational duties in Japan in the future to operate separately
from any British Commonwealth force.[7] 'We must insist', it said,
'that this contribution [to the occupation] is being made by
Australia as a separate belligerent of Japan, and that our force will
operate under an Australian commander who will be subject only to
the Supreme Allied Commander'. It subsequently approached
Washington direct with this request.

This technique of the direct approach to the Americans,
bypassing Britain, had previously worked on the issue of obtaining
separate Australian representation at the surrender ceremony in
Tokyo Bay: but this time the Australian attitude of intransigence
worried the Americans almost as much as it embarrassed the
British. Washington had already noted earlier in the year that 'under
the assertive leadership of Dr HV Evatt Australia is determined to
play as large a part as she can in the Pacific settlement and is to a
large degree carrying New Zealand along with her'.[8] Evatt reinforced his country's claims on the occupation by constant recourse

to 'the active field cooperation of Australian and US forces who for three years fought almost alone against Japan', thus ignoring like many others the British effort in South East Asia, let alone the vast Chinese deployment.[9] He undoubtedly expressed a view widely held in Australia that the events of the war had established a new and different relationship with the Americans. The US had replaced Britain as Australia's major ally and protector.

Evatt made a public statement on 25 August which raised the temperature dramatically. He described the moves for greater recognition of Australia's nationhood, and implied opposition to this from the mother country. The dispute about attendance at the Tokyo surrender ceremony was recalled, and the complaint that the UK had agreed to the Potsdam Declaration without consulting Australia was revived. 'There is still a deplorable tendency now that the fighting is over', he said, 'to relegate Australia to subordinate status and either not consult it at all or to consult it in a perfunctory way and not on a footing of equality'. Attlee cabled the Australian Prime Minister, Chifley, to defuse the situation and to stop 'the constant stream of public criticism', which Fraser in New Zealand also deprecated as being quite unjustifiable behaviour.[10]

Against this turbulent background the British Chiefs of Staff were predictably horrified at the Australian stance on an independent occupation role. They told Attlee on 30 August that the adoption of the Australian proposal would be a deplorable example of lack of unity within the Commonwealth, and asked that the Australians be pressed to think again, in the interests of both Australia itself and the whole Commonwealth.[11] As a compromise solution they suggested that the UK should offer to place the whole British Commonwealth Force under an Australian commander, who could be jointly responsible to the Australian and the British Governments through their respective Chiefs of Staff. This new organisation would be a new and valuable link in post-war Empire defence machinery which might have special attraction for the Australians. They thought that this part of the bargain might have an even greater attraction for the Australians than the concession on command.

The Cabinet endorsed this approach and messages were sent on 31 August, which made two additional points: first, that a joint force of corps size under a single commander would carry much more weight with the Americans in Japan than two commanders of lower rank in command of smaller forces and acting independently; and secondly, that if an Australian officer were appointed as inter-service commander-in-chief, the Australians might also wish to provide the bulk of the headquarters personnel.

The proposals received an extremely dusty answer in a telegram from Chifley to Attlee on 10 September.[12] There was first an offended retort to the suggested threat to the Commonwealth image. The Australian Government 'fully recognises and has advocated the importance of the maintenance of British Commonwealth prestige in the Pacific.. our war effort is convincing evidence of what we have done to further the cause of the British Commonwealth in the Pacific . . .' Then there was a somewhat petty objection to the concept of a single Commonwealth force, on the grounds that since Canada and South Africa were not participating and the British Pacific Fleet would be under US command, the force would not be fully representative of the Commonwealth anyway, nor would it be unified under a single commander. Then came the final blow:

> 'we have informed General MacArthur of our wish to organise an independent Australian force for Japan . . . we have no doubt that he will cooperate fully with us in allocating to the Australian force a role appropriate to our status and the contribution we have made to victory in the Pacific . . . we regret therefore that we are unable to concur to your proposals and wish to adhere to the arrangements for an independent Australian force'.

The Chiefs of Staff were understandably depressed. While on all counts they believed that it remained highly desirable that the Australian force should form part of a combined Commonwealth force, the Australian reply was quite unequivocal, and the issue seemed now to be out of the Chiefs' hands. It looked as if planning would have to proceed without the Australians on the basis of a British–Indian–New Zealand force under British command.

But there was one last hope. Evatt was then in London, and the Chiefs suggested to Attlee that he should take the opportunity to tell him 'how disappointed we were at what appears to be a retrograde step taken by the Australians from the point of view of British Commonwealth post-war defence', in a final attempt to get Chifley and Evatt to change their minds.[13]

Chifley was a strong, practical and shrewd working-class leader, highly respected by Evatt (British diplomatic representatives remarked that Evatt seemed notably subdued in Chifley's presence): but although he was inflexible in carrying through a cause which he believed was just, he had little experience of, or taste for, international affairs. Evatt, on the other hand, imaginative, vigorous, intellectually brilliant, used to pursuing Australian interests on the international scene, saw opportunity in adopting an altered attitude on the issue when Attlee spoke to him, and intervened with Chifley.

Chifley accordingly sent a further message on 21 September to say that he had reconsidered his decision at Evatt's request.[14] He still believed that the Australian desire for an independent role was entirely justified, and properly conformed with the development of status of the Dominions since the Statute of Westminster (this invocation of the constitutional position showed how seriously the issue had been regarded in Canberra). But, since maintenance requirements would be better and more economically arranged as part of a single force, he was persuaded to agree to the British Commonwealth Occupation Force (BCOF) proposal after all, provided that the commander would be an Australian and that he would be responsible operationally directly through the Joint Chiefs of Staff in Australia.

This reply was clearly drafted by Evatt. His intervention and the *volte face* which followed were undoubtedly strongly influenced by the position already taken up by the Australian Defence Committee. They had told the Government at the end of August bluntly that it was quite impossible to set up and maintain an Australian force wholly from Australian resources, if that was really the Government's intention.[15] It would be necessary to provide shipping resources and to establish separate Australian base installations, repair and maintenance facilities, with the provision by Australia of all supplies, stores, and fuel which would be required. These had hitherto largely been supplied to the Australian forces in the South West Pacific by the US forces. 'With the resources at present available to us, an independent Australian force in Japan can be maintained and supplied only with considerable assistance from US and UK authorities.' On the other hand, a combined Commonwealth force would be self-sufficient. The Committee, observed somewhat tartly that no mention of the overall maintenance aspect involved had yet been made to the UK Government, and suggested that it should be introduced immediately into the consideration of the Australian Government's proposals. 'This would be preferable to taking the matter up with the UK Government after receipt of its decision', said the Committee, rightly wishing to avoid subsequent embarrassment.

Recognising that a turnabout was probably unavoidable on these logistic grounds, Evatt saw that other advantages might be obtained from a more conciliatory response. In the course of the exchanges in London, therefore, he sought and received UK support for the continued inclusion of Australia in the proposals then being discussed for control arrangements for Japan. Although these were modified many times in the succeeding months, he was able to tell the Australian Parliament in March 1946 that Australia's status in the Pacific councils was now fully recognised: by his own appointment as chairman of the Far East Commission in Washington; by MacMahon Ball's representation of Australia, the UK, New Zealand and India on the Allied Council for Japan; by Sir William Webb's appointment as President of the International Military Tribunal for the Far East; and, not least of all, by the appointment of an Australian general to command the British Commonwealth Occupation Force in Japan.

General Hollis, the Deputy Chief Staff Officer to the British Prime Minister in his role as Minister of Defence, had heard that it was due to Evatt's efforts that the Australian Government had rescinded its previous decision on the occupation issue, and he suggested that Attlee might write a note to Evatt to thank him for his personal help in the matter. Attlee did so on 25 September.[16] 'We are glad that we shall all be joined together in a single force', he said. 'I think', said Evatt in reply, 'that an important result may now be achieved by our government'.[17]

As part of the agreement and as a further gesture to Australian aspirations, the responsibility for making the arrangements for BCOF with the Americans was handed over to the Australian Government, which was given the authority to act on behalf of all the Commonwealth governments concerned. Evatt was determined to extract the most personal kudos and national satisfaction from this agreement, and obtained Attlee's concurrence to the announcement of it being made first from Australia, with a concluding paragraph reading 'The final arrangements for the organisation and control of the British Commonwealth forces in Japan have followed direct discussions which the Australian Minister for External Affairs has had in London with the United Kingdom authorities. They are designed to recognise the special position of Australia in view of the Australian share in the defeat of Japan and the Australian interest in the settlement of Pacific questions'.

In giving his final agreement to the unified force, Chifley had made the point that it was of vital importance for the maintenance of the prestige of the British Commonwealth in the Pacific that the force should be organised and despatched to Japan as soon as possible. His government was anxious that the Australian component should get there with the least avoidable delay. Three Royal Australian Navy (RAN) ships were already in Tokyo Bay, the organisation of the Royal Australian Air Force (RAAF) component had reached an advanced stage, and the initial Army component was being raised immediately. But he had not envisaged that there would still be a long and trying period of discussion and negotiation between the Australians and the Americans, and within the US Government itself, with many doubts and uncertainties before a firm basis was reached for BCOF to take up its role in Japan.

The Americans had already given some thought to the pattern of the Allied occupation. On 18 August 1945, President Truman had approved a policy paper drawn up by the State-War-Navy Coordination Committee (SWNCC) and endorsed by the Joint Chiefs of Staff which was to set the scene for the occupation.[18] In effect it laid an obligation on the other major Allies – the UK, China and the Soviet Union – to participate with the US in the occupation and military government of Japan and to assume a share of the burden through substantial contributions to the occupation forces. The underlying objective was, of course, and was stated to be, a desire to get get back to the US as many American soldiers as possible consonant with security and American maintenance of the dominant role: and to limit US expenditure on the occupation. It was continually emphasised that the occupation should be carried out under a single central administration and that any suggestion of splitting the country up into separate national zones with their own administrations – as had happened in Germany – was out of the question.

The Russians were already bidding for their own area of occupation in Japan proper. On 16 August Stalin had sent Truman a request to include in the region of surrender of the Japanese armed forces to Soviet troops the northern part of the island of Hokkaido.

'This,' he said, 'has a special meaning for . . . Russian public opinion . . . The Japanese in 1919-21 held under occupation of their
troops the whole Soviet Far East . . . Russian public opinion would
be seriously offended if Russian troops would not have an occupation region in some part of the territory of Japan proper'.[19] Truman
made it clear in his reply on 17 August that MacArthur had the
responsibility to accomplish the surrender of Japanese forces on all
the islands of Japan proper, including Hokkaido, and said 'General
MacArthur will employ Allied token forces, which of course include
Soviet forces, in so much of a temporary occupation of Japan proper as he considers it necessary to occupy in order to accomplish our
Allied surrender terms'.[20] Further requests for Hokkaido were made
subsequently, but they were ignored by Truman and finally subsided.

Britain had already indicated its proposals for an occupation
force and was busy making its own bid to influence the arrangements for the control of Japan. In a 'tentative' proposal to the State
Department dated 18 August for various Allied Councils and
Committees, the British said that 'the prefecture of Tokyo should be
garrisoned jointly by US, Russian, Chinese and British forces as
directed by the Supreme Commander, but the area should not be
zoned on the Berlin model'.[21] Civil administration should be an
American responsibility and while all occupational duties in Japan
other than in Tokyo should be undertaken by US forces, a suitable
location should be allotted for the British air contingent and a port
should be allotted for the headquarters of the British naval forces in
Japanese waters. These suggestions were carefully ignored by the
Americans as the consideration of Allied participation proceeded.

On 15 September Marshall advised MacArthur that the matter
of Allied occupation forces in Japan was under active discussion.[22]
He recalled that a principle of the present American policy approved
by Truman was that a number of the Allies should contribute forces
for the occupation 'in order to share the burden, impress the
Japanese with the number of nations involved in their defeat, and
obviate any feeling that the war was between Orientals and
Occidentals'. Russian, Chinese and British contingents had been
specifically mentioned in stated US policy. He added that it was for
consideration whether others such as the French, the Dutch and the
Philippines should be invited to take part. There was considerable
feeling becoming evident in the US, including the introduction of a
resolution in Congress, that others of the Allies should bear their

proportional share of the occupation burden. Against this background, Marshall asked MacArthur for his views on the problem of Allied occupation forces and his suggestions for the participation of the British, whose indication of the provision of four Empire brigades was the only offer so far, and which the Joint Chiefs of Staff had welcomed in principle.

The US commanders in the field had already become confused in their view of the occupation requirements. On 14 September General Eichelberger was reported as saying that 400,000 American troops would be sufficient for the occupation and that it would not be necessary to bring British or Empire troops to Japan (although he would be glad to meet them socially!), but he considered that the US occupation force would be withdrawn within a year.[23] On 17 September MacArthur said that, working through the Japanese government, it would be possible to accomplish the surrender terms with a force of as little as 200,000 after disarmament had been completed, compared with the several million troops who would have been required if an Allied military government had been set up on German lines. Truman, the State Department and Marshall reacted angrily at these declarations: 'in a highly explosive Congressional situation which may jeopardise an orderly occupation and replacement policy' they were worried about the adverse effect that the Eichelberger and MacArthur statements would have on their efforts to continue the draft to provide replacements and on the political position of the US in the Far East at that particular time.[24] MacArthur, rebuked, was contrite, and disowned any responsibility for Eichelberger's words: but contradictory statements continued to be made. On 25 September a spokesman for MacArthur said that the occupation might last many years: and in October MacArthur was reported as saying that he expected to have only 60,000 men in Japan by March 1946.[25]

MacArthur's reply to Marshall's enquiry about Allied involvement made it clear that he had no objection to the participation of the forces of any or all of the nations mentioned, provided that they were completely integrated into the army of occupation under the Supreme Commander for the Allied Powers (SCAP) and his US higher commanders.[26] Allied forces should under no circumstances constitute independent units with specific geographical locations – 'a divided command here would be fatal'. As for the British, they should not be treated as a single unit under a British commander.

'Each Dominion force should be of its own nationality – Australian, New Zealand or English', and its supply should be the responsibility of its own government. MacArthur was determined that other nationalities should be dispersed throughout his command and kept in their place. He was also sympathetic to the idea of an independent Australian command, provided that it was integrated with his own.

At this point he unexpectedly received the direct approach from the Australian Prime Minister, which canvassed the idea of overall commander-in-chief for the Commonwealth forces, with a line of communication to the Commonwealth governments through the Australian channels of command.[27] MacArthur described this plan to Marshall as being 'completely impracticable and [it] would lead inevitably to confusion', and refrained from replying.[28] His unfavourable comments were based largely on the implication that, if they were agreed, similar arrangements would have to be set up for the Chinese, the Russians and any other Allied participants, which would have been an administrative nightmare.

The availability of Allied troops for the occupation and the effect of their participation on the US manpower requirement became increasingly important in Washington, where the political pressures for the return of US soldiers to the US and for the limitation of US expenditure on the occupation continued to mount. Various more or less desperate solutions also crept into consideration from time to time: for example, on 3 October Marshall advised MacArthur[29] that one suggestion was to organise the major portion of the occupation force for Japan, Korea and the Ryukyus along the lines of a super military police force with highly mobile tactical units in reserve instead of the present lines of combat organisation. This would be commanded by US personnel, but most subordinate positions would be held by Japanese in Japan and Koreans in Korea, with US regimental combat teams in reserve. This bizarre proposal was dismissed by MacArthur, as far as Japan was concerned, with the comment that it would in effect mean a practical lifting of military occupation, substituting for combat troops a type of police force largely composed of enemy nationals. 'I believe', he said, 'such a force should not be considered under any circumstances until the surrender terms have been complied with', which it was then thought might well take a number of years.[30] But the proposal illustrates the concern felt in the US at the continued retention of large American forces in the Far East, which continued to preoccupy the politicians in Washington: in early 1947, the House Appropriations Committee even suggested the raising of a foreign legion to take over the US role in Japan, which elicited a withering retort from MacArthur: 'If the United States cannot support its occupational responsibilities with its own manpower, it should withdraw therefrom.'[31]

Throughout his exchanges with Marshall in Washington, MacArthur repeated his conviction that 'the United States should exercise the predominant control', and that 'the forces of the other United Nations should be of token size and in no case should exceed a Division for any one country' and should be completely integrated into the Army of Occupation under the operational control of US commanders.[32]

Further discussions between MacArthur and Washington led to a proposal being made on 11 October by the Joint Chiefs of Staff State/War/Navy Coordinating Committee (SWNCC) for the deployment of Allied contingents to the effect that, if the United States were to maintain the controlling voice in the occupation, US participation in the occupation forces would have to be at least equal to that of all other nations combined.[33] On SCAP's latest estimate that 200,000 men were required to occupy Japan and enforce the surrender terms, provision of Allied contingents of 90,000 to 100,000 men would enable the US to reduce its force to 100,000, with the caveat that any reduction in the overall total required would require proportional reductions in both US and Allied totals if the United States were to keep the dominant voice. With this objective in view, the Secretary of State was asked to enter into negotiations as soon as possible with China, Great Britain and Russia to provide 30,000 men each, to be integrated operationally into the US forces.

While these manpower considerations made it desirable in one sense to secure participation by Russia and China, the political problems were more sensitive. Reports from Moscow in October indicated that Stalin would not be prepared to place Russian force under MacArthur's command. His territorial objectives had been achieved by the recovery of Manchuria and the areas lost to Japan in 1905. His aim to secure a voice in occupied Japan was now directed towards the establishment of an Allied control council in which the USSR would share control with the US, Britain and China.

Secretary of State Byrnes went so far as to suggest in Washington in early November that, because of the difficulty and delicacy of the discussions with the USSR to obtain agreement on the control arrangements for Japan, it might be as well to avoid complicating the debate by dropping the requests for forces from the other Allies altogether. He had told Harriman, the US Ambassador in Moscow, in October that his own disposition, like that of the Soviet Government, was to discourage the use of other than US forces in the occupation.[34] He was swiftly reminded by the War Department of the policy established for Allied participation under Presidential agreement.[35] Formal proposals had already been made by the Australians on behalf of the Commonwealth and Washington's manpower planning had proceeded on the basis that Allied participation would reduce the requirement for US forces to 50 per cent of the total, with a comparable reduction in the size of the army as a whole. The War Department warned that any change in this assumption would require a complete revision of plans, which would by implication be unacceptable to the President.

In order to protect the United States from subsequent Soviet accusations, Byrnes thereupon instructed Harriman in Moscow on 17 November to inform Stalin formally through Molotov that the British Commonwealth had offered a force of 30,000 men, details of which were under discussion, and that the US would be willing to have a similar force from the USSR.[36] As expected, this invitation was not accepted. Stalin was still not prepared to place a Soviet force in Japan under SCAP command and he had previously gone as far as to say, perhaps in the hope of discouraging others from accepting the invitation which he had refused, that in his view the problem created for MacArthur in employing Allied forces would be of such magnitude and difficulty as to make undesirable any Allied participation in the occupation force.[37]

As far as China was concerned, Generalissimo Chiang Kai-shek had expressed a desire to make available one army of three divisions (30,000 men) for the occupation and it had been contemplated that this force could be transported to Japan after 1 December.[38] Indeed, tentative plans for siting this force in the Nagoya area were discussed in Tokyo and a provisional allocation of territory was made. However, as his domestic situation worsened, the Generalissimo had second thoughts and advised with regret that, due to internal conditions in China, Chinese forces for Japan could not be provided for several months.[39] The securing of liberated areas in China had a higher priority. He still wanted Chinese forces to participate should his internal situation permit, but the increasing threat and eventual domination of the Chinese Communist armies ensured that this hoped-for state was never reached. (Perhaps to deceive the Communists, the Chinese Ministry of Information made an extraordinary and isolated statement on 23 May 1946 that the Chinese 3rd Army under General Chou Fu-cheng, which had fought in Yunnan and North Burma and had since been stationed in Indo-China, would embark at Haiphong in June to take part in the Allied occupation of Japan, landing at Yokohama and being allotted a zone of occupation by MacArthur.[40] It never happened).

So, as November was reached, the only offer from any of the other Allied powers for provision of occupation forces had come from the British Commonwealth. In the light of the Russian and Chinese positions and the lack of interest or capability on the part of the other Allies, it was clear that the Commonwealth was to be the only non-American participant. A proposal to include a forma-tion of 50,000 Filipino scouts in the occupation forces which had been approved by the US Congress in October had come to nothing: and a final desperate invitation from Byrnes to China as late as 26 December met with no greater success than before. But the negoti-ation of the arrangements for BCOF were to drag on for a long time yet. The concentration of the components of the force, how-ever, was already well under way.

3

Preparing the Force for Japan

In South East Asia Command Mountbatten was facing immense problems following the surrender. The area under his jurisdiction had been extended to include the Netherlands East Indies, Borneo and Hong Kong, previously covered by the South West Pacific Command. The task of re-occupying Japanese-held territory, disarming over half a million Japanese military personnel and releasing and repatriating some 123,000 Allied prisoners-of-war and internees, was a formidable one. It was exacerbated by the fact that acceptance of surrender was not certain, especially in Malaya, where the Japanese commander, Itagaki, was 'breathing defiance' and possible resistance might be encountered.

Moreover, in the Netherlands East Indies and Indo-China, nationalist movements armed and trained by the Japanese were opposing the return of their former colonial rulers. British and Indian formations were reluctantly becoming involved in these conflicts in the course of their enforcement of the surrender. In Java and south Indo-China, indeed, the ultimate irony was reached when a number of Japanese units were allowed for a time to keep their arms in order to help the British and Indian divisions restore and maintain order pending the re-establishment of the original regimes.

Against this background Mountbatten had to provide the two brigade groups required for the occupation of Japan. It had been directed that one brigade was to be from the British troops and one from the British/Indian troops under his command. With the manpower pressures increasing elsewhere, it was clear that these two brigades would have to be formed from units readily available in

India and not yet committed to operations. At the same time, for political and sentimental reasons, it was considered important that units with the maximum war experience should be chosen.

It was judged necessary to establish at the outset a force head-quarters for these two brigades which would in effect act as a divisional headquarters. The force, initially known as Force 152, was later named BRINDJAP (British and Indian Troops Japan). The commander selected for BRINDJAP was Major-General D Tennant Cowan CB CBE DSO MC, known throughout SEAC as 'Punch' Cowan. He had served with distinction throughout the Burma campaign from the 1942 retreat to the 1945 victory as com-mander of 17th Indian Division, known to the Japanese as well as the British and Indians from its divisional sign as the famous 'Black Cat' division.

It was decided that the British brigade would be taken from 2nd British Division which had been withdrawn from Burma in April and May 1945, together with 36th British Division, after the long campaign had developed into a pursuit of the defeated Japanese armies. After rest, reinforcement and training in India, 2nd Division was under orders to go to Malaya following the sur-render, to take the place of other formations being sucked into the operations in Java: but its 5 Brigade was reconstituted for the Japanese occupation and was held back in India, leaving 4 and 6 Brigades to move on to Malaya.

Some care was taken to ensure that 5 Brigade fairly represent-ed the various parts of the United Kingdom. It already contained an English battalion, 2nd Battalion The Dorsetshire Regiment (the Dorsets), and a Scottish battalion, 1st Battalion The Queen's Own Cameron Highlanders (the Camerons). A Welsh battalion, 2nd Battalion The Royal Welch Fusiliers (the Welch Fusiliers), was drawn from 36 Divison to take the place of the third English battal-ion (7th Battalion The Worcestershire Regiment) in the brigade. Brigadier R S McNaught, who had already commanded 4 and 6 Brigades of 2nd Division in action, was selected as the brigade com-mander.

The Dorsets and the Camerons had served with 2nd Division in the fierce battles at Kohima in 1944, had then advanced to Tamu, crossed the Chindwin, captured Ye-U, forced the Irrawaddy and raced on to Mandalay. In 13 months they had advanced nearly 800 miles over very difficult country, mostly on foot.

The Welch Fusiliers had served with 36th Division in 1944 and 1945, initially in the Arakan and subsequently in northern Burma as part of the Northern Combat Area Command under General Stilwell, where they joined in the advance down the so-called 'railway corridor' to Mandalay.

All three battalions had a high proportion of their strength due for repatriation after over three years' service overseas and these men were stood down and replaced by reinforcements from various sources. The Camerons and the Welch Fusiliers received drafts of about 600 men each remustered from the Royal Navy and the RAF, whom their core of regular officers and NCOs had then to convert into infantrymen. The Dorsets were reinforced by substantial transfers from other battalions in 2nd Division.

The Indian brigade was selected with the same care to provide units with the maximum combat experience and at the same time to represent as many of the martial classes and areas of India as possible. Headquarters 268 Indian Infantry Brigade, which had fought in Burma during the 1944-45 campaign, was re-formed to command the three battalions selected. These were 5th Battalion The 1st Punjab Regiment (the Punjabis), 1st Battalion The Mahratta Light Infantry (the Mahrattas) and 2nd Battalion The 5th Royal Gurkha Rifles (the Gurkhas).

The Punjabis had taken part in the early withdrawal from Burma in 1942, and had returned to serve with 26th Indian Division in the 1943 and 1944 Arakan campaigns. After training in combined operations they had joined in the landings on Ramree Island and at Rangoon in 1945. The battalion represented most of the martial races of northern India – Rajputs, Punjabi Mussalmans, Hazarawals and Sikhs : and as was typical of the Punjab Regiment, the senior infantry regiment of the Indian Army, with a history going back to 1759, the companies were formed on an all-Muslim or all-Hindu basis.

The Mahrattas were the only battalion in BRINDJAP not to have fought against the Japanese, although many other Mahratta battalions had: but they represented a high-caste Hindu martial race from south west India, and their own credentials were based on a long and active experience of war. They had originally sailed overseas in 1941 to the Middle East and had fought as part of the 8th Indian Division in the Western Desert and subsequently in Italy. There they were constantly engaged in action until the German surrender in the north and won a Victoria Cross in the final decisive battle of the campaign, the crossing of the Senio. When the European war ended, the Mahrattas were embarked at Taranto and had arrived back in the regimental centre at Belgaum in July.

The inclusion of the Gurkha battalion was testimony to the special place occupied in the Indian Army by the Gurkhas from the independent kingdom of Nepal. The battalion had fought in Burma from the start of the Japanese invasion in 1942 until late in 1944 as part of 17th Indian Division and during this period won three Victoria Crosses, two of them in the same action in the Imphal area on successive days in June 1944.

268 Indian Brigade was special in another way. Its commander, Brigadier K S Thimayya DSO, had been the first Indian to command a brigade in action, and was in command of 36 Indian Infantry Brigade of the 26th Indian Division when it captured Rangoon in 1945. He had also represented India at the Japanese surrender ceremony in Singapore on 12 September 1945.

Force troops included the 7th Light Cavalry (7 Cavalry), an Indian cavalry regiment, consisting of Jats, Sikhs and Punjabi Mussalmans from northern India. 7 Cavalry fought in their tanks in Burma from Imphal in 1944 to the final race to Rangoon in 1945. In just over a year they advanced 1,000 miles and won three Distinguished Service Orders and many other decorations. For its expedition to Japan the regiment exchanged its tanks for Daimler armoured cars. Artillery and engineer units together with the other supporting arms and services were mainly from 2nd Division, and had shared in its campaigns.

The Indian Army was an all-volunteer force of over two million men. The majority, as the Commander-in-Chief, India, General Auchinleck, advised the Chiefs of Staff at the end of the war, had no wish to be demobilised and would serve as long as required. Life in the Army was a good deal more economically secure and comfortable than in the dusty villages of India. The Indian units were therefore fortunate to have no worries on account of release or repatriation. They had a wealth of old soldiers who settled down to the business of peacetime soldiering far more quickly than the British brigade, a British commanding officer noted enviously.[1]

So the components of BRINDJAP began to come together from various locations in India to camp at Nasik, near Bombay, in preparation for embarkation for Japan. The extensive battle experience of the heavily-decorated units and the distinction of their commanders were evidence of SEAC's determination to provide a force of high quality for the occupation and of the expectation that the situation in Japan demanded such a contribution. That expectation was to be somewhat shaken in months to come.

Meanwhile the New Zealand Government was implementing its decision to provide a brigade for the occupation. Its only immediate source of trained and experienced troops was the New Zealand Division in Italy, which had fought a hard and successful war through the Middle East desert campaigns and up the Italian peninsula. The end of the European war had found them in Trieste facing Tito's partisans in an atmosphere of suspicion and mistrust. They had moved from Trieste to rest near Perugia while plans for New Zealand troops to join the Allied forces in the Pacific to continue the war with Japan were discussed, and then happily discarded.

It was decided to constitute the contingent for the occupation as a self-contained brigade group of three battalions with a field battery, engineer and service corps companies, a hospital and other support units, and to build this up around the existing 9 NZ Infantry Brigade of the New Zealand Division. This consisted of 22 and 27 NZ Infantry Battalions and the New Zealand Divisional Cavalry Regiment, which had been converted to infantry in October 1944 for the winter battles of the Italian campaign (although still retaining their black berets and their form of organisation in squadrons and troops). The Government had hoped originally that the contingent, now christened J Force, could be formed on a voluntary basis, but it was soon realised that insufficient volunteers would be forthcoming and that compulsion was the only means of achieving the required strength (although this caused some political uproar in New Zealand). It was therefore decided that the units would be made up initially from single men drawn from the 13th, 14th and 15th Reinforcements (the last still on its way from Egypt). They had seen little or no actual fighting and none of them had served more than 12 months overseas. It was decided that personnel would only be required to serve in Japan for six months and would then be replaced by volunteers from New Zealand. The idea of such an excursion on the way home was more attractive than the previous expectation of being sent to India en route to the Japanese war, although a direct return home would have been preferred by all ranks.

In October J Force settled down in Florence, initially under command of Brigadier Gentry and then Brigadier K L Stewart OBE DSO, to await its move to Japan, which finally took place four months later. Stewart had the difficult job of bringing together the original units, forming them into an effective force, and endowing it with new spirit. (There was a strong Maori element in the new units: in the Divisional Cavalry Regiment one of the squadrons now consisted entirely of Maoris). Meanwhile, a recruiting campaign for the relief force was initiated in New Zealand in February 1946: volunteers between 20 and 40 were called for, to serve for a term of 12 to 18 months, with a minimum of six months in Japan, and the first draft entered camp to start training in March.

The Australian approach to the assignment of ground forces for Japan was quite different. Instead of allocating existing formations to the task, as had been the case with the British, Indian and New Zealand contingents, the Australian Government decided to raise an entirely new formation from volunteers from units throughout the Australian Army's operational areas. The complications of the immediate post-war tasks – the repatriation of released Australian prisoners of war and the start of demobilisation, which began only six weeks after VJ Day – caused some delay, but on 25 September 1945 authority was given to raise a new 34 Australian Infantry Brigade Group. Brigadier R H Nimmo from Headquarters 1st Army in New Guinea was appointed to command, and volunteers were called for from the divisions serving in forward areas for a minimum period of service of twelve months in Japan. The new 65th Australian Infantry Battalion was to be formed from volunteers from the 7th Australian Division in Balikpapan, North Borneo, and the 2/40th Battalion in Timor; the new 66th Battalion was to come from volunteers from the 9th Division in Labuan and Tarakan; and the new 67th Battalion was to receive volunteers from the 3rd Division in Bougainville, the 6th Division in Wewak and the 11th Division in Rabaul.

These were divisions with considerable experience in various theatres of war. The 6th, 7th and 9th Divisions had all seen extensive service in the Middle East and following their return to Australia in 1942 had been heavily engaged in the Papua and New Guinea campaigns prior to the final landings in Borneo. The 3rd and 11th Divisions had been similarly committed to the campaigns in New Guinea and New Britain from 1943 onward.

It was decided to concentrate the new 34 Brigade at Morotai, a major Allied base in the Halmahera islands, where General Blamey, the Australian Commander-in-Chief, had accepted the surrender of all the Japanese forces in the Netherlands East Indies some weeks before. There was no shortage of volunteers: the colonel appointed to command the new 66th Battalion, for instance, had applications from over 120 officers for the 34 vacancies he had to fill. The standard was high, and many applicants were decorated. They were mostly single, had some time to go before they could expect to be discharged, and wanted to see more of the world. But the process of selection and their transportation from their different areas was a laborious and lengthy task: the units concerned were, after all, scattered along a chain of islands 3000 miles long. However, by the end of October 34 Brigade had assembled at Morotai.

It was decided to add an armoured component to the Brigade to enhance its capability, and volunteers were called for from 4 Armoured Brigade, part of the 1st Armoured Division in Australia. The Brigade had waited with mounting impatience for overseas service through four years of war (it had been ruefully called 'the Anchored Brigade') without satisfaction, and the volunteers were quickly forthcoming. The men were brought together at Puckapunyal in Victoria in an independent squadron which in February 1946 was issued with new Staghound armoured cars and christened 1 Australian Armoured Car Squadron. Other supporting units, including a field battery and a hospital, were also assembled in Australia.

The formation of the British Commonwealth Air Component, to be known as BCAIR, was even more geographically complicated. It was decided that the UK would contribute a fighter wing, a transport squadron and a communications flight; Australia a fighter wing; and New Zealand a fighter squadron. An initial suggestion that the UK should also provide two Mosquito squadrons was dropped during negotiations with the Americans (see Chapter 4), when it was also decided that one of the squadrons in the UK fighter wing should be provided by the Royal Indian Air Force.

Air Vice-Marshal C A Bouchier CB CBE DFC, Royal Air Force, was appointed to command BCAIR, and subsequently, as a consolation prize for the British, he was designated as Deputy to the Commander-in-Chief BCOF. His headquarters were first assembled in September 1945 in Madras and then moved to Singapore, leaving a skeleton headquarters behind.

11 and 17 Squadrons RAF were selected as the two British fighter squadrons for BCAIR, and 4 Squadron RIAF as the Indian Air Force contribution. All three squadrons were equipped with Spitfires. 11 and 17 Squadrons had been supporting 14th Army in Burma up to the end of the war there, and following the surrender had moved to Singapore, and then onward to Kuala Lumpur in January 1946. 4 Squadron RIAF, which had also flown in Burma, had returned to South India for redeployment. A communications flight equipped with Dakotas and Austers, together with a mobile field hospital, were added to the strength from RAF resources in India.

81 Wing RAAF was selected to constitute the Australian element. It consisted of 76, 77 and 82 Fighter Squadrons, which had been actively engaged in operations in New Guinea and the islands since 1942, and in June had moved to Labuan, where the squadrons continued to operate against Japanese targets in North Borneo until the end of the war. Up to that point, the squadrons had flown Kittyhawk aircraft but in September 1945, in preparation for Japan, were re-equipped with Mustangs. In addition to the fighter squadrons, the Wing included 381 Base Squadron and 481 Maintenance Squadron: and 5 Airfield Construction Squadron was also allotted to BCAIR from the RAAF, in view of the anticipated need to make Japanese airfields fit and serviceable for use by BCAIR. All had volunteered for a minimum of twelve months' service in Japan.

The remaining BCAIR element was the New Zealand squadron for Japan. 14 Squadron, the oldest operational squadron in the RNZAF, was reformed in Auckland to fill this role in December 1945. Volunteers were raised specifically to join the squadron for the occupation task, mainly men with considerable war experience as air and ground crew. Over 60 fighter pilots volunteered for duty in Japan – half were New Zealanders returning from service with the RAF in almost all theatres of operations, while the other half came from RNZAF squadrons in the South West Pacific. There was a lengthy process of selection for the 24 pilots actually required, and this comprised formation flying, air-to-air combat, air-to-air and air-to-ground gunnery, and bombing, together with (to the dismay of the pilots) ceremonial drill. The squadron was formed as an autonomous unit at Ardmore, a fighter station south of Auckland, with its own ground support and transport units, and was equipped with FG-1D Corsair aircraft, a type which many of the pilots had been flying in the Pacific theatre.

As it awaited its movement orders, the Air Component, although scattered over a very wide area, was now organisationally complete.

4

Negotiating with the Americans

As the BCOF units assembled at Nasik and Morotai, in Italy and at the various air bases in South East Asia and the South West Pacific, action slowly began to get under way on the implementation of the arrangements for Allied participation in the occupation.

On 19 October the US War Department gave the State Department in Washington a summary[1] of the situation as far as it was known to them regarding the provision of Allied forces for the occupation of Japan. The British Chiefs of Staff had indicated informally to them that a four-brigade contingent would be supplied from British, Indian, Australian and New Zealand forces; but there was also the direct Australian approach to MacArthur for the Australian force to serve directly under his command rather than as part of the 'British Empire' contingent envisaged by the British, which the Americans had found somewhat embarrassing. The Russians and the Chinese still seemed unlikely to take part, but MacArthur was pressing for a contribution of 30,000 men from each of the three major Allies in order to allow the Americans to reduce their manpower commitment to half the occupation force. MacArthur envisaged a two-area organisation in Japan, with a US Army corps headquarters in each area, and with appropriate Allied elements in each area and token forces from each power in Tokyo; but he would not make firm plans for deployment until he had been advised of the composition, strength and date of arrival of the Allied forces. However, the War Department's principal concern was to stress that no formal proposal had yet been made by any of the Allied powers and to complain that the State Department had not yet initiated any conversations with the Allies. The US Chiefs of Staff had told the British that they expected a formal proposal on troops for Japan and also Korea.

To bring further pressure to bear on the State Department, the War Department also provided guidelines which had been already drawn up by the Joint Staff Planners for an agreement with a foreign nation (whichever it might be) on participation in the Japanese occupation, indicating the points which they considered should be covered.[2] These laid down that the foreign force should be integrated within the overall Occupation Force under the command and control of SCAP, but in formations under its own commanders and with SCAP having the right to locate and move the force wherever he saw fit. No exclusive area of control should be allocated to the force and there should be provision for withdrawal of the force on written notice by either side. It would be the responsibility of the foreign government concerned to arrange for the equipment, transport to and from Japan, and the supply and maintenance of its forces there.

No doubt at the instigation of the State Department, smarting at the War Department criticism, a formal proposal for the use of British Commonwealth Occupation Forces in Japan arrived the next day (20 October) at the State Department from the Australian Government 'acting on behalf of the Governments of the United Kingdom, Australia, New Zealand and India'.[3]

This proposed the composition of the force in the following specific terms:

'(A) Land Forces – One British and one British/Indian Brigade with a proportion of supporting arms and administrative troops organised as a group under an Indian Army Commander. One Australian Brigade and one New Zealand Brigade similarly organised as a group under an Australian or New Zealand Commander. It is proposed to consider later whether a second Australian Brigade be raised.

(B) Air Forces – An air contingent organised as a Tactical Group under an integrated Group Headquarters. This would be composed as follows – British: 1 Fighter Wing, 2 Mosquito Squadrons, 1 Transport Squadron; Australian: 3 Mustang Fighter Squadrons; New Zealand: 1 Squadron of type unknown.'

As agreed in the long debate between the UK and the Dominion Governments, the proposal named an Australian as Commander-in-Chief of the British Commonwealth Occupation Force (BCOF).[4] He was Lieutenant General John Northcott CB MVO. Northcott was the Chief of the Australian General Staff and therefore the most senior soldier in the Australian forces. He was probably the oldest serving soldier as well, having been born in 1890, only 10 years after the sexagenarian MacArthur. He had been wounded at Gallipoli in 1915 and had thereafter taken no further part in active service in the First World War. He had attended the Staff College at Camberley and the Imperial Defence College in London between the wars and was therefore at home in the British military scene. In the Second World War he had briefly commanded an Australian armoured division and then the 2nd Australian Corps, but in 1942 he was promoted to Chief of the General Staff and had remained in that post through to the end of the war, in a capacity which had offered him regular contact with MacArthur and his staff.

It had also been agreed between the various Commonwealth governments during the formulation of the proposal that the individual governments would be responsible for the requirements of their own contingents for the initial period of occupation duty (up to 1 August 1946) but that thereafter Australia would be the main source of supply and that the Australian services would accept responsibility for the maintenance of BCOF as a whole, with the costs being shared.

The Australian Government proposed that, while Northcott would be under the control of SCAP for operational matters and should have direct access to him for that purpose, he should for policy and administrative matters be responsible to the British Commonwealth Governments concerned through the Joint Chiefs of Staff in Australia (JCOSA) and through Australian Government machinery. JCOSA was a new Commonwealth organisation to be set up in Melbourne, consisting of the Australian Chiefs of Staff together with representatives of those of the UK and New Zealand and of the Commander-in-Chief, India. Their instructions to BCOF would be issued by the Australian Chiefs of Staff, thus giving the whole operation the Australian emphasis which Evatt had sought throughout.

Approval for BCOF's participation was sought on this basis.

Details of role, location and other arrangements could be left to be completed direct between Northcott and MacArthur, but the point was made that, while some part in the occupation of Tokyo Prefecture was desired, a separate Zone of Occupation was not sought for BCOF. A port should be included in the area allotted to BCOF and three airfields would be required, located alongside the land forces.

The US Government was asked to agree to this proposal, which would be 'a further practical manifestation to Japan and the world at large of that cooperation between the British and American peoples and their forces which have marked their common war effort as members of the United Nations'. This underlined the symbolic importance attached by the British to participation in the occupation by the Commonwealth governments, and there were high hopes in some quarters of the real benefits which might accrue. Churchill (now out of office) was upset by the apparent reluctance of the Foreign Office to press for joint US–UK control in Japan and in a letter to Bevin in November[5] underlined his own touching belief in the continuing strength of British influence:

> '. . . Although the United States is far more powerful than the British Commonwealth [in the joint occupation], we must always insist upon coming in on equal terms. We should press for joint occupation at all points in question rather than accept the exclusive possession by the United States. We have so much to give that I have little doubt that, for the sake of a general settlement, they would agree to joint occupation throughout'.

This was far-fetched: the dominance of the US had effectively already been accepted by the Commonwealth. But the US Government was asked for an early reply to the Australian proposal on behalf of the Commonwealth 'in order that organisation and movement of forces may be proceeded with as soon as possible'. It was hardly conceivable at that stage that the first elements of BCOF would not land in Japan for another four months.

The Americans, however, still remained deeply concerned at the lack of contribution from Russia and China to spread the load of the occupation. Although particular stress had been laid on the desirability of 'Orientals' taking part in the occupation, it now seemed unlikely that Chiang Kai-shek would ever be in a position to furnish a Chinese contingent, even though SCAP had provisionally allotted the Nagoya area for one.

Secretary Byrnes was continuing to attempt to reach a more favourable conclusion with Russia. This would not only relieve the US of a proportion of its manpower and expenditure commitments without affecting MacArthur's overall power of command, but would also achieve a degree of US-Soviet cooperation which could be of considerable help in establishing a joint approach to the tricky question of the control machinery in Japan and the ultimate peace settlement. Soviet participation in the occupation had become part of the complicated pattern of US-Soviet relationships both in the Far East and in Europe as well. Until it was determined whether or not the USSR would participate in Japan, the Americans were not prepared to respond to the Australian proposal, since its intention remained to restrict the numbers of Allied forces to no more than 50 per cent of US strengths.

There was a strong reaction from MacArthur to the Australian proposal in relation to the command and control arrangements, under which General Northcott's responsibilities as Commander-in-Chief of BCOF for policy and administrative matters would be to JCOSA. MacArthur expressed the view on 20 November that these suggestions were fundamentally impracticable unless Japan was to be divided into definite spheres of control by the various foreign contingents.[6] 'There are other features from a military standpoint . . .' he said, 'which make the proposed Australian setup unworkable. Basis principles are involved in the matter and I therefore do not believe that the problem can be approached on the basis of making concessions for reasons of expediency'.

After the final approach to Moscow for a Russian involvement in the occupation had failed, the State Department eventually replied to the Australian proposal on 23 November, accepting the participation of BCOF in general, but leaving the exact arrangements for the force and its movement to be decided in further discussions with representatives of the Australian Government.[7] The two main points of disagreement, however, remained: the Americans did not want an overall Force Commander and they wanted the channels of communication for policy as well as operations to be through the US Government and the US Chiefs of Staff.

Moreover, there was still disquiet among the Commonwealth

partners, especially on the part of New Zealand, at the determination of the US to integrate BCOF operationally into the US forces, and the harmful effects this would have on its identity and independence. But Evatt, then in Washington, recommended that the US position be accepted. The Russian attitude was in everyone's minds. 'If we resist, the US will probably take up the position that the Russians will insist on a share of the occupation on the same lines, and this we know the US cannot accept in the present circumstances'.[8] Evatt was convinced that Northcott would be able to make entirely satisfactory arrangements on the spot with MacArthur.

General Northcott and his Australian staff officers from the skeleton BCOF headquarters which had been established initially in Melbourne, accordingly went to Tokyo in mid-December to resolve these problems and to thrash out the detailed plans for the entry of BCOF into Japan. There were many practical logistic issues to be dealt with. SCAP had, for example, already issued a warning on 29 November in connection with an informal advice that the Australian Government wanted to begin movement of the brigade at Morotai, together with an RAAF component, about 15 December. 'This unit, it is reported to me,' he said, 'is outfitted for tropical service only and has no winter clothing or gear with it. It should not move until it is completely serviced for winter campaign. I cannot from American resources supply deficiencies along this line. This matter is important as it cannot fail to lead to friction and recriminations if these troops are sent forward unequipped for winter service'. And due to the limited availability of minefree ports, he added that it was inadvisable to set any dates for the entry of Australian troops into Japan until times and places for landings had been agreed with SCAP.

The resolution of these issues did not take long, and SCAP was able to report to Washington that tentative agreement had been reached on 18 December on the composition and role of the Force, subject to approval of the governments concerned.[9] BCOF would be a component of the occupation forces under SCAP; its duties would include the military control of Hiroshima Prefecture and the demilitarisation and disposition of Japanese installations and armaments there, but the Prefecture would not constitute a national zone.

Although the ground force would be under the operational control of the US Eighth Army, it would be preserved as a self-contained corps of two-division strength, with the Commander-in-Chief BCOF as the corps commander, responsible for the maintenance and interior administration of the force as a whole. Alongside the British and Indian Division, the Australian and New Zealand formations would function as independent brigade groups, the idea of an ANZAC division put forward in the October proposal having been discarded. The Royal Navy Port Party would function as a small but independent unit under the operational control of the US naval authority for the operation of the port of Kure only, and the Kure Navy Yard would remain firmly under US control. There would be provision for BCOF to be represented in Tokyo Prefecture by a detachment of battalion strength drawn from each national contingent.

The point regarding the channel of communication on policy matters, however, remained unresolved: the channels for major policies affecting the Force should still, in MacArthur's view, be via the US Government and US Chiefs of Staff. Two further issues surfaced: at 43,600, the total size proposed for BCOF was higher than the ceiling of 30,000 previously suggested by SCAP for each Allied component; while the size of the air force element proposed (six RAF squadrons, three RAAF squadrons and one RNZAF squadron) was regarded by SCAP as being in excess of tactical requirements, especially if they were to be co-located with the ground forces. In the case of the ground forces, the requirement that BCOF should be fully self-sufficient in fact meant that there would need to be a much higher proportion of base and support units than would normally have been necessary for a formation of army corps size.

It took another month to reach final agreement. The RAF strength was reduced to two fighter squadrons and one transport squadron, and one RIAF squadron was added. The overall total strength of the Force was to remain at roughly 43,000 (in the event, it never exceeded 37,000). Further riders were added to allow for reductions in BCOF from time to time in line with progressive reductions in US forces (to keep MacArthur's balance right) and to provide for the review of the size of BCOF in the light of any future arrangements which might be made for Chinese or Russian participation. As Northcott said later, 'this second and unpredictable factor undoubtedly delayed the final agreement'.[10] But the major change was the acceptance by the US that the channel of communication on policy and administrative issues should be via JCOSA to the Australian Government, a victory won by continual lobbying in Washington by Evatt over the past months.

The text of the final agreement was completed on 24 January 1946 and simultaneous press releases were issued on 31 January.[11] The planning dates for the movement of BCOF envisaged the first elements of the Australian component arriving in February 1946, with the leading elements of BRINDJAP and the New Zealand brigade arriving in March. MacArthur made a warm statement of welcome, referring particularly to his special relationship with the Australian contingent in the Pacific campaign and foreshadowing the corresponding reduction in US forces on which he had been so pressed by Washington. BCOF's presence would 'materially broaden the base along international lines of a burden which up to this time has of necessity been carried to a large extent unilaterally by United States forces and cannot fail to be of overall beneficial effect. It will enable a diminution in our own strength, and will thereby bring welcome relief to many individuals'. The necessary US force in Japan had originally been established as one Marine division and four Army divisions: the arrival of BCOF would enable the release of the Marine division and its return to the US.

It had taken over three months to get the green light for the arrangements for BCOF's involvement, and four months from the original agreement in principle by the US to their participation. Apart from the political delays connected with the need to clarify other potential Allied participation, a further factor contributing to the delay was the administrative chaos in SCAP Headquarters Tokyo. The US forces had arrived as soldiers equipped for the final assault and were not prepared for their role as civil governors: and it took time to adjust to this function. Until some equilibrium was established, there was a stream of chaotic events within the headquarters for the first six months – 'false information, false messages, people hearing one thing, interpreting another, issuing instructions under the name of the Commander which later the Commander violently opposed'.[12] Indeed, years later one of MacArthur's senior staff officers went as far as to admit that in those early days they could have benefited from the assistance of experienced British colonial civil servants.[13] Whatever the reasons, the protracted nature of the inter-governmental negotiations and the delays and uncertainty which accompanied them had, as Northcott admitted, 'most adversely affected the mounting and movement of Japan of the Force'.[14]

5
The Long Wait

The units making up BCOF had been forming up in their assembly areas since September 1945, and the long delay in establishing the basis for their involvement in the occupation was tedious and dispiriting. It was not easy to maintain the initial burst of enthusiasm with which everyone had embarked on an enterprise which had seemed to combine the mystery of an unknown country with the importance of sealing the victory.

The assembly area for Headquarters – BRINDJAP – after arrival in Japan to be designated the British and Indian Division (BRINDIV) – and its component brigades was at Satpur and Mashrul Camps, outside the town of Nasik, about 90 miles northeast of Bombay. The camps were largely tented and had been used for the transit of units in past years since they were convenient for embarkation at the port of Bombay. The climate was pleasant at that time of year: the location on the edge of the south Indian plateau at an altitude of 2,000 feet made for hot days and reasonably cool nights. However, the site was treeless, extremely dusty, remote from any major city and lacking in suitable amenities for the troops, and it was therefore not a desirable place for a protracted stay.

For the British troops in particular Nasik was an uncomfortable station. Most of the reinforcements for the battalions had recently arrived in many cases on unpopular transfer from the RAF and the Royal Navy, to take the place of long-service men going home on repatriation. Nasik was their first and only taste of India and they did not like it. As one officer recalled, the soldiers'

44

'rare excursions into Bombay had opened their eyes to the
fact that as far as the British civilian community was concerned soldiers below commissioned rank didn't exist. This
the troops bitterly resented. They had come to expect more
than the brothels and arrack stews where they were expected to take their recreation'.[1]

Although their attitude toughened as time went on, they were desperately keen to leave India.

The experienced NCOs who were so vital for the training of
reinforcements to battalion standard and had postponed their repatriation to go to Japan were also dismayed by the lengthened delay.
The proximity of Nasik to Deolali, the principal departure point for
soldiers returning to the UK, increased their restlessness aand a
number withdrew their deferment and opted for repatriation.
Meanwhile, spit and polish was the order of the day as the battalions prepared to show the flag in Japan. As one NCO recalled, 'out
came the white blanco, bayonets were polished with sand until they
shone, woodwork of the Lee Enfields was gleaming with boot polish, and cap badges reflected the sun!'.[2]

The Indian battalions had a different set of problems to face.
Although they were generally glad to be back in India, and the most
fortunate of all in being able to take some leave at home, only the
Mahrattas were within easy reach of their native country. However,
they for their part had been spoilt for the tents of Mashrul by the
villas of Italy and the friendly and sometimes intimate relationships
they had formed in the Italian towns and villages. Many of the men
still used the odd Italian word in their daily speech.

But political pressures were beginning to build up. The end of
the war had made the Indian public aware of the existence of the
Indian National Army (INA) which had been recruited by the
Japanese, primarily from Indian prisoners of war in Singapore and
Malaya. Under the leadership of Subhas Chandra Bose, they had
taken part in the Burma campaign on the side of the Japanese
against their former comrades, in many cases in the cause of Indian
nationalism, but more often to escape the hardships of life as prisoners of the Japanese. The Indian Army had, of course, been aware
of the INA since 1944: as its members began to surrender or were
captured in battle, they were brought back to India and segregated
into different categories according to the gravity of the offences

known against them for action in due course. Now the time for this had come, and the Government of India announced in August 1945 that, while there would be no attempt to punish the rank and file, the leaders and those accused of atrocities would be court-martialled.

Indian Congress politicians seized on this as an opportunity to exploit animosity to British rule to the utmost. Amid emotional uproar the INA became a symbol of national unity and its heroic deeds (largely imaginary) an article of faith. When it was announced in October that the trial of the first three INA officers, all regular holders of the King's Commission in the Indian Army, was to start in November at the Red Fort in Delhi, the wave of hysterical nationalism reached new heights and the INA became identified with the cause of Congress itself. The strain on soldiers serving in the Indian Army and loyal to their oath of allegiance increased. Auchinleck said at the time 'there is a growing feeling [among the Indian ranks] of sympathy for the INA and an increasing tendency to disregard the brutalities committed by some of its members as well as the forswearing by all of them of their original allegiance'.[3]

Subsequent lenient treatment of the three officers and most other offenders, culminating in general amnesty, had beneficial political results but did nothing to alleviate the unease of the serving soldiers in their confusion of loyalties. The long delay at Nasik did not help, although its isolation reduced the effect of the unfavourable publicity. While the spirit of the combatant units remained generally high, the morale of the integrated units and headquarters troops suffered significantly.

Auchinleck's appreciation of the internal security situation in India on 1 December 1945, forwarded to the Chiefs of Staff in the UK, carried a strong sense of foreboding.[4] In his view, the Congress INA campaign had had a deeply unsettling effect on the Armed Forces generally and made them receptive to Congress doctrine. The Forces could not understand why Government had not taken firm action against the agitators and were beginning to worry about the treatment which a Congress government might mete out to those now serving. The enormous expansion of the Armed Forces during the war, with the creation of a large number of technical and administrative units, had introduced a high proportion of politically conscious and better educated men: and the possibility of a major breakdown in discipline was increased because of the great many war-promoted and inexperienced Viceroy's Commissioned Officers and NCOs. Commissioned Indian officers were particularly affected: as Auchinleck recognised, most of them were quite naturally nationalistically inclined and he thought they might be overpersuaded by Congress propaganda. It was a reflection of the oddness of the situation that Brigadier Thimayya's elder brother had been a staff officer in the INA and had been captured at Rangoon by Thimayya's brigade.

Surprisingly, the explosive disturbance caused by the Royal Indian Navy mutiny in Bombay on 19 February 1946 had little effect on the troops at Nasik, which in terms of Indian distances was close by. The mutineers were inspired by a collection of real grievances (bad food, low pay, ill-treatment by their officers) but inflamed by the added political emotions of Congress and the Muslim League. Army units had to be called in to suppress the mutiny. Before it was brought to an end on 23 February major civil disturbances had erupted in the city in sympathy with the mutineers, leading to considerable looting and damage, and over 200 killed. Fortunately it was not necessary to call on BRINDJAP resources to deal with the mutiny, although a fellow Mahratta battalion was deployed from the regimental depot at Belgaum. But the Indian Army had never had much respect for the Indian Navy at the best of times: it was an upstart service, without the tradition and continuity of the Army. The bustle of impending departure at Nasik, with the advance party already on their way to Japan, obscured any feeling of support or sympathy. Oddly enough, while the mutiny passed BCOF by without any apparent effect, it was remarked elsewhere: in 1952 Communists in Japan used the commemoration of the sixth anniversary of the mutiny as an excuse for an outbreak of violence against their own government for its acceptance of colonial rule by the Americans, which they claimed was similar to that previously existing in British India.[5]

The posting to Japan was generally welcomed by the Indian contingent, and it was seen to be a good career move for the regular officer in the Indian Army. The Indian officers knew that they had established a good record in the war and their confidence had grown as a result. The days of the British Raj were obviously numbered, and those whose experience developed further after the end of the war would clearly be in the best position to assume the leadership of a newly independent Indian Army.

As far as the Australian Army contingent was concerned, Morotai was in some ways a more pleasant place to wait than Nasik. It was a mountainous jungle-clad island just north of the Equator with a limited coastal plain under cultivation. US forces had landed there in September 1944 in a final step towards the invasion of the Philippines and it was used later in 1945 by the 7th and 9th Australian Divisions as a staging post for the campaign in Borneo. The areas occupied by the BCOF contingent had recently been vacated by US troops returning home and were mostly on the beach front. From the tent lines there was a fine view of the sea, Halmahera with its smoking volcano and a myriad of small islands. Fruit and fish were readily available. 'Every tent had its hand of bananas hanging at the tent pole, and every unit had its pet monkeys', a soldier remembered. But there were drawbacks, notably the risk of malaria and other insect-borne diseases, and Morotai was hot, humid and boring. Life under canvas was not luxurious, amenities were few, and there was no city within 1000 miles. Reminders of the war were everywhere: abandoned and rusting vehicles and equipment, Japanese prisoners engaged on labouring tasks, even a local war crimes court which the troops could attend as spectators to hear of the grisly cruelties committed by their defeated enemies.

The expectation had been that the brigade would move on to Japan shortly after assembling in October 1945, and the enforced delay was resented by the troops, many of whom had been in jungle combat for some time and had volunteered for this further task. It was strongly believed that MacArthur was purposely delaying the arrival of BCOF (although we now know that not to be true) and the troops became increasingly restive. In the words of one officer, they 'got sick of doing nothing but parade-ground type of training for which Australian troops are not noted'. In fact this constant attention to drill and turn-out resulted in a highly satisfactory standard of performance. 'We even polished the inside of the metal buckles on our chinstraps', recalled one soldier.[6]

Throughout November and December there were a large number of withdrawals from the force due to the delayed move, and by early December the brigade was under strength by over 2000 personnel. A further invitation to units in Australia for volunteers had only limited success and direct recruiting was introduced there, which attracted among others a number of ex-soldiers already discontented with civilian life. These reinforcements, however, did not join the force in Morotai but in due course went direct to Japan.

On 11 January the increasing restiveness in Morotai culminated in a protest parade mounted by the men on the brigade parade ground which acquired some fame in Australian Army history. Although it was held against the specific orders of their officers and senior NCOs, the parade was well-disciplined, properly organised complete with bands, public address system and spokesmen. Units marched on to markers formed up on the parade ground, and the drill was of a high standard. 'It was the best brigade parade ever', reported a non-participating officer.[7] A formal presentation was made of a list of questions on the continuing delay in movement to Japan and related conditions of service, after which the troops marched off in an orderly manner to their lines. In response to this the Minister of the Army, Frank Forde, visited the force on 23 January, promising that the Government would adhere to the conditions stated and that everything was being done to speed up departure. As the participants had no doubt realised, disciplinary action against an entire brigade was not feasible and it was recognised that there were good grounds for complaint. The opportunity was therefore offered for men to withdraw from the force if they wished, and a few did so. Northcott later commented that 'it was a tribute to their commanders and to the troops themselves that the wastage due to sickness and boredom was not greater'.[8]

The RAAF contingent waiting in Labuan was equally affected by the boredom and discomfort of waiting in demoralising tropical conditions without news of their departure. The situation was not helped by an unwise statement at the end of September from Air Commodore Scherger, who had been appointed Air Officer Commanding of the RAAF force for Japan, to the effect that the unit would be transferred from Borneo to Japan within a month. While they did not achieve the splendour of the Morotai parade, a number of 'stop-work' meetings took place to emphasise their discontent as the months ticked by, and the Australian press sponsored the cause of 'our forgotten airmen' with alacrity. A large number of 81 Wing personnel had in fact decided not to volunteer for Japan and were being replaced from Australia, and this created added turbulence.

However, the contingent was kept busy with the re-equipment of the squadrons with Mustang aircraft in place of their Kittyhawks, and the conversion of those pilots and ground staff who had volunteered for Japan to the new aircraft. This proved to be lengthier and more difficult than expected: the Mustang, although a first-class aircraft, had some vices, the worst of which was a tendency to swing sharply on take-off and landing because of the torque effect of the powerful Merlin engine. This led to a number of accidents (luckily none fatal) during the extended period of flying conversion and training over the period up to December.

Some Kittyhawk flying was continued by pilots who had elected for discharge or return to Australia. The last operational mission was flown on 6 October on tactical reconaissance over Borneo, when a large number of Japanese troops were sighted heading south towards Tambuna, all carrying heavy packs – part of the difficult process of concentration of surrendered Japanese personnel prior to their repatriation.

The New Zealand brigade was best placed to come to terms with the long wait. J Force, as it was created in October, had much work to do in terms of marching out all those not going to Japan and integrating the reinforcements to take their place. There was also a major task in guarding the enormous dumps of equipment being formed by whole units disbanding and going home to New Zealand. But despite the arduous Italian winter, the environment was civilised and friendly. It was no hardship to wait in and around Florence, although the interminably delayed departure lowered morale and 'added to a feeling of indifference in the expedition'.[9]

The New Zealand Government was itself becoming restless at the delay and Fraser, the Prime Minister, sent Chifley a message of impatience and concern for the ultimate value of the exercise: '. . . in view of the time which has elapsed since the first tentative announcement was made . . . and the way in which negotiations have dragged, the enthusiasm for it has flagged very considerably in New Zealand. There is a general feeling that this Force is not needed and it appears questionable whether . . . it is likely to yield any increase in British Commonwealth prestige'.[10] This was a perceptive although pessimistic assessment. However, it provoked a swift visit in January by Northcott to New Zealand to discuss the results of his conferences with MacArthur and the part the New Zealand air and army components would play in BCOF. With this encouragement and Northcott's assurances (somewhat ill-informed, as it later transpired) that the BCOF area was excellent and that it boasted good accommodation and a good climate, the New Zealand Government decided to go on. The desire to be seen as a good Commonwealth member by Britain, combined with the desire to be seen by the US as pulling its weight, overcame the doubts in the end.

But many others had similar doubts. As a Sydney paper pointed out, 'military ardour is apt to wane as war recedes into the background'. BCOF should have followed the Americans into Japan within two or three months at the latest, and the delays implied that it was neither needed nor wanted. But 'prestige demands that the armed forces of the British Empire, which next to those of the US played the leading role in overturning Japan, shall be strongly represented in that country . . . the Japanese must not be left with the idea that the Americans alone defeated them'.[11]

6

On Japanese Soil

In accordance with the Northcott-MacArthur agreement, the different formations of BCOF finally started their long and separate journeys to Japan in February 1946. The Royal Navy port partly arrived by sea in Kure on 1 February (the day after the agreement was announced publicly) to prepare for the working of the port for BCOF. Advance parties from Bombay and Morotai followed by air, and throughout February, March, April and May the troopships and aircraft carriers began to arrive in an intricate pattern from the East Indies, from India, Burma and Ceylon, from Malaya and Singapore, from Italy, and from Australia and New Zealand. It was a complicated and elaborate feat of organisation and because of the adverse weather conditions at that time of year, especially in the North Pacific, many of the troops had an eventful voyage to Japan.[1] 'We crossed the Equator five times', recalled one Australian soldier sailing up from Sydney.

As their ships slowly wound their way through the wintry waters of the Inland Sea towards Kure, the troops huddled deeper into their newly-issued greatcoats and wondered what the future held for them in this mysterious and defeated country. At the same time there was a feeling of great relief that the need for a final invasion had been averted: most shared the emotions of a sergeant in the Dorsets who said '. . . as the numerous small islands slid past I could only . . . think how grateful I was that the dropping of the atom bomb had saved the lives of thousands of Allied troops who would have had to storm these island bastions of Japan'.[2] The view of the intensive cultivation and the steeply terraced hillsides provided another unexpected insight. 'It's no wonder', men said, 'that they wanted more room.'

The sea was always busy with a cloud of small fishing boats, but the first Japanese sighted at close quarters was usually the pilot, whose little boat would appear suddenly out of the mist to run alongside, and his busy upholstered figure would clamber up the ladder to the deck and then to the bridge. It seemed odd that the invaders were still dependent on the invaded to find their way ashore.

In contrast to the scenic beauty of the Inland Sea and the coast itself, Kure, the port designated as the port of entry and base port for BCOF, was a dispiriting sight. High explosive and incendiary bombing raids had destroyed the naval base, the largest in Japan, together with much of the town. Along the waterfront, in the words of a newly-arrived Australian, 'the battered remains of half a dozen warships, including two battleships, stood out against the foreshore, itself a tangled mass of churned-up earth and masonry, festooned with twisted steel . . . Kure is defunct'.[3] The winter snow accentuated the desolation of the scene. The docks, however, were coming back to life and work was already in hand on the disarming and refitting of Japanese naval vessels to render them capable of taking part in the repatriation of Japanese surrendered personnel from the different theatres of war.

Hiroshima, the capital of the Prefecture and 20 miles from Kure, was a vastly more depressing sight of complete demolition. The only buildings still standing were those of reinforced concrete and even they were badly cracked and damaged by the blast. Otherwise the remainder of what had been the city was a wilderness of broken glass, tiles, furniture, pillars, graves and shrines. Trees were charred stumps and steel electric lamp poles heeled over at crazy angles. Sightseers were particularly struck by the vast number of rusted fire-scorched bicycle frames and melted masses of bottles. The rubble of the devastated city had been neatly piled on the blocks between the roads to allow clear passage for traffic; trams were running, crowded to overflowing; and an active shanty town was springing up on the ruined blocks, especially around the railway station.

As the Australian brigade, the first complete formation to arrive hard on the heels of the naval port party, began to take over from the US Eighth Army in the various occupation locations in the

Prefecture, it found the discomfort of unheated barracks, aggravated by snow on the hills and the bleak climate, and the complete lack of amenities in the area a sharp disappointment. The men had spent many months, some even years, in tropical heat and the contrast was an unpleasant shock.

In the middle of the general gloom, one officer had a particular consolation on arrival: he had brought with him the entire contents of a Japanese army pay office which he had acquired in the Bougainville campaign, and found to his delight from the reception officers that the money was at that time still legal tender in occupied Japan.[4]

The first units of the British Commonwealth Base which was to support and maintain the Force arrived at the same time as the Australian brigade, and started to establish the supply and transport organisation needed. Because of the serious effect on the troops of the continuing uncertainty and delay, Northcott had accepted the obvious difficulty and had taken a gamble in moving combat troops in ahead of the staff organisation required to administer them.[5] But as other contingents began to arrive, it swiftly became obvious that accommodation and facilities were inadequate for the 37,000 troops of BCOF. The earlier reconnaissances had been poor and superficial; they had assumed that sufficient space would be available in the Prefecture for men and *matériel* and had taken no account of the sorry condition of buildings and the dire state of communications. The situation would have been even worse if the force had mustered the 43,000 troops originally envisaged in the discussion with the Americans.

Within a few days of taking over, therefore, Northcott decided to press for the extension of his 'somewhat limited and devastated area'.[6] After considerable discussion with JCOSA and SCAP, the Prefectures of Yamaguchi, Okayama, Shimane and Tottori, and the entire island of Shikoku consisting of the Prefectures of Ehime, Kochi, Kagawa and Tokushima, were added to BCOF's area of responsibility. SCAP, having ensured beyond question that BCOF took no part in the military government, did not object to US troops exchanging routine occupation duties for the return home.

The airfield at Iwakuni in Yamaguchi Prefecture, just over the border from Hiroshima, had already been designated as BCOF's air port of entry for BCAIR, the Force's air component, which was

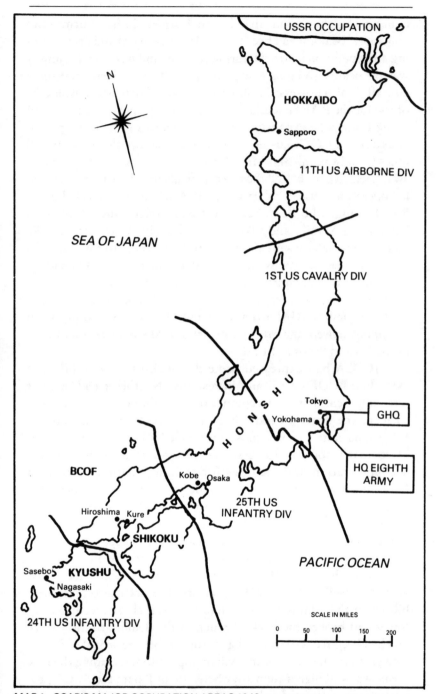

MAP 1. SCAP'S MAJOR OCCUPATION AREAS 1946

coming together from airfields in Borneo, India, Burma and Singapore. Iwakuni had been a large Japanese naval and army training and operational airfield during the war, and its concrete runway was the nearest to Hong Kong which could accept heavy transport aircraft. It also possessed a slipway for flying boats which would be of use for the RAF Sunderlands operating transport services out of Hong Kong. The expansion of the BCOF area now firmly placed Iwakuni in BCOF's custody, and added the airfields of Bofu (30 miles from Iwakuni) and Miho (on the north coast nearly 100 miles away), which gave BCOF the three airfields they had always wanted for operational use. The arrival of BCAIR's aircraft was led by 81 RAAF Wing, who flew their Mustangs directly into Bofu from Labuan via Manila and Okinawa. Unhappily 3 aircraft from 82 Squadron were lost with all pilots on the final approach in treacherous weather conditions into this unfamiliar airfield. 14 Squadron RNZAF arrived complete with their 24 Corsairs, stores and transport by sea on the carrier HMS *Glory* and went on to Iwakuni, while 4 Squadron RIAF from India and 11 and 17 Squadrons from Singapore arrived similarly by the carrier HMS *Vengeance* and were offloaded and flown to Miho.

JCOSA had expressed some doubts on the desirability of extending BCOF's area, and in response Northcott had made it forcefully clear that the acceptance of the additional areas was vital to meet the Force's needs. It had now been realised that the Hiroshima/Kure area was most unsuitable for locating large bodies of combat troops. It was essential to move to areas with better accommodation and facilities for training. Within Hiroshima Prefecture it was impossible to provide satisfactory quarters for the greater part of the New Zealand brigade, and there were no barracks for several British and Indian units. Many other units were in buildings unsuitable for other than temporary occupancy.

At the same time, there was no question of needing any increase in the size of the force. The acceptance of the additional areas was well within BCOF's capacity. The occupation responsibilities in the additional areas had been largely reduced: the US forces had broken the back of much of the demilitarisation work and had been reduced to small garrisons before the arrival of BCOF. The proportion of troops to civilian population, including the new areas, was still higher than anywhere else in Japan: the BCOF proportion was estimated to be 1 : 500 in comparison with the average

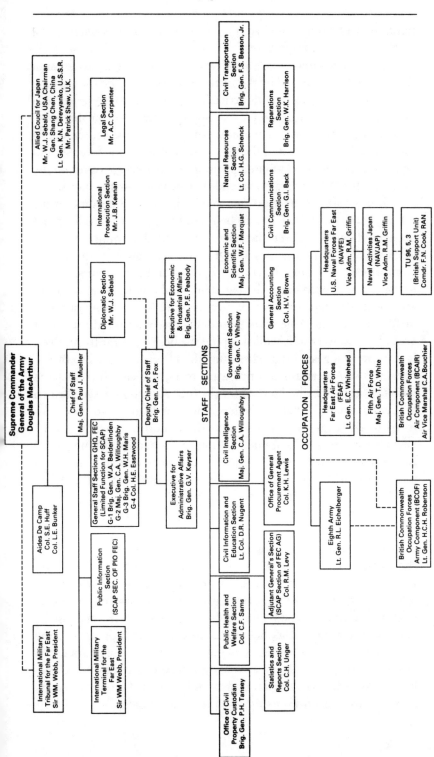

Fig. 6.1 SCAP Organisation

figure of 1 : 800 in the US zones, which went up to as much as 1 : 1100 in the largest prefectures.

Northcott's impatience at JCOSA's questioning of the decision was probably aggravated by the silent suggestion that he should have known all this before BCOF arrived, and he vigorously rejected a proposal that the Governments should be consulted on the issue. 'Government policy in the matter was approved in the acceptance of the original agreement and the local distribution of the force should be for my decision as I am in a position to take into account all the factors.'[7] JCOSA backed down and there was no further query.

But the size of the total area now to be covered meant that the different units of BCOF had to be spread thinly, with little contact between them. Moreover, the larger area added nothing in the way of city facilities or amenities. BCOF's area remained provincial and comfortless, far from the centres of power and entertainment, and much of it had been badly damaged by bombing. Its rural isolation and the devastated condition of its cities gave rise to many rumours in BCOF that the Americans had deliberately awarded the worst area of Japan to BCOF, while keeping the best parts for themselves. It was even suggested that Hiroshima had been allocated to BCOF because the Americans did not want to be too closely associated with the target they had picked for the first atom bomb. One British officer commented that 'we believed that the British had been banished to the edge of Japan so that the Americans would not be embarrassed by our discipline, bearing and general air of purpose'.[8] An Australian officer said 'we soon learnt that we had a thankless job in one of the worst areas in Japan . . . our part in the Allied occupation force was to be the Cinderella'.[9]

Despite these assumptions, the choice had not in fact been left to the whim of the Americans. Northcott later explained that his discussions with MacArthur had originally examined three options: the northern island of Hokkaido, the Kobe-Osaka area, and Hiroshima Prefecture.[10] All of them satisfied the basic criteria, among which the most important was the possession of a working port and usable airfields. Hokkaido had been rejected because its climate was regarded as being too cold for the Indians and the Australians. (It would in fact also have been even more remote than Honshu). The Kobe-Osaka area had been considered by Northcott himself to have had too large a population to be controlled by BCOF. This had left Hiroshima as the initial choice.

Again, at the time of considering the take-over of further areas in March, the British had advised JCOSA that politically and commercially it would be preferable to include the Kobe-Osaka area rather than the territories to the north west of the present area which were being suggested.[11] Northcott was asked to discuss the possibility of extending to Kobe, Osaka and Kyoto and, on 18 March, received the American reaction: they had no objection to him taking over the areas, but the ports had not been cleared of mines. Clearance had been left to the Japanese, but they had made little progress. Northcott still had his own objections dating from the original discussions with SCAP. Because the areas were so densely populated, he thought they were certain to give trouble should disturbances arise from economic reasons, which would probably demand additional resources. He was anxious that BCOF should be allotted contiguous areas, to avoid the administrative difficulty and the complications of control of the civilian population which would arise if prefectures were split between separate forces. This attitude was unfortunate. While Northcott's objections may have had some military validity, his reluctance in fact cost the Commonwealth their chance for a location of real advantage which might well have provided the political and commercial benefits impossible to secure from the rural isolation of Hiroshima. It is of interest in passing to note that either Northcott's ideas on Japan's geography were shaky or that he wished to give the impression of a larger fiefdom than he actually had. His valedictory despatch drew attention to the fact that 'BCOF occupied half of Honshu, and Shikoku island', whereas the actual area of Honshu which the force occupied was not much more than a quarter.[12]

So the opportunity to press for the more desirable platform desired by the British for the cultivation of their interests was not pursued, and BCOF's formations were deployed in their allocated areas of western Honshu and Shikoku. The Australian brigade, as first arrivals, were dispersed throughout Hiroshima Prefecture, while HQ BCOF together with the British Commonwealth Base, itself largely staffed by Australians at the outset, remained in the Kure-Hiro area. The British and Indian Division (BRINDIV), which arrived next, was allocated to Okayama, Shimane, Tottori and the island of Shikoku: and Yamaguchi was allotted to the New Zealand brigade, which was the last to arrive.

Whatever the difficulties of accommodation and the discom-

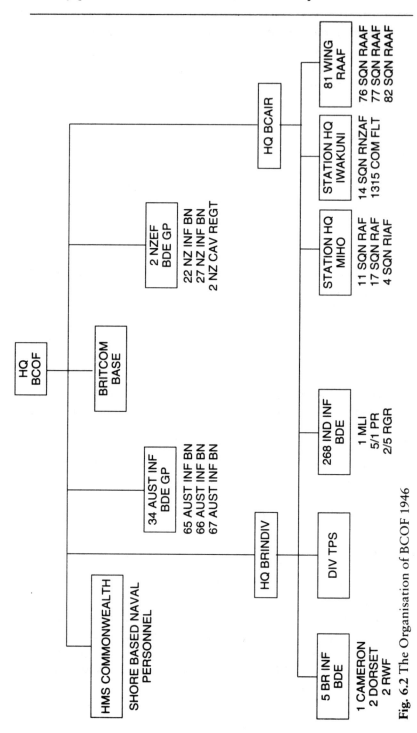

Fig. 6.2 The Organisation of BCOF 1946

fort of the weather, there was a feeling of great satisfaction within the Force as each contingent finally arrived. A sergeant in the Dorsets recalled that when he and his fellow sergeants escorted the regimental colours down the troopship gangway on to Japanese soil to head the battalion's march into Kure, 'it was the proudest moment of my life'.[13]

Hiroshima and Kure were both depressing scenes of ruin and destruction, although in the case of the latter the picture was relieved by the pretty little grey-tiled houses of its suburbs. In fact, after the first sightseeing curiosity had been satisfied at Hiroshima, many officers and men preferred to avoid the town, not because there was any fear of radiation (the danger was unknown at that time) but because of the doubts and depression it caused. However, the remainder of BCOF's area was largely rural, a patchwork of villages set in valleys separated by steep hills, each with its neat terraces of cultivation; and a complicated coastline of little inlets and tiny beaches with a string of fishing hamlets.

As the units passed through Kure and Hiro, the nearby BCOF base, and on to their different destinations, the poor state of internal communications in the country was appreciated for the first time. Trains were the best means of transport. They were invariably crowded, with Japanese hanging out of doorways and lying on the top of carriages; but special coaches were provided for occupation troops. The roads were in a very bad state and the poor surfaces and the weaknesses of the bridges in the countryside meant that the brand-new armoured vehicles of 7 Cavalry and the specially-formed Australian Armoured Car Squadron could only be used on the short stretches of bitumen in town areas. Experience soon showed that even the relatively light weight of a ¼-ton jeep would often smash through a typical wooden bridge and cut the road until repairs had been effected. Long detours were often unavoidable and in one typical case a journey of 150 miles was required to cover a direct distance of 80 miles. Such difficulty of communication accentuated the remoteness and separation of the units.

This in many ways appealed to unit commanders. In the case of the Mahrattas, who were stationed at Hamada in Shimane Prefecture on the north coast, their Brigade Headquarters were at Matsue, 80 miles along the coast to the north east. Since they were normally used to being within four miles of their brigade headquarters at the most, this gave rise to an unusual freedom and independence.

Even within battalions there was a wide spread of deployment. For example, 67 Australian Infantry Battalion had its headquarters east of Hiroshima, but its companies were detached: at an early stage one was as far west as Otake, 40 miles from the city. With a local brewery dedicated to supplying the needs of that company, and a fleet of small motor boats available for its use, the absence of conventional amenities was not noticed and the independence of action was welcomed.

By June 1946 the initial deployment of BCOF was complete.[14] In general, units were located on or near the coast because of the mountainous nature of the interior. The coastal roads were better and water-borne transport was available. Protection of the coastline was to be an important task. HQ BCOF itself, together with two companies of 65 Australian Infantry Battalion and the Australian military hospital, was established on Etajima, a small island in the Inland Sea off Kure, in the buildings of the former Japanese Naval Academy.

HQ 34 Australian Brigade, which was responsible for Hiroshima Prefecture, was at Hiro, together with the bulk of 66 Battalion, the armoured car squadron, and supporting troops. 65 Battalion was based at Onomichi, and 67 Battalion was at Kataichi with the Australian field battery. The remaining Australian infantry companies, with various supporting units, were deployed along the coast of Hiroshima Prefecture at Fukuyama and Hiroshima itself.

The British Commonwealth Base (BRITCOM Base), the centre for supply and administrative services, by now a substantial unit with a strength of over 6,700 officers and men, was established at Kure, together with HQ BCOF Signals and the Indian military hospital, as well as the Royal Naval Port Party.

BRINDIV was responsible for Okayama, Shimane and Tottori Prefectures and the island of Shikoku. Its divisional headquarters, divisional troops and support units, including a field battery and the British military hospital, were located at Okayama. Okayama was a substantial city and major railway junction, but it had been badly firebombed, and the whole of the city centre had been burnt to the ground. (One officer described it as a great doughnut of the American variety surrounded by rice fields). 7 Cavalry, the divisional armoured car regiment, was stationed at Kurashiki and Uno in Okayama Prefecture.

268 Indian Infantry Brigade Headquarters were located at

Matsue, and the brigade was deployed throughout Shimane, Tottori and Okayama Prefectures, with the Mahrattas at Hamada, the Punjabis at Tottori city, and the Gurkhas at Okayama city as divisional reserve alongside BRINDIV Headquarters. Shimane and Tottori were real backwaters, and their significance to the occupation rested on two factors: they were food surplus areas and helped to feed the starving cities, but with black market channels competing fiercely with legitimate government sources of supply; and they faced Korea and were the natural target for illegal entry by Koreans.

5 British Brigade was deployed throughout the island of Shikoku, another remote rural area considered to be the least developed of all Japan. Brigade headquarters were at Kochi: the Dorsets were at Gomen, the Welch Fusiliers at Tokushima, and the Camerons split between Kochi and Matsuyama. Supporting troops, including an Indian field battery, were at Wadashima and Takamatsu.

Yamaguchi Prefecture was occupied by the New Zealand brigade, now known as 2 New Zealand Expeditionary Force (2 NZEF) Japan. Its headquarters were at Chofu at the south western tip of the main island of Honshu, and its infantry battalions(22 and 27 Battalions), its cavalry regiment(2 NZ Div Cav)and various supporting units were scattered round the coast of the prefecture from Otake in the east to Hagi in the north west, with the bulk of 27 Battalion inland at Yamaguchi city. The New Zealand military hospital was located at Kiwa.

Much of BCAIR was concentrated in Yamaguchi Prefecture, at the air bases at Iwakuni and Bofu. Iwakuni housed BCAIR Headquarters, 14 Squadron RNZAF and the RAF communications flight, while 81 Wing RAAF was located 45 miles to the west at Bofu, with 76, 77 and 82 Squadrons RAAF. 11 and 17 Squadrons RAF and 4 Squadron RIAF were at the third station at Miho, on the north coast in Tottori Prefecture, about 100 miles from Iwakuni.

The territory now occupied by BCOF covered nine of Japan's 46 prefectures, with an area of 20,000 square miles. This was about one-seventh of the total land area of the country, and had a population variously estimated at between 10 and 15 million, out of a total population of about 80 million. BCOF's strength at the outset was 35,436, and rose to over 37,000 at its peak, which was around 20 per cent of SCAP's total occupation forces at the time. Although the original agreement with the Americans had dictated that the various components of BCOF fell under the operational control of the different land, sea and air commands of the US in Japan, the Force still retained a cohesion of its own. It was a well-equipped, experienced and well-trained formation, self-contained, with its armoured units and artillery, its own air force, and its own infrastructure, with occasional naval support. It represented a unique combination of Commonwealth countries drawn together for a unique purpose. What in fact was it going to do?

7

The Task

SCAP's military government plan, which was subsequently append-
ed to BCOF's Occupation Instruction No.4 of 26 March 1946, said
that military control of Japan had been established not only to carry
into effect the surrender terms but also to further the achievement of
'the ultimate objectives of the occupation'. These objectives and the
means to achieve them were set out at the beginning.[1] Although
SCAP's actual planning in detail for the occupation had been characterised as 'the product of a number of sometimes conflicting and
largely autonomous planning agencies and agents, rather than
deriving from any single or coordinated source', the main thrust of
MacArthur's plan for Japan was clear: the demolition of militarism
and the construction of a new and economically healthy nation
founded on democratic principles.[2] This was to be achieved by
retaining the Emperor as a constitutional monarch along British
lines and by preserving and working through the established structure of government.

The more limited objectives of BCOF were stated differently
and more briefly early in the preparation of the Force. They were to
represent worthily the British Commonwealth in the occupation of
Japan; to maintain and enhance British Commonwealth prestige
and influence in the eyes of the Japanese and our Allies; and to
illustrate to, and impress upon, the Japanese people as far as possible the democratic way and purpose in life. They were idealistic
objectives which assumed that BCOF would actually be in a position to exert the influence and set the example desired.

General Northcott, after inspecting BRINDJAP in India in

65

January 1946, had stated the task in more soldierly terms, yet with a continuing regard for the ideals involved. He said

> 'Our job in Japan is to play our part in winning the peace which is just as important as the task we had in winning the war . . . For the first time we form a completely integrated British Commonwealth Force . . . We have to take over the occupation of a large area in southern Japan called the Hiroshima Prefecture. It is an area stiff with armaments, coastal defences, ammunition works, naval workshops and so on. The whole area is to be demilitarised and we have to do it. We have to supervise the Japanese who will do the labour and see that they do not put anything over us. It is a man-size job and it will take us some time to complete it. Another most important task which is the object of this force is to occupy this country and to show the Japanese what it means to enjoy the personal freedom we know but of which they have not the slightest understanding . . .'

and he concluded 'As representatives of the British Empire your behaviour, discipline, military efficiency and the whole manner in which you comport yourselves both on parade and off duty will be a great example to this cowed and defeated nation'.[3]

The actual military role allotted to BCOF was specified as the safeguarding of all Allied installations and of all Japanese installations awaiting demilitarisation; the demilitarisation and disposal of Japanese installations and armaments; and the military control of the BCOF area, but excluding military government. This last limitation was more specifically defined on 7 March 1946 in one of BCOF's earliest instructions, which made it clear that all military government in the BCOF zone was to be carried out exclusively by US military government units operating under HQ Eighth Army. It was this key policy restriction which was to deprive BCOF of the opportunity to play a full part in developing the wider objectives of the Allied occupation.

Military government at the local level was in fact something of a misnomer. The Japanese government machinery had as a central pillar of US policy been kept in place for the administration of the country, and functioned on SCAP instructions (SCAPINS) issued by MacArthur and his staff in Tokyo. (Over 6,000 SCAPINS emerged

from Tokyo during the period of the occupation, written in a special
jargon which the irreverent called SCAPINESE). Apart from some
minor administrative functions, local military government units
were charged primarily with a surveillance task, to ensure that
SCAPINS were properly implemented at the working level in the
prefectures.

In the BCOF area the units were 76 Military Government
Company, based in Kure, which supervised Hiroshima, Shimane
and Yamaguchi prefectures; and 91 Military Government Company,
based in Takamatsu, which supervised Shikoku island. BCOF units
were reminded that it would be the commanding officers of these
military government units who would procure from the Japanese
Government for BCOF all necessary labour, accommodation, ware-
housing and storage space, although BCOF would be allowed to
procure labour direct from Japanese labour offices when the need
arose and no military government unit was available.

In fact BCOF's first job, before it could address any of its military tasks, was an intensely practical one. The most pressing need
was the improvement of the poor standard of living of the Force.
Accommodation was generally in ramshackle wooden barrack
buildings with no heating and often with holes in the walls and
ceilings. In most cases they lacked lighting and proper sanitary and
kitchen facilities. Some had been unoccupied for up to nine months.
The arrival of BCOF unfortunately coincided with directives from
SCAP which withdrew from occupation forces the right of 'pre-
emption' of supplies and materials (that is to say, the right which
had existed up till then to grab whatever was required without for-
mality), and prohibited the use of timber by occupation troops –
both considerable handicaps to the speedy improvement of conditions. As late arrivals, BCOF units were sensitive to the comparison
with the US forces. 'We didn't like seeing the Americans well set up
and materials going to the Japanese, while we lived in the greatest
discomfort', recorded one battalion commander.[4]

It took many weeks and the efforts of many hundred Japanese
labourers under supervision to restore the buildings to a minimum
standard. A major works programme was subsequently established
to enhance existing buildings to the desired level of acceptability,
and to construct new permanent barracks for 25,000 all ranks, with
materials, labour and furnishings to be supplied by the Japanese
Government. This was a considerable challenge to the specialist

engineer units and also to unit quartermasters, who found themselves engaged in construction works of a size they had never dreamt
of before: it was an exciting time for the professionals.

In June 1946 Northcott left BCOF to take up the less stressful
and more prestigious appointment of Governor of New South
Wales, with a luxurious official residence in a uniquely beautiful
location on the north shore of Sydney Harbour, an improvement
even over his quarter on the pretty island of Etajima, opposite Kure
in the Inland Sea. He had been greatly respected as a gentlemanly
soldier, a man of honour and discretion with an orderly mind,
although perhaps a little dour. His determination to visit and speak
to as many of the units destined for BCOF as possible during the
long wait had been highly regarded by the troops. Some of his officers had thought he appeared apologetic about his lack of command
experience in battle, but his personal skills were never in doubt.[5]
Now he had become the first Australian to be appointed as governor
of an Australian state.

Northcott's early departure only seven months after taking up
the post of Commander-in-Chief, and only three months after
arrival in Japan, reflected a feeling in Canberra that, once the original agreement had been reached with MacArthur, his gifts justified
a wider field of deployment than a limited military environment:
and Chifley decided that he should be released from BCOF for the
appointment. Northcott was surprised, but accepted his new
responsibilities willingly and his subsequent success in the post,
which he held until 1957, undoubtedly encouraged the appointment
of other Australian-born governors.

He was replaced on 16 June by Lieutenant General Horace
Robertson, who was an experienced and well-decorated commander
with a record stretching back to the First World War, and with more
recent service in the Middle East and the Pacific in the Second World
War. His last appointment had been GOC 6th Australian Division
in Wewak. 'Red Robbie' (so-called because of his flaming red hair
and moustache) was a very different kettle of fish from Northcott.
The two commanders' hobbies as they recorded them in 'Who's
Who' gave an amusing but accurate clue to their different personal-
ities: Northcott listed gardening and bowls, while Robertson quoted
game fishing and rifle shooting. Robertson was an ambitious, arrogant and egotistical commander who relished 'cutting a dash, with
his glinting monocle and swaggering walk'.[6] He had in his varied

career acquired a reputation for high-handedness and intolerance, and his arrival was greeted with some trepidation and disquiet by those who knew him.[7] There were many stories about his insistence on protocol and respect: entire cinema performances, for instance, had been cancelled because the soldier audiences had not stood to attention on the general's arrival; junior officers daring to address him would be completely ignored. Officers who had served with him in the desert said scathingly that he was the author of two books: one was called 'Famous people who have met me', and the other 'How I would defeat Rommel'. But his forceful personality gave BCOF a needed impetus at a difficult time.

Northcott was able to say in his valedictory despatch that the deployment of the Force had been achieved successfully.[8] BRIT-COM Base in Kure was functioning satisfactorily in spite of inadequate accommodation for stores and personnel, and the enlarged area of occupation had been taken over without difficulty. The administrative task of welding together the various national land and air contingents was complicated enough, if only in terms of the different procedures in operation: for example, a military policeman checking drivers' work tickets had to be prepared to cope with any one of twelve different forms.

The arrangements for command and control of BCOF by the novel JCOSA organisation in Australia produced a vastly higher degree of complication. Under JCOSA the executive responsibility for the maintenance and administration of the Force lay with Australia, but requisitions had to be passed from Australia to the other countries concerned for special items such as Indian food-stuffs and uniforms, and for reinforcements as and when they became necessary. There was uncomfortable jockeying for position and competition for authority between the Australian Chiefs and the representatives of Britain, New Zealand and India who togeth-er made up JCOSA. From the BCOF point of view, it could be frustrating. Northcott noted that, with at least four Governments, their Chiefs of Staff, their Treasuries and their other Departments of State being directly concerned, decisions on policy matters were subject to a delay of at least six weeks.

In May a small unit had been set up in Tokyo under the name of the British Commonwealth Sub Area Tokyo (BRICOSAT), to coordinate all BCOF elements in the Tokyo – Yokohama area (prin-cipally the guard battalion) and to provide logistic support for the

Commonwealth missions there. This was a tiresome additional commitment, complicated by civilian arrivals for which BCOF had not been organised. By March 1947 there were 12 British Commonwealth civil missions to be looked after, including the Commonwealth members of the Allied Council for Japan and their staffs, and the Australian Economic and Scientific Mission, in addition to the normal diplomatic representatives.

It was an uncomfortable time for the troops for a long while. Amenities were limited. All their rations had to be provided from Australia in accordance with the sensible SCAP directive which prohibited the occupation forces from using local sources, and the supply of food was unreliable. The hunger and living conditions of the Japanese themselves were 'bloody horrendous', said one Australian infantryman. 'They were living under rubble like rabbits.'[9] Communications other than by train were appalling. Leave hostels and centres were non-existent. Morale in those early months was low.

Complaints began to mount both within the Force and outside. In July 1946 a visiting Australian banker was reported in the press as saying that Kure was a shambles and that the Commander-in-Chief was 'terribly worried'.[10] The British forces' lot was 'a pretty sad one' compared with that of the Americans. Press correspondents provided wide publicity for the poor living conditions. 'A walk through some of the British barracks reminds one of a tour through a gaol', said one reporter.[11] The diet was bad. Senior officers were criticised for living in luxurious accommodation completely detached from their men. There was no news and no entertainment. A soldier writing home complained of 'living virtually under jungle conditions'.[12]

The lack of amenities was particularly acute with the Australians in the Kure base area, who compared themselves unfavourably not only with the Americans but also with the British, who already had service clubs in operation. They suffered from living in the ruins of a devastated dock area; they frequently had to work long hours while ships were unloaded; and their constant routine work in the Base prevented them from enjoying the leave or temporary change of station available to troops in other locations. 'In our men', said one officer on his return to Australia in July 1946, 'their shabby clothes, their limited amenities, their drive to defeat idleness by adventures into prohibited darkness and its dangers . . .

have produced and will produce a sense of inferiority working to the discredit of Australia.'[13]

On taking over from Northcott, Robertson quickly came to appreciate the effect of these conditions on his other problem areas. 'The most pressing need of BCOF', he said, 'is amenities – not the amenities of gifts for individual soldiers, but the civilised surroundings which keep men normal'.[14] The drive to improve existing barracks and build new ones was given new impetus. Action was put in hand to provide leave centres and clubs, and forces' newspaper and radio facilities were set up. But the most important advance was the approval given in mid-1946 for wives and their families to join their menfolk in Japan. Existing houses were taken over from the Japanese for their accommodation and a programme was set in hand for the construction of new housing estates purpose-built for family occupation. Although there were delays in implementing the organisation, the first British and Indian wives arrived in Japan in late 1946 and were followed by wives from Australia in March 1947. (It was ironic that the British gave priority to families to move to Japan from Palestine and India, because of the concern over their security in the unsettled conditions prevailing in those British-protected territories: occupied Japan was considered safer!) The New Zealand Government declined to allow families to join their forces, perhaps foreseeing that the occupation might come to an end earlier than this might suggest.

At the outset there were substantial military tasks to be tackled. Demilitarisation was an important and immediate requirement. There was an immense amount of military equipment, ammunition and warlike stores in the BCOF area and the task of tracing, identification and disposal was a lengthy and complicated process. Besides warehouses and dumps, huge quantities of explosives were stacked in tunnels and caves in the hills. Maps of some of these were supplied by the Japanese, but others had to be searched for and found by infantry patrols and then transported to destruction sites, where the work was carried out by Japanese under BCOF supervision. By August 1946 36 ammunition dumps had been reported in the BCOF area, containing over 225,000 tons of bulk explosives, projectiles and bombs, as well as seven dumps containing about 17,000 tons of war gases, including mustard gas.[15] Within the first few months a total of over 75,000 tons of ammunition were found and destroyed by burning or dumping at sea. A special 2,500 ton ship was acquired later for the disposal of mustard-gas and lewisite filled shells, bombs and containers at sea.

The disposal of naval equipment was another significant task. Commonwealth naval vessels destroyed 25 submarines, including 4 large ocean-going types, by sinking them in the deep water of the Bungo Strait by gunfire or demolition charges; while 203 complete midget submarines, 65 partly-built submarines and over 500 gun barrels were found, collected and cut up for scrap. In addition, thousands of tons of stores and equipment, including 4,000 machine tools, were located in 'bewildering mixed dumps'. Some were taken into use by BCOF and some were deemed to be suitable for reparations, while a great deal was handed back to the Japanese Home Ministry for civilian use in accordance with SCAP instructions.

Demilitarisation was a specific assignment which could be dealt with and accomplished. It was sometimes hazardous but, for the troops involved, a clearly necessary job which made them feel that they were making a positive and valuable contribution to the occupation, even though it sometimes went to extreme lengths. 'One of our duties', reported a Welch Fusilier, 'was disposing of samurai swords into the sea. It was forbidden to keep them'.[16] It seemed a terrible waste, particularly when many other units were later allowed to retain them as souvenirs.

The other immediate task to be undertaken – the supervision of the three repatriation centres at ports in the BCOF area, at Ujina (the port of Hiroshima), Senzaki and Otake – was an equally important one. These centres were run by Japanese civilian staff under the Ministry of Health and Social Welfare, but were guarded and overseen by companies of either Australian or New Zealand infantry, in whose respective brigade areas the centres were located. About 700,000 Japanese surrendered personnel, including civilians from overseas territories which had been occupied by the Japanese, passed through the BCOF repatriation centres – 350,000 through Ujina, 100,000 through Senzaki and 250,000 through Otake. About 65,000 of these and thousands of others formerly resident in Japan were then repatriated outwards to their original homes in China, Formosa, Korea and the Ryukyu islands, often against their will and by compulsion.

BCOF had to supply guards on the trains carrying the outgoing families from their former Japanese homes to the repatriation centres when the trains entered the BCOF area, to ensure their safe delivery: and this sometimes distressing duty lasted until November 1946, when it was taken over by the Japanese civil police. In the early days the consignments occasionally included suspected war criminals being returned for trial to the scene of their crimes, which gave the guards a sense of quiet satisfaction, although it was often difficult to visualise these sombre-suited civilians with their horn-rimmed spectacles and homburg hats as instruments of violence and terror.

The surrendered personnel being returned to Japan were carried in special shipping made available by SCAP. Initially it was intended that they should all be Japanese ships, but in view of the shortage of these, additional ships were made available by the US. The fleet engaged on this task was a motley collection ranging from battered Japanese aircraft carriers with gaping bomb holes in their flight decks to rusty American Liberty ships. At times the congestion at the ports was such that there were up to six ships fully loaded standing off waiting to discharge their cargoes to the repatriation centres. These human cargoes were often in an advanced state of deterioration. A British officer visiting one such ship reported

'. . . this ship carried officers and men from one of the infantry battalions in Borneo. Practically all the men were suffering from malnutrition, and dysentery and such-like diseases . . . We met a major, the officer commanding the troops on board, and the chief medical officer, who told us that during the fortnight's voyage 25 men had died, the twenty fifth that morning. We were taken down to the mess decks where the men were living, and I felt physically sick at what I saw. Into a small deck were crowded like sardines hundreds upon hundreds of Japs – yellow, bloated in some cases, withered in others . . . huddled, some with blankets over their shoulders, some eating their rice cakes from mess tins with chop sticks . . . like animals, unshaven and inhumanly ugly. The sight, however, was not a quarter as bad as the smell . . . All the troops were the same and I was again assured that this troopship was very undercrowded compared with most'.[17]

Sometimes there were unusual passengers who were better off than the others. On one occasion an Australian officer boarding a

Japanese carrier at Otake, with its giant hangar packed with soldiers, was conducted to a wardroom full of naval officers and offered a glass of beer. Soon afterwards, a Japanese army general bustled into the wardroom, wearing several rows of medal ribbons, with a group of his staff officers in attendance, each making a studied entrance with a smile. On seeing the Australian, the general stopped, and his officers formed a circle around him, hiding him from view. When a moment later they fell back, releasing him to full view again, his rows of ribbons had vanished, leaving only the loops which had supported them. High rank still elicited protection among the Japanese, but found no favour with the Australians. When on disembarkation the general tried to use two of his batmen to carry his kit, he was abruptly told by the nearest guard to carry it himself.[18]

When a voyage was less than six days, the personnel were quarantined for a further six days on arrival in Japan. In all other cases it was assumed that diseases would have become apparent before return. On disembarkation all personnel were counted and checked against nominal rolls and then examined by customs and intelligence personnel. War criminals were identified when possible and were handed over to the War Crimes Commission in Tokyo. All drugs (and there was always a good deal of opium), excessive quantities of tobacco, badges of rank and Allied equipment were confiscated. There followed a medical inspection which included a DDT spray and vaccination. All personnel were then sent off by special trains and their discharge was completed on reaching their destination. In many cases those returning had had no news from home for years, and maps were made available showing the areas devastated by bombing so that they could see whether their homes still existed. If they did not, an alternative destination was determined. The process was well-organised and seemed to work satisfactorily.

The occupation troops were the first visible sign to the returning Japanese of the defeat of their country. It was considered essential in BCOF that the troops carried themselves as conquerors, well turned out, strict but fair. Japanese discipline was impressive: all Japanese officers and soldiers were required to salute Allied personnel in uniform and it was common for an Australian private soldier to be saluted and bowed to at a range of several hundred yards across the expanse of a parade ground.

Japanese soldiers had, of course, been brought up to believe that death in battle for the Emperor was the highest form of honour to which they could aspire, and that to become a prisoner was by contrast the worst kind of dishonour that could be experienced, and indeed should in the ultimate by avoided by suicide. It helped the repatriates to overcome their instinctive shame and the shock of the circumstances of their return to see the many Japanese notices of welcome and to hear the softly repeated '*Go-kuro sama deshita*' (thank you for all your trouble) from the women volunteers handing out tea at the centres. The compliance of the surrendered personnel was absolute. Up to the time the last repatriation centre in the BCOF area closed on 15 December 1946 and the last of the 700,000 had left, there was no incident of any kind involving conflict or dissent. They were just glad to get home.

The supervision of the general election in April 1946 was a further task of importance both to occupied and occupiers. It was the first to be carried out under the new democratic regime of SCAP and the new constitution he had introduced and it was the first in which women in Japan had the vote. The UK Liaison Mission in Tokyo was somewhat dismissive of the event: there was 'none of the electric atmosphere associated with general elections in our own country', it reported in March 1946. 'The people are unmoved by the manifestos of the various political parties . . . [they are] only too aware that none of the problems which really affect their pockets, their stomachs and their roofs can be solved by putting a cross against the names of a lot of uninspiring and for the most part inexperienced candidates.'[19] Nevertheless the people turned out in their millions: 75 percent of those entitled cast their votes, including more than 13 million women.

By arrangement with Military Government BCOF provided 45 observer teams in its area to cover the campaign prior to the election and to watch over the polling stations to ensure that it was carried out in a free and fair manner. Afterwards MacArthur commented on 'the splendid cooperation of the BCOF in the Kure area, since they were not charged with this or any military government responsibility but nevertheless most ably and whole-heartedly assisted American forces in their election observation duties'. This was a sharp reminder to BCOF that military government was nothing to do with them, and in reporting it Northcott had commented ruefully that this showed the true status of BCOF in the government of Japan: 'we assist the American forces'.[20] The two essential links with the Japanese people – that is, Military Government and the Counter-Intelligence Corps – were staffed and controlled entirely by Americans. All BCOF could do was to carry out SCAP Directives and to ensure that they were obeyed.

It became increasingly important in the first year of the occupation to control illegal immigration, mainly involving Koreans, the former colonial subjects of Japan. There was a large and turbulent Korean community in Japan totalling about three million. A healthy antagonism existed between the Japanese and the Koreans, and after the end of the war a large number of Koreans asked to be returned to their homeland, which had at last been freed from its situation as a Japanese colony. However, when the time came they found conditions even worse there and many tried constantly to get back to Japan. It had been decided that they would not be readmitted. In view of this, a busy activity grew up in illegal immigration, which the occupation forces had to prevent in conjunction with the Japanese police.

This anti-immigration task had many compensations. The infantry units who were involved assumed a maritime function which they found a pleasant change from their other duties and which had a refreshing operational flavour. In Shimane Prefecture, for example, although the Mahrattas found it easy enough to catch the Koreans after they had landed because they were always burdened by rucksacks, babies and other impedimenta, the vessels concerned usually managed to escape. The battalion was therefore allocated a 170-ton sea rescue boat capable of 33 knots, together with a Japanese crew of 17, for sea patrols which, in collaboration with the RAF from Miho on surveillance, proved to be most effective in capturing the offending vessels.

The Koreans who had remained in Japan (and there were many in the south west of the country) gave the occupation troops more trouble than the Japanese. At the end of the war they adopted an attitude of arrogant superiority to the Japanese, imagining themselves to be above the law in the first flush of their newly-won independence. They were heavily implicated in big black market rackets and illegal imports, as well as taking the lead in labour disputes and other attempts to further their own ends through a highly organised pressure group formed under the title 'League of Koreans Resident in Japan'. BCOF troops were from time to time called out to deal with large groups of Koreans demonstrating against some aspect of the regime which they felt to be against their interests, and made many arrests of Koreans for black market offences – 6,000 in the first six months of BCOF's occupation.

Regular attempts were made to discover hidden arms which accidental discoveries, unguarded conversations or malicious informers suggested still existed, especially in the rural communities. These were rarely found. A typical operation by the Gurkhas in November 1946 in reaction to armed robbery at a dump at Sangenya led to searches of neighbouring villages, which revealed several old flintlocks, an unlicensed sword, one live rifle round, some empty rifle cartridges, and a number of small knives, some of which were marked 'property of the US Government' – hardly an exciting haul, and certainly not evidence of a potential armed revolution. Although a number of men and women were arrested, it was noted that the attitude of the villagers was one of indifference or polite interest and there were no signs of fear at any time – all typical reactions of the Japanese rural population to the occupation forces.

Once the demilitarisation and repatriation activities were completed, apart from patrols and flag marches in their respective areas, the infantry brigades spent a good deal of time in practising or taking part in ceremonial parades. These parades and guard-mounting gave the occupation force some prominence in the eyes of both the Japanese and the Americans. The events also had significance for BCOF as an entity. A flag-raising ceremony in Kure in April 1946 displayed the national flags of the four countries together for the first time; the first Anzac Day commemoration ceremony in Kure was attended by 2,000 representatives of all BCOF elements; and the Empire Day celebrations which took place in Tokyo in 1946 served to remind MacArthur, who attended with his wife, that the Empire was not dead.

The month of guard duty in Tokyo which each infantry battalion performed in rotation with the other battalions of BCOF was a high spot in the lives of the soldiers. The guard battalion was based at Ebisu, in somewhat gloomy barracks a few miles from the centre of the city. Guards were mounted day and night on various key points, including the British Embassy, Radio Tokyo, and the Britcom Sub Area offices in Empire House: but the most important and prominent of all was the Imperial Palace. A Welch Fusilier officer said 'we never knew whether we were supposed to keep the people out or the Emperor in'.[21] Nevertheless, to mount guard on the Emperor himself seemed to the soldiers to be the very summit of occupation duty. For those who had fought through the jungles and swamps for years against a feared and respected enemy, there was an almost mystical significance in penetrating to his very heart. When Australian infantry mounted the first BCOF guard there, Northcott noted its historical importance: they 'thus reached the end of the long hard road to Tokyo . . . and it was very fitting that they should share these guard duties, post by post, with soldiers of the First US Cavalry Division, demonstrating to the Japanese people the cooperation which exists between our military forces'.[22]

The Plaza in front of the Imperial Palace was the location for many special BCOF parades. They provided unique opportunities for BCOF troops to show off their undoubtedly superior standards of drill and discipline in front of large crowds of spectators, both American and Japanese, to the clicking of a thousand cameras. The beating of retreat was a popular spectacle and Thimayya organised one such parade there, involving the bands of all three Indian battalions in full dress uniforms. The Welch Fusiliers put on a special show by carrying out a formal trooping of their colour during their stay, and the Gurkhas performed a King's Birthday parade there in June 1947. They fired a *'feu de joie'* for the first time since 1938.

Operational activities all played a useful part in the implementation of SCAP directives and 'showing the flag', whether by patrols or by ceremonial parades, seemed to be worthwhile in establishing the presence of the occupation forces. Detailed plans were drawn up to deal with threats to internal security, whether by civilian riots, demonstrations against the occupation, open conflict between civilian groups, or attacks on the occupation forces by organised civilian or quasi-military forces. Although a state of peace prevailed, a degree of preparedness was maintained. But on the whole it only involved the infantry battalions, leaving the remainder of the Force disengaged and less able to find a role once the initial demilitarisation activities were completed. Since a more positive involvement in the administration of Japan had been denied to them, it was felt that perhaps BCOF's best contribution to the process of democratisation in Japan might be by setting an example of the quality of a truly democratic way of life through individual and collective action.

But this was where the Force was beginning to run into trouble.

As a correspondent to the Australian press noted, 'the utter tedious-
ness of garrison life imposes a trial on the moral stability of a
man'.[23] Although conditions were improving, discipline was under
some strain and lapses were quickly picked up by the press. In
November 1946, for example, the *Chicago Tribune*, a newspaper
well-known for its anti-British sentiments and those of its propri-
etor, Colonel McCormick, reported a high-ranking Japanese police
official in Tokyo as saying that the Australian troops were the worst-
behaved in Japan, and added its own view that they were out of
control and should be sent home. Although it had rated the British
troops as the best behaved, and better than the Americans, it added
gratuitously that it would be a good idea to send the British home
too – 'they contributed nothing to the victory over Japan'. The
Australian Minister for the Army rejected these reports robustly,
saying 'I quite realise that Australian soldiers would not be pushed
around by the Japanese authorities – and rightly so'.[24] Robertson
commented more discreetly on the Tribune story, saying 'there are
always one or two who are a discredit to the Force, but the general
standard of the troops is good'.[25]

A major obstacle to the development of beneficial contacts
along civilised lines lay in the official BCOF policy of non-fraternisation. As we shall see, this was much more restrictive than the
practices followed by the US forces. Indeed the prohibition of a normal association between troops and civilians perversely encouraged
contacts of a more shadowy nature, and as a consequence, relations with the civilian population became an increasing problem.

8

Relations with the Americans

The American attitude at top level towards the involvement of BCOF was somewhat ambiguous. The commanders were aware of the manpower savings they were able to make and the repatriation of troops to the US which was made possible by virtue of the arrival of reinforcements. But there was still determination to keep the occupation American and resentment of any attempt to dilute this.

The Australians, who had served in the South West Pacific theatre under MacArthur, had of course the best credentials. Australia had after all acted as host to MacArthur and his family after his flight from Corregidor, and thereafter to the many thousands of US military personnel who had protected the country from Japanese invasion: and it had served as the springboard from which the island campaign had been launched. Indeed, it was under MacArthur that the Australians had achieved the first victory on land against the Japanese at Milne Bay in 1942. The New Zealanders by association enjoyed the same niche of affection and respect with MacArthur and his commanders.

For his part, MacArthur had achieved a position of authority and esteem in Australia. The Labor government under Curtin was pleased and relieved to have him as Supreme Commander of all Allied forces in the South West Pacific. Curtin had set the scene with his famous statement of 27 December 1941: 'Australia looks to America, free of any pangs as to our traditional links or kinship with the United Kingdom'. It almost seemed at times that the Labor leadership had abdicated national responsibility to MacArthur. MacArthur's British liaison officer later reported him as saying

80

'Curtin had indicated that Australia was ready to move to us away from the British Empire', adding laconically himself 'Curtin and company more or less offered him the country on a platter'.[1] Although, as the threat receded, Australia became more wary of American ambition in the Pacific and sought to rebuild ties with Britain, the Government was happy to let their men serve under MacArthur in Japan.

The Australian military were not so blind in their admiration. They had had to come to the rescue of the Americans in a number of combat situations and had not received the credit. They had noted that whenever GIs were doing the fighting MacArthur's communiqués identified them as 'American', but when it was Diggers who were engaged, they merely became 'Allied'.[2] Their commanders in New Guinea had complained with such force to Curtin that he had to ask MacArthur to allow greater coverage of the Australian part in his military operations. They resented the fact that, despite the outstanding performance by Australian forces in the New Guinea campaign, MacArthur was determined to keep the Pacific campaign for the Americans and, while he forged ahead to his main objective, the Philippines, had relegated the Australians to the unglamorous and arduous task of dealing with the 160,000 Japanese left in New Guinea, New Britain and Bougainville. MacArthur's reference to this difficult and dangerous assignment as merely 'mopping up' drew a particularly resentful reaction from the troops involved.

However, MacArthur felt he had a special relationship with the Australians, and frequently referred to it in his florid communiqués. His original statement in January 1946 which welcomed the announcement about BCOF's participation in the occupation said '. .. The Australian contingent served under my personal command with brilliant honor during the long and arduous campaigns on the road back and I take a special personal pride in again being associated with it . . .'.[3] Undoubtedly Northcott's previous friendly association in Australia and the South West Pacific with MacArthur and his staff officers, with General Eichelberger and with many other senior officers, had eased the negotiations in December and had secured a ready spirit of cooperation at this level.

But the British and Indian Division was something else, unfamiliar and strange. MacArthur was often accused of anti-British feeling, perhaps wrongly. He was proud of his Scottish ancestry and referred to it freely: he had supported the lone British stand against the Nazis in 1940 and had strongly advocated the need to keep the bastion of freedom in the United Kingdom fully supplied by the United States before it was too late. 'Such coordinated help as may be regarded as proper by our leaders', he said at the time, 'should be synchronised with the British effort so that the English-speaking peoples of the world will not be broken in detail.'[4] And his admiration for British fighting units, their professional excellence and their martial bearing was expressed generously in later years.[5]

Nevertheless, as the war with Japan developed he became bitterly opposed, for understandably selfish reasons, to the influence of the British Government in general and Churchill in particular on the US Administration, which established and firmly maintained the Allied policy giving the defeat of Germany priority over the defeat of Japan. The competition for Allied resources, he felt, was unfairly weighted against him by Britain, whose representatives he believed were constantly conspiring against him in Washington and the Allied councils of war.[6]

There was also a solid anti-British wedge of opinion and influence in his command and among his colleagues. 'Vinegar Joe' Stilwell had come to take up command of the US Tenth Army under MacArthur for the assault on Japan after his recall from the China-Burma-India theatre, where the Anglophobia he had first developed in the First World War had reached hysterical proportions: 'the more I see of the Limeys, the worse I hate them' and 'the bastardly hypocrites do their best to cut our throats on all occasions' were two of his choicest phrases to have entered the records at that time.[7]

Admiral King's resentment of the British had already been well in evidence in his determination to keep the British Pacific Fleet out of the final stages of the onslaught on the Japanese homeland and his unsuccessful endeavours to sideline them into the Borneo campaign. Even when American naval commanders were unable to avoid British participation in the air attacks on Japan in the final months of the war, they ensured, as Admiral Halsey subsequently admitted, that they were allocated 'unimportant targets' to reserve the prize targets for American aircraft.[8]

Many US personnel, moreover, were affected by the anti-colonialist attitudes which they had honourably inherited and which had been vigorously propounded by President Roosevelt and others. SEAC had been translated as 'Save England's Asiatic Colonies' by

unsympathetic Washington warriors. Some Australians had difficulty in explaining to Americans that they were not colonial subjects
but citizens of an independent self-governing Dominion.[9] Indeed, in
those days many of them still felt they were, and described themselves as, British.[10]

The major impact of the Burma campaign on the Japanese
empire had been totally ignored. As far as the Americans were concerned the object of operations in that theatre had been purely to
keep the supply route open to China and to Chiang Kai-shek's
armies, which were pinning down so many Japanese troops. It had
always been difficult and frustrating for the British to get across
the message of their efforts in South East Asia to their own people
(14th Army was always the 'forgotten army'), let alone to the
Americans. In July 1945 Churchill had in fact called for a brief from
Ismay for him to use at Potsdam, to inform and remind the Allies of
the Imperial war effort in the war against Japan. This noted particularly, while recognising the invaluable contributions of Australia
and New Zealand, that 'during the last 18 months Burma has been
the scene of sustained land fighting on the largest scale which has yet
been witnessed in the Japanese war. Imperial troops have liberated
an area of some 160,000 square miles with a population of some
9,500,000, killing over 90,000 Japanese and suffering some 63,000
casualties . . .'[11]

Against this background, to receive in Japan suddenly a
colourful mixture of British and Indian units, with their exotic professional accoutrements – kilts, hackles, kukris, mascot goats – was
something of a culture shock to the few Americans who came into
contact with them. Their bands, parades, trooping of the colour, all
fostered the image of unreality. What was this Indian army largely
officered by white Britons but some colonial vestige?

As it turned out, contacts at the working level were few and far
between, except with the military government teams who were
based at each prefectural headquarters throughout the BCOF area.
Although the signs outside their offices in English said 'Allied
Military Government', the Japanese characters accompanying the
inscription always read 'American Military Government', leaving
no doubt as to the true nature of the operation.

There seemed indeed to be a silent conspiracy to ignore the
presence of BCOF in Japan altogether. MacArthur's biographer
makes just one mention of the British there – 'the 38,000 Tommies'

(sic) who shared the occupation with 152,000 GIs by the end of 1946 were referred to once and never again.[12] Willoughby's map of occupied Japan showed no divisional or brigade signs in the area allocated to BCOF, although his SCAP organisation chart included a mention.[13]

For the American occupationnaires stationed in Tokyo, the BCOF battalions who took it in turn to provide a guard detachment there as provided for in the Northcott-MacArthur agreement, were a positive reminder of Commonwealth participation. There also developed a limited amount of interchange on army training courses, and several combined training exercises took place in which BCAIR squadrons supported the US Air Force. The occasional visits paid to US-occupied ports by ships of the British Pacific Fleet in support of BCOF provided the best opportunity for close contact: but for the majority of the US occupation forces, BCOF did not exist.

BCOF's opportunities to establish relations with the Americans on the ground were limited for reasons of geography, and the differences in the attitudes and quality of the troops were another obstacle. By the end of September 1945 the US Eighth Army had moved over 230,000 men into Japan, and the Sixth Army about the same. But by the end of the year, as a result of a high-speed repatriation and demobilisation programme, the Eighth Army was down to less than 200,000, most of them fresh reinforcements from the United States, and the Sixth Army had vanished altogether. Gascoigne, Head of the UK Liaison Mission in Tokyo, recorded some damning comments on the occupationnaires at the time of the arrival of BCOF's vanguard,

> 'A considerable proportion of the American troops now in Japan is made up of youthful novices without either the background of battle or the personal experience of the Japanese as inhuman fanatic enemies. They are restless, disinterested, and spend their spare time . . . collecting souvenirs, speculating on their early repatriation and worst of all in undignified fraternisation. The mediocre quality of these replacements has resulted in the deterioration of the general standard of discipline within Occupation units.'

Gascoigne   hoped   that   the   advent   of   well-disciplined

Commonwealth forces might do much to raise the general level of Japanese respect for their victors.[14]

BCOF's initial opinions reinforced those of the Mission. When the advance party of the Punjabis shared a barracks at Tottori for seven days with the US unit they were to relieve, the contrast was enormous. 'The US troops lounged about the barracks, ill-dressed and unkempt, almost like a crowd of unemployed', said a BCOF liaison officer. 'The Indian unit was a model of spick and span discipline.'[15]

MacArthur never visited BCOF himself. This was noted and resented by the Commonwealth troops: but it was entirely normal. Although he was *de facto* ruler of the whole country, up to the time of the Korean war he maintained an imperial solitude and only left Tokyo twice (once to go to Seoul and once to Manila, returning on the same day in each case). Indeed his knowledge of Tokyo itself was largely confined to his residence in the American Embassy, his office in the Dai-Ichi Building and the route connecting them. He had already assumed the position and the trappings of a latter-day shogun which he was to occupy for the next five years, surrounded by his faithful 'Bataan gang' of generals and backed by 5,000 enthusiastic followers in his headquarters. He was, in Manchester's words, 'the last of the great colonial overlords, remote and unapproachable by all except a few natives': and he had already embarked on that massive programme of reform which was intended to transform Japanese society and the Japanese nation.

A new democratic constitution; female suffrage and the encouragement of women's rights; the purging of the militarists and their supporters from all public office; the enfranchisement of tenant farmers; the break-up of the *zaibatsu*, the powerful industrial combines; the unionisation of labour; the liberalisation of schools; these were fundamental changes which were intended to form the basis for Japan's return to the society of free nations. Not all of them worked perfectly, and not all of them endured, but in general they succeeded in bringing about the renaissance of a friendly nation: and the process of putting them into place was an urgent and overriding task in which MacArthur would brook no interference, either from the instruments of apparent Allied control, the Far Eastern Commission in Washington and the Allied Council for Japan in Tokyo, or indeed from his own government. After all, the

President had told him 'your authority is supreme'. Without such a dominating and single-minded approach, it seems unlikely that Japan could have undergone the metamorphosis from demoralised and defeated enemy to reliable friend and ally.

Against the background of the furious speed and intensity of MacArthur's programmes, it is hardly surprising that BCOF received little attention. MacArthur's only personal contact with the Force was by occasional attendance at ceremonies in Tokyo and through the frequent visits made to him by Robertson, who as Commander-in-Chief BCOF was entitled to direct access and made the maximum use of that right. It was astonishing, almost shocking, that Cowan, the only British general commanding occupation troops, left Japan after 15 months and numerous visits to Tokyo, with his ambition to meet MacArthur unfulfilled. In fact Robertson would have undoubtedly discouraged or even prevented such a meeting: he was excessively jealous of his position *vis-à-vis* MacArthur and was always on the alert to preserve and forward his interests, both as a commander and as an individual. For their part General Eichelberger, under whose Eighth Army operational command BCOF had been placed, and his senior commanders made brief and infrequent visits to the Force.

As far as MacArthur was concerned, BCOF had to be content with occasional warm words of encouragement from the Dai-Ichi Building. An anniversary message in February 1947 was typically flamboyant,

> 'The BCOF has today completed its first year of occupation duty in Japan. Its units have shown themselves as splendid in peace as they were in war. They are discharging their missions here with everlasting credit to the great nations they represent. I am very proud to have them in my command and very grateful for their loyal service.'[16]

The infantry battalions' principal opportunity to meet their American opposite numbers came when they left their self-contained and isolated life for the periodic guard duty visits to Tokyo and its sleazy bright lights. Their opinion of US troops was never very high – 'they had given up soldiering', said one British officer[17], and according to an Australian NCO were 'indulging themselves to the hilt'.[18] An Australian sapper visiting Beppu on leave had noted how young and naive seemed the men of the US infantry division stationed in Kyushu.[19] Other differences were apparent. 'The Americans seemed very impressed with the formal and highly disciplined way in which we behaved', said a Welch Fusilier warrant officer visiting an American supply depot,' in particular the respect which we had been trained to show to all officers'.[20] A Dorset sergeant whose platoon shared guard duty at an airfield outside Tokyo with the US 8th Army Air Force said '. . . their discipline of course was much more lax than our service demanded. I relented to a certain extent but drew the line at beer and women in the billet all night!'[21] But the life style was comfortable and the food was 'like Christmas every day'.

The open fraternisation with the Japanese everywhere was a shock for BCOF personnel visiting the American area (the difference in policies is examined in detail later). But the American soldiers were welcoming and hospitable, sharing their clubs, canteens and shops with enthusiasm. There were many recorded instances of this warm hospitality. The Gurkhas were elated at being invited to a 'Stateside County Fair' at the US Red Cross Club during a Tokyo guard stint, which was open to all ranks, with free drinks, ice cream and popcorn – a series of unfamiliar delights. A Welch Fusilier told his colonel with amazement that an American corporal had taken him to the PX for an all-day treat and refused to let him pay for anything. The standard of the Americans' amenities was so high that BCOF troops, like Allied troops in many other theatres, felt like poor relations. Many units in BRINDIV had a specific reason to feel inferior: their summer uniform was the jungle green they had worn in South East Asia Command (unlike the khaki worn by the Australians and New Zealanders). Since the American troops only wore green for fatigue duty, the British and Indian troops always looked to the American eye as if they were on fatigues.

Apart from the Tokyo guard and occasional local leave at hostels in the US area, there was little other opportunity to mix. MacArthur was blamed (as figureheads always are) for the remoteness of the BCOF occupation area, for BCOF's relegation to a minor role and for the denial of a proper share for them in the military government. A popular BCOF parody characterised their frustration and annoyance:

Our General which art in Toyko
MacArthur be thy name.
Thy kingdom be off limits to BCOF troops
As it is in Tokyo.
Give us this day our daily Directive
And forgive us our trespassing in the American zone
As we forgive our postal for jettisoning our mail
And lead us not into re-engagement,
But deliver us from Kure
For SCAP is thy kingdom
And thou art Almighty for the period of the occupation.[22]

9

A Wider Responsibility?

British Government hopes that its representation on the Far East Commission and the Allied Council for Japan might exercise some influence on the conduct of the occupation had soon been shown to be unfounded in the face of MacArthur's determined grip on the control of Japan.

Quite apart from its isolation and lack of amenities, the BCOF area did nothing to assist the political and commercial aspirations of the British Government, even after the addition of the extra Honshu prefectures and Shikoku. The ceremonial guard and the small BRICOSAT outstation in Tokyo, together with the Commander-in-Chief's occasional residence there, had little effect in making the Commonwealth presence felt. In August 1946, General Gairdner, the British Prime Minister's special representative with SCAP, decided to make another attempt. Gairdner had originally been appointed by Churchill to join MacArthur after his landing in the Philippines, and had stayed with him ever since, continuing into the occupation period as Attlee's representative after the latter's election success in 1945.

In his report to Attlee of 23 August 1946 Gairdner said: 'The British Commonwealth troops have got a poor area to occupy. In addition the amenities provided for them are so far in no way comparable to American standards. It was a great pity that when Northcott made the original agreement with MacArthur he did not insist on Kobe being included in the British area. I pointed this out last December but apparently it was thought even then to be too late. While our bargaining position is not so good as it was then, I still think that a very good case could be made for Kobe to become the British port. We always had large interests there ourselves and anyhow it is ridiculous that a great sea power like ourselves should have no commercial port when I understand that China is going to be given the use of Nagoya [As we have noted, this did not happen: there was no Chinese share in the occupation.] It must be borne in mind that every British soldier relieves an American soldier for the USA and that is a bargaining counter of considerable value'.[1]

This led to an enquiry from Attlee to JCOSA, and their reply on 11 September relayed a far more positive and optimistic reaction from the Commander-in-Chief BCOF than Northcott's original attitude at the time of the discussion of additional areas in March 1946.[2] In direct contradiction of Northcott's previous views, Robertson said that he could take over Kobe, Osaka and Kyoto in addition to his existing areas without any increase in BCOF strength and that he would be ready to do so from 1 January 1947, or even earlier, to avoid winter moves. In reporting this JCOSA recalled that MacArthur had been asked at the end of June if the present areas were permanent. He had replied in effect that there were no permanent areas as there were in occupied Germany. The present dispositions in Japan were just as accidental as deployment in the line of battle, he said, and that when repatriation was completed in the autumn changes could be made. Robertson should discuss with Eighth Army as to where he would like to go.

Subsequent discussion with Eighth Army and staff at SCAP, however, had led Robertson to believe that they would strongly oppose any changes, chiefly on the grounds of the infrastructure already provided for American dependents in the areas in question. Payment in US dollars would be demanded for American *matériel* and equipment in houses, clubs and other accommodation, and removal of their dependents, with the accompanying department stores, clubs and other extensive amenities, would be a major task which would become more difficult with every week that passed.

In spite of this likely opposition, Robertson still believed that MacArthur would adhere to his undertaking if the request were to be made at the highest inter-governmental level, although he recognised that the US dependent housing issue would remain a tremendous physical obstacle. He hoped that there would be some further reaction to his report in London and Canberra, and for the time being refrained from pursuing the matter with MacArthur directly, contenting himself with discussing with SCAP staff the establishment of a small supply base at Kobe for the provision of rations to the BCOF leave hostels in Kobe and Kyoto.

He was at the same time trying hard to obtain some involvement, however small, in the military government. The issue was discussed at a general conference with JCOSA on 24 September 1946, and JCOSA poured cold water on his ambitions with the statement that 'although the advantages of taking over a share in the military government are quite clear, the accepted Government policy is against BCOF taking such action'.[3] This was an astoundingly passive and unimaginative attitude to adopt, and there is no evidence that Commonwealth governments were consulted on the desirability of a change in policy. It is highly likely that, in spite of the Foreign Office's original subservient acceptance of American domination, the British Government would have welcomed some improvement in the British position in Japan if it could have been achieved without further resources being needed.

Even so, Robertson managed to make a tiny infiltration by seconding a three-man team to each military government unit in his area, with the excuse that this would assist in overcoming procurement difficulties and would also train personnel 'in case of an emergency'. He felt that 'there should be no objection to BCOF participation in military government on this basis provided the overall control remained as at present with GHQ'. There was none; the Americans realised that this was no threat to their domain. The total number of BCOF personnel seconded to military government never exceeded 50 all ranks.

In the middle of October, Robertson told Gascoigne in Tokyo that the time was most favourable for a governmental approach to the Americans on the inclusion at least of Kobe in the BCOF area. He had found out confidentially from Eichelberger that the total strength of US troops in Japan and Korea was down to about 100,000, compared with the established strength for Japan alone of 140,000. Eichelberger was said to be at his wits' end to know how to carry on the occupation, and might be thankful for an offer to take over more territory.[4] Opinion in London suggested that, in view of discussions on possible withdrawal of the British brigade, this would need careful handling: but it was eventually decided to act on Robertson's suggestion and ask the Australian Government to consider making an approach to the Americans for the acquisition of

Kobe. The military advantages of an important centre with facilities of a standard equal to those enjoyed by US troops and a considerable enhancement of prestige were accompanied by the longer-term attraction of establishing a firm footing of anticipated economic and commercial benefit to all the Commonwealth countries.

In the event, the possibility of this extension to the BCOF zone was never pursued with the Americans. As Gairdner told the Chiefs of Staff later on a visit to London in February 1947, there was little hope of extending the BCOF area in view of the then impending withdrawal of the British brigade and the possible withdrawal of other national contingents. With such likely reductions from his force, Robertson could not claim to be able to take over additional areas, and the matter was dropped. The objections by SCAP staff and the threat of the consequential costs would have probably prevailed in any event. It was regrettable that it was Northcott who had had the opportunity in March to take Osaka and Kobe and had refused it, rather than Robertson, who would have undoubtedly accepted it.

The nagging desire to extend BCOF's responsibilities persisted. On 29 October, Robertson delivered a speech at the opening of the new British Infantry School at Matsuyama. He called on all British troops to show the Japanese that the system they had followed in the past was not the right one, and to set an example of the highest democratic principles in their dealings with the Japanese. The re-education of the Japanese people would take years, and it was still too early to judge the extent of progress since the beginning of the occupation. The British press, ignorant of what had already happened, chose to interpret this stirring call as a preliminary bid for British participation in military government, and Robertson undoubtedly encouraged the thought. But there was no prospect of any advancement of the British interest.[5]

10

Reactions to Japan

Japan and the Japanese were a study in contrasts. The first sight of Japan for the arriving troops had been the grey and ugly desolation of Kure and the neighbouring desert of Hiroshima. Their barracks were often dreary and forbidding. The people were equally drab in their dingy black or grey clothing. However, once out of the towns and away from the ramshackle suburbs, the scene changed. Every piece of available land was utilised for food. Hills up to a slope of 45 degrees bore crops, and even the half metre strips along the road-sides were cultivated. 'So different from all our open land in Australia', said one infantry officer.[1] This intensive farming brought another marked difference in its train: the universal use of human excreta as fertiliser in the fields. The wooden-wheeled night-soil carts (the 'honey carts', as the soldiers called them), hand drawn or pulled by oxen, were a constant menace to traffic and Western nostrils alike.

But the miniature charm of the villages and the exquisite countryside were irresistible. Some early reactions were lyrical. A British officer wrote in the spring of 1946 'there is no doubt that this . . . is the most beautiful country I have ever seen. Cherry blossom in abundance . . . and the most lovely wild flowers . . . all along this coast there are the most delightful little bays and beaches. The colour of everything is so beautiful here'.[2] 'The farm houses are fairy islands in seas of fallowed fields . . . glistening chocolate-coloured roofs and dazzling white walls, framed by feathery pines . . .' said an Australian interpreter, equally overcome.[3]

A naval officer from a French warship which was briefly visiting Japan in the middle of 1946 as a token of French support for the occupation, was just as enthusiastic: 'the mountain landscapes are splendid: torrents, waterfalls, dense forests, paddy fields in the valleys, and around 100 metres the well-known Japanese meadows, their gentle slopes covered with delicate pink or dark blue flowers, huge deserted and charming expanses. This captivating country is very much like our own land, with several special characteristics which give it its originality: the paddy fields, the trees everywhere, on the plains groves of enormous bamboos with their delicate tracery of pale green foliage, with a touch of yellow'.[4]

The Frenchman at least had Pierre Loti as forerunner and guide: but nothing had prepared the BCOF troops for the beauty of this strange and original land. While many of the troops had deplored their remoteness from the cities, broken and comfortless as these were, others realised the compensations. One RAF man said 'we were far better off in a comparatively rural area, than in any of the big cities, full of squalor and hunger'.[5]

For the BCOF men who had been serving in tropical or semi-tropical areas for years, the climate in their part of Japan was something of a shock. Many had disembarked in snow and icy rain and had had to endure extreme discomfort in unheated and windowless barracks in winter conditions. For most of the Australians it was in fact the first time they had ever seen snow. The spring was a season of pleasant relief, but was followed in June by the rainy season known as *tsuyu*, a period of increasing warmth and humidity when the daily rains and continuous clammy heat not only exhausted the troops but also caused outbreaks of virulent disease among the civilian population, which led to strict controls on movement and endless courses of inoculations. After the rainy season came the typhoons which raged erratically through the summer and were a constant threat to BCOF buildings and the farmers' crops. The golden second half of summer and the beginning of autumn were the climatic high spots of the year; but they were soon followed by frosty nights and then by the ice and heavy snowfalls of the winter once more.

As for the people, the attitude which the occupation forces were to adopt towards them had been impersonally prescribed in BCOF instructions.[6] They were to be treated in such a way as to develop respect for and confidence in the troops; they were to be completely free from interference with their individual and property rights; and historical, cultural and religious objects and installations were to be carefully protected and preserved. Occupation troops were to observe the obligations imposed upon them by international law and the rules of land warfare – a somewhat threatening reminder that peace had not yet been negotiated.

But these basic rules could not provide for the reality of contact with the civilian population, who seemed to present a series of further contrasts. The first Japanese the occupying troops saw properly were the men working in the docks and the surrounding area in Kure. They took little notice of the troops passing and continued their work with expressionless faces. Most of them were dressed in some mixture of cast-off uniform and all wore the traditional short-peaked cap that gave them a semi-military appearance. 'I remember feeling little sympathy for the local men who were labouring on the wharf', said a New Zealander. 'We had fought them for years and had learnt to hate them and even fear them . . . It took time for the prejudices to break down'.[7] It was common practice for the young soldiers to spit on the wharf at Kure when they arrived.

The awful conditions under which the people were living in the towns and cities, however, had quite a different effect on most of the men. Families were living in appalling conditions, crowded into shacks and dugouts, living in hallways and on pavements, lacking the basic necessities of life. An Australian sapper recalled his reaction on arrival in Kure: as his truck turned the corner from the docks towards the transit camp, there was a young girl on the opposite corner naked to the waist, with a baby at her breast. She seemed totally disoriented. In the background there was the once-city of Kure, 'flattened like a pancake'. 'That one sight drove every bit of hatred for the Japanese from me', he said.[8]

Even a New Zealand pilot, like his comrades especially hostile towards the Japanese because of their normal practice of executing captured Allied pilots, could not avoid a feeling of pity when he caught a supposed saboteur on the airfield at Iwakuni and found that he had been scavenging in the squadron rubbish container and was running away with the prize of a small bag of used tea leaves.[9]

The ability of the Japanese to withstand the hardships of those early days and their readiness to adjust to the abrupt change in their fortunes were a constant source of amazement. The sense of national discipline and obedience to the Emperor had apparently enabled them to change direction without difficulty towards the rebuilding of their country on a peaceful basis. They accepted without complaint a relatively benevolent occupation which functioned through the familiar machinery of their own government, and which provided a new security to a people bewildered by unexpected defeat. There seemed to be hardly any resentment of the tremendous damage suffered by Japan or of the atom bomb itself: they were accepted as being acts of war in a war started by Japan. A British officer noted that 'after the dirt, disease and poverty of the Indian sub-continent one began to realise the discipline and hardiness of the local culture'.[10]

The troops' strongest impression at the outset was of the vast numbers of Japanese and their apparent imperviousness to the occupation. Men, women and children wandered everywhere, some in kimonos, others in drab Western-style dress, most clip-clopping on wooden *geta* sandals. Women carried infants on their backs or else a huge pack or basket, as if they were beasts of burden. Battered and unpainted buses and trams, running on stinking gas-producing engines, with broken or boarded windows, were so crowded with passengers that it seemed impossible either to get on or get off.

Although the inhabitants of what was left of Hiroshima were noticeably and understandably more stolid and sullen, the city dwellers generally were cooperative, and those who entered the service of the occupation, which was a boon in the conditions of poverty then prevailing, were naturally enough industrious and reliable. For their part, the country dwellers were generally speaking better off than the townspeople, whose access to food over and above the official ration of rice and wheat or barley was restricted and often depended on the black market.

In country areas, when troops passed, the older men would frequently smile, bow and raise their hats, although younger men would sometimes stand and leer and take delight in minor embarrassments such as a stalled engine. However, the general acceptance of the occupation and the passivity of the people was reassuring, although an occasional wave of emotion could not be suppressed. A British officer wrote

'the Japanese men I dislike intensely . . . I felt a little out of place sitting [in a train] surrounded by these slit-eyed cunning looking men who stared at me all the time, peering through their specs with an expression that read curiosity and dislike! I should loathe to have been a prisoner in Japanese hands as I can see the bestiality in their faces. However, when I asked the way or name of the station they were very polite and after a curt bow and indrawing of the breath through the teeth, told me . . .'[11]

An understandable lack of understanding of Japanese ways and memories of the war often produced an extreme reaction and it was difficult to bridge the gap of understanding between East and West. 'I made it my business in my rare off-duty time to try to delve into the Japanese mind', said a Dorsets sergeant, 'but I soon realised that I could devote a lifetime to this subject and still get nowhere!'.[12]

Japanese officialdom presented yet another face. It had been decreed from the beginning of the occupation that, in order to accomplish the occupation with the least possible expenditure of Allied manpower and resources, SCAP would conduct government through the existing Japanese administrative machinery, and so the local government structure remained in being. Although they were denied any involvement in the actual military government, BCOF units had continuous contact with local authorities, mainly the mayors and the chiefs of police, in the implementation of their occupation activities, especially the gathering of intelligence information and the prevention of illegal immigration.

There were occasional links of common experience. The Mayor of Okayama, for example, turned out to have been a senior officer in the Japanese invasion of Burma from Indo-China in 1942, and to have commanded the very troops to have defeated the British at the battle of the Sittang Bend. The Gurkhas in Okayama had been part of that defeated British army, and the battle was refought at an extraordinary ceremonial dinner arranged between some of the officers and the Mayor. The fact that he had lost his wife and family in the fire-bombing of Okayama strangely did not affect the cordiality of the occasion.

BCOF personnel continued to be amazed by the diligence with which the Japanese carried out to the extreme the Emperor's directive to cooperate with the occupation forces. On one occasion two small boys were reported to the Director of Education in Matsue for having thrown stones at a passing jeep with soldiers aboard. The stones missed their target and the soldiers were quite unaware of the incident. But the parents and the Director of Education presented themselves to the local headquarters to make a formal and ceremonial apology, and strict instructions were issued by the Education Department to all schools on the need for proper respect for the occupation forces.

The police were all-powerful: 'the people were far more frightened of the police than they were of the occupation forces', said a British NCO.[13] The officials were excessively helpful and embarrassingly polite. One British officer reported 'the Japanese here have been most cooperative, almost overdoing it. The Chief of Police is the 'big' man of the town : a monkey-like little man in his black and gold uniform and sword. He does and arranges practically everything for us. The Mayor and town officials are also most helpful. All the same I could never conjure up any love for these little men – I am sure they are completely double-faced – so scrupulously polite with their bowing and scraping.'[14] The failure to appreciate the Japanese way of doing things is reflected in another account of this kind of contact: 'they are polite to the extent of sitting and fanning you if it happens to be hot! . . . talking to these Japanese officials is a long and tedious business. Whereas we can usually answer a question in a short sentence or even one word, the Japanese has to go round and round the point first, eventually giving the answer . . . it tries one's patience somewhat . . .' It was, of course, good policy for the local officials to keep on the right side of the occupation: they could safeguard their own positions and use BCOF to help them get things done.[15] There were even cases where the local authorities played the local BCOF unit off against the local US military government in situations where they could see some advantage.

The Japanese female seemed to be of a different race from their menfolk. An Australian interpreter, Allan Clifton, commented on 'the calm resignation that has been the lot of Japanese women for centuries, a life that has ennobled and dignified them far beyond the men of their race'.[16] Japanese women in those days were demure and decorous in public, their eyes on the ground. They would look up shyly but with every impression of interest, and would hang on every word the menfolk said, commenting so flatteringly that the Westerner, unused to such compliments and deference, would be captivated. As the Australian journalist George Caiger has said, 'Japanese women are the world's champions at inflating men's egos. Having had no legal rights for centuries, they have had to become adept at handling their menfolk. The absence of legal rights doesn't mean that they have no influence . . . they get their way almost as much as their Western sisters . . .'.[17] Acquiring the right to vote in 1946, and exercising it to the full, enhanced their independence but did not diminish their appeal.

In the early years of the occupation the women had little opportunity to dress in a suitably feminine way. Over half the female population wore *mompei*, the loose trousers tied at the ankle. Skirts were fairly common. Kimonos were sometimes seen in the streets but were usually kept for special occasions and indoor wear. Mompei were regulation wear for the hard manual labour that the women had to carry out: carrying big loads of firewood, stacking railway sleepers, heaving earth for road works.

The natural charm and kindliness of the women overcame these superficial handicaps. They were more actively friendly than the men. Many, especially with children on their backs, would wave vigorously to passing troops while their menfolk merely looked on. A BCOF intelligence review in late 1946 noted that 'the Japanese woman is now definitely beginning to take advantage of her newly-found freedom, a state of mind which the Japanese male does not regard with any enthusiasm'.[18] Few of the younger women would openly greet troops publicly, but like their elder sisters they always seemed more kindly disposed than the men. It may have been because they had been fed lurid propaganda tales of the barbarity of the foreigners who eventually landed on their shores, whom they then found on the whole gentlemanly and pleasant. It may just have been because they were glad that the killing had come to an end.

At first many of the people had appeared shy, afraid and distrustful of the British forces even though the area occupied by BCOF had previously been occupied by US troops. As the occupation progressed, however, a number of BCOF observers noted that 'the civilian attitude has deteriorated in respect to occupation troops'.[19] Now the Japanese had generally grown accustomed to the presence of the British forces and there were some instances of men treating occupation forces 'in a disrespectful manner'. One symptom noted was the use to occupation troops of the sort of non-honorific Japanese normally used to servants. It was felt that the Japanese were beginning to take their humane treatment for granted and 'as always, familiarity is breeding some measure of contempt'.[20] One Western pressman reported that he had watched the Japanese 'change from apprehensive wretches to nearly their old arrogant selves as they began to realise that they were destined for the softest occupation ever'.[21]

There were a number of ex-POWs among the BCOF units who reacted vigorously when the attitude of the Japanese (sometimes misleadingly) seemed to deteriorate. The survivors of Japanese captivity divided into two groups: those who would never forgive the Japanese for their conduct, and those who were ready to forgive and forget. Most fell into the latter category. One ex-POW, a former journalist, said: 'I saw the ones who tortured me stand trial. They are dead. They were individuals, not a people'.[22] For him and most of his comrades, the score had been settled: and a view of Hiroshima was enough to confirm the expiation of the Japanese people.

Notwithstanding the attitude of their elders, it was the children who formed the firmest and fastest bridge between occupier and occupied. They were cheerful, exuberant, inquisitive and open-hearted, with a complete lack of fear. They would always shout a spontaneous greeting to the soldiers, they would wave from houses and from the fields, they would run beside trucks handing flowers to the troops. A British naval officer noted that all the children seemed to know two words of English, 'Hello' and 'Goodbye', but used them quite indiscriminately. 'It is surprisingly disconcerting on arrival in a village', he noted, 'to be greeted by dozens of children all shouting 'Goodbye'. Is this entirely fortuitous or is some subtle propaganda being instilled into the young?'[23] Of course the children would ask for gum and chocolate, especially in the towns and cities, but most of the time they would be happy with a smile. BCOF troops were always touched by the friendship of the children, which often led in due course to amiable contact with their families. 'I had a lot of time for the kids', they would say. One of his staff officers[24] tells how General 'Punch' Cowan arrived in Japan in a mood of extreme bitterness against the Japanese. He had spent three years on active service fighting them in Burma, from the early defeats to the final victory, and his only son, like 'Punch' an officer in the Gurkhas, had died of wounds received in the taking of Mandalay in 1945. But within a month of arrival his mood had completely changed. 'How can I blame these children and their families for what has happened?' he said. It was a transformation.

11
The Seamy Side

Armies of occupation in wartime have to endure the stresses of a hostile environment. There is a constant need to be alert, to meet the threat of external attack or internal resistance, or both. Cooperation is not easy with a civilian population itself sensitive to charges of collaboration and the possible penalties attached. There is a tendency for local hostility to increase with time, especially if the external threat is also growing. The life of the occupation troops is circumscribed and the opportunity for friendly contact with the local population is limited.

Occupation of a defeated country in the aftermath of a surrender which is accepted passively by the whole nation is by comparison an easy task. Then the problem becomes one of morale, of discipline, of controlling rather than encouraging friendly contact with the local population for fear of the slackness which it may bring in its train.

An Australian officer has said that the two main areas of concern in BCOF were the black market and women.[1] To some extent these both sprang from the same root cause: the extreme shortage of food and luxury goods in the cities, where conditions were desperate. It was common to see scavengers on army rubbish dumps and in the harbours round Allied ships, and Japanese workers in occupation establishments constantly rummaged through garbage and sweepings. A cigarette end thrown in the gutter was immediately snapped up. One Australian unit in Kure asked its commanding officer for the cookhouse slops to be given to camp workers instead of to contractors who were selling them for human consumption anyway.

The black market was born when troops quickly found that they were able to trade their canteen goods for large amounts of Japanese yen. Although it was an offence for Japanese to have occupation force goods, either by gift or by purchase, there were always huddles of would-be traders outside or near the camps and barracks. Chocolates, cigarettes and condensed milk were always in great demand. It was apparent, said a NZEF report in late 1946, that 'a large proportion of the troops consider the disposal of canteen goods and army property to be a desirable way of augmenting their income'.[2] In fact many soldiers never found it necessary to draw any pay. 'You could have what you liked for a cake of soap', said an Australian infantryman.[3]

Regular checks were made by searches at unit gates or in the railway stations, and Japanese caught with occupation goods were likely to be gaoled, and if employed by BCOF would also be dismissed and black-listed so that they could not return to Allied employment. Occupation troops found to be involved were court-martialled and faced return to their home country and dishonourable discharge, although the soldiers concerned were rarely apprehended owing to the lack of evidence for identification. The Japanese usually would not or could not identify their military accomplices.

JCOSA noted with concern in one of their 1946 reports that black marketing was 'very prevalent' in the BCOF area, and that numerous raids and arrests had been made.[4] But the risks and penalties were acceptable for the big-time operators, who built up considerable business in trading in foodstuffs, clothing and petrol in partnership with occupation personnel in key supply positions.

Moreover, SCAP's financial policy had laid down a fixed rate of exchange for the Japanese yen in which BCOF troops were paid: but the purchasing power of the yen outside Service canteens and institutes bore less and less relation to this fixed rate, which actively encouraged black market transactions in rations and canteen stores. One of the signs of the substantial illegal dealings of the troops was the large amounts of yen they were depositing in their pay accounts. It was therefore decided to introduce British Armed Forces Vouchers as the only legal tender, which would be used for all pay and allowances and for all purchases of services, stores and supplies in BCOF, and to limit conversion of yen already held to the amounts drawn from paymasters by each individual over the previous six months. This had the effect of rendering excessive amounts of yen valueless overnight and served as a useful deterrent for the future. It did not eradicate 'wogging' (the slang for black marketing canteen goods) but it drove out much of the illegal activity into barter and other forms of exchange.

This often took the shape of the second 'area of concern': women. In the early days young women would offer themselves at street corners or at railway stations in exchange for food. There were usually clusters of girls around the gates to barracks and camps in the cities. Kure, being an important naval base and sea port, had always housed a large population of prostitutes to cater for the sailors before the occupation. This was now considerably increased as a result of the economic conditions. There were throughout the area also a significant number of women who had been the girl friends of the American troops previously in residence and had become accustomed to a regular supply of food and other comforts. They were now ready to take on their Allied successors.

It was little wonder that these temptations proved too much for the troops: drill, sport and flag marches were not enough. The normal civilian recreation facilities which troops could expect under peace-time conditions were not available and they had to rely almost entirely on Service amenities. In the early months, the provision of local leave and recreation centres was difficult because all suitable European-type hotels on Honshu were in the US zone of occupation and had already been taken over by US forces. Moreover, the official policy of non-fraternisation prohibited normal social contact with Japanese families in their homes.

The most immediate effect of all these circumstances was an extremely high rate of VD. Wide sexual promiscuity and poor facilities for diagnosis and treatment had already produced a very serious VD problem among the Japanese population, and this was soon transmitted to the occupation troops. As early as March 1946, when only part of BCOF had arrived, 286 cases of VD had occurred in the Force (matched only by the large number of malaria relapses, which were to be expected when so many troops had been on suppressive atebrine in the tropics before arrival). In June, the Commander-in-Chief noted with concern the practical effects: the large number of cases, especially Australian, had resulted in an increased work burden for their comrades, a need for extra beds in the Australian hospital, and a demand for large quantities of high-cost drugs; and he instituted a programme of new measures to combat the situation. Amenities were to be improved urgently; education in sexual hygiene was to be increased; there were to be personal talks by all commanders, and sterner disciplinary measures were to be taken. In fact, while offending officers were to be returned to their country of origin, the punishment for other ranks was often limited to 15 days confined to barracks and no beer ration! Anything more severe might well have had catastrophic effects on BCOF's strength. However, these measures failed to produce the desired result. As a British battalion commander said, 'the boys will do it!'

Had BCOF adopted an organised system of medical inspection and control of brothels, along the lines established by the Japanese Army, the problem might have been largely eliminated: but fear of unfavourable publicity and fierce reaction in the home countries ensured that this never happened. In fact a sensible attempt to implement such a plan on a limited basis in BRITCOM Base nearly took place but was frustrated by local commanders.[5] The Camerons reported what must have been a typical experience, when their local Chief of Police urged them to adopt the Japanese Army arrangement in the interests of a guaranteed freedom from disease: the merits of the scheme were recognised but it was rejected, with regret.[6] Nevertheless there were a few commanding officers who were sufficiently concerned about their troops' health to tolerate discreet arrangements on an unofficial basis, with the encouragement of their medical officers, who took on the regular examination of those involved. This in one case provoked violent reaction: when an Australian infantry battalion set up an unofficial 'butterfly house' near its barracks in Kataichi, the battalion padre, after complaining to Brigade Headquarters without satisfaction, contrived to have the building destroyed by fire. In the face of such Biblical retribution, the operation was terminated.

By the end of December 1946 the total of VD cases had grown to 8090, of which the Australian contingent were responsible for 4504 – 55 per cent of the total, which was well above the 32 per cent of the force which the Australian contingent represented. This unfavourable ratio was partly due to the fact that the Australian contingent's area of occupation was Hiroshima Prefecture. Northcott had expressed his regret that the Australians had to continue to hold 'the ashes of Hiroshima and Kure', appreciating that 'as an Australian I could and would not favour them at the expense of other contingents'.[7] (An Australian Army publication had already noted the situation with the headline 'Australia takes the Ashes'). But as the main centres of civilian population in the BCOF zone with the greatest pressure of hunger and poverty, the cities of Hiroshima and Kure were the most hazardous stations for BCOF troops in terms of exposure to VD and the temptations of the black market: and the high proportion of administrative and support units located in the area were at greater risk than the more strictly disciplined infantry brigades.

There had also been a change in the composition of the Australian and New Zealand contingents. Most of the older and more experienced men who had taken part in the beginnings of the occupation had returned home for discharge and had been replaced by drafts recruited specifically for service in Japan. Among these there were a number of ex-servicemen who had not been able to settle into civilian life. Many were men who had missed the war because they were too young or in reserved occupations. Going to the war had always been a means of escape from Antipodean remoteness and parochial seclusion, an avenue of access to the world outside. Signing up for Japan restored that means of escape for boys who thought their last chance of excitement and travel had vanished with the end of the war.

There were disturbing reports of unruly behaviour at the reinforcement camps in Australia, especially at Bathurst in New South Wales, and of cries of protest from the local communities. Soldiers already serving in Japan complained of the poor standard of some of the reinforcements: they were 'loud-mouthed larrikins and law-breakers' unlike the well-behaved and well-disciplined members of the original brigade.[8] Indeed, the Sydney police warned BCOF HQ of several well-known criminals who had actually signed on in order to participate in the pickings from the black market in Japan.

It was difficult to maintain stability, although the infantry battalions were better able to sort out the problems. 67 Battalion, for example, a highly decorated unit, set up a special company officered entirely by holders of the Military Cross, to induct their reinforcements, and concluded that there was nothing wrong with the new men – any blame lay with their commanders in training and *en route*. Regimental discipline held well and was consistently enforced. Field punishment with the unit ('chasing the bugle', as it was called) meant pack drill morning and afternoon, and having to parade in full kit whenever the bugle sounded from the guard room between reveille and 'lights out': and it was usually enough to keep the wilder ones under control. But there was still a gap between old and new, a feeling of class distinction, a superiority on the part of the men who had seen combat, and a sense of loss and frustration on the part of those who came too late. (The veterans used to refer to the new boys as 'hairpins' – on the analogy of hairtriggers which are over-sensitive and pull too easily).

One of the important differences lay in the expectations of the different groups. The publicity used for recruitment in Australia and New Zealand was far too rosy. It made service in Japan sound enticing – 'like a Cook's tour', said one disillusioned Digger – and the contrast with actual conditions was a powerful shock. The wartime soldiers were conditioned to the stark realities of Army life, the discomfort, poor food and cramped quarters. The men who volunteered after the war had a difficult period of adjustment before the improvement in conditions caught up with their original expectations.

Serious crime was limited, but there was a steady stream of robberies, sometimes with violence, committed against the civilian population, as well as occasional rape and sexual offences. Excessive drinking was often involved. Naval ratings ashore at Kure were particularly prone to committing thefts from Japanese shops and other acts of a more or less violent nature, and struck fear into the hearts of Japanese of both sexes as they roamed the streets in their rowdy gangs. Soldiers would sometimes find themselves protecting civilians from naval attack. Offenders were dealt with severely and convicted criminals were removed from Japan: prompt action was important not only to maintain law and order but also to increase the confidence of the civil population.

The military police were busy men. The 34 Brigade MPs in Hiroshima Prefecture, who were the busiest of all, were highly effective, and acquired an excellent reputation for justice and consideration with Japanese and BCOF personnel alike. 'They didn't interfere unless you were outrightly in the wrong, doing something illegal or fighting or very drunk', said one connoisseur.[9] Interpreter Clifton rated them as the best unit in BCOF and 'fine ambassadors' for Australia.[10] The British MPs were deemed to be far too formal, lacking in understanding and over-keen on enforcing dress regulations, while the American MPs met in Tokyo and Kobe were considered to be immature and far too ready with firearms.[11]

While the usual machinery of courts-martial and military punishment existed for offences by members of the occupation Force, BCOF Provost Courts were set up to try Japanese for offences against the occupation, such as black marketing, theft, violence and disobedience of SCAP's military directives. In the first nine months of the 2 NZEF Provost Court's operation, for instance, when it was sitting alternately in Shimonoseki and Yamaguchi, it heard 330 charges, and handed down sentences ranging from four years' imprisonment and heavy fines for disobedience of directives to deferred sentences and probation for young people convicted of less serious offences.

The courts were also directed to try offences by Allied nationals against Japanese law, and found themselves frequently hearing charges against Chinese civilians, often long-term residents in Japan, who had discovered that their newly-recognised status as Allied nationals gave them great mobility and wider access to successful black market activities.

Courts were always open to the civilian population, which attended in large numbers. Their operation was almost the only way open for BCOF to demonstrate to the Japanese the workings of democracy. However trivial the charge, an officer was always available to defend the accused, and Japanese counsel were encouraged to appear if desired. A further extension of court activities which aroused much local interest and surprise was the introduction by the New Zealanders of children's sessions with the aim of reform rather than punishment.

Sometimes particular cases and their treatment in the BCOF courts could be turned to the advantage of the occupation's broader purposes. There was a specific example of this on 17 September 1946 when a Japanese civilian, Suzukawa, was put on trial before a BCAIR Provost Court in Iwakuni on a charge of murdering a member of the occupation force.[12] Signalman Paul, an Indian serving with the Air Formation Signals at the Iwakuni air base, had posed as a military policeman to get access to a house on the pretext that it was a brothel which he was inspecting. He had been drinking and tried to rape the lady of the house. Suzukawa, a friend of the family, restrained Paul with a judo grip and in the struggle Paul's neck was broken. It was obvious that Suzukawa would be acquitted and it was decided that he should be tried publicly, so that the local Japanese could see British justice in action and appreciate that they had the same rights and privileges in a British court as British nationals. The trial was held in the Lotus Dance Hall in Iwakuni in order to allow as many locals to attend as possible, and 300 people packed the building. The verdict of acquittal was received with great emotion by both the accused and the spectators, and the court was praised for the excellence of its humane judgment. According to the local press, this was the best example of democracy in action so far. Every Japanese knew that had a civilian in a country occupied by the Japanese killed a Japanese serviceman, no matter how, he would not have lived long enough to come to trial. (Paul's fellow signalmen thought he was an undesirable character who probably deserved his fate).

Such excitements were luckily rare. A different kind of problem with a different kind of attendant excitement was the permanent risk of fire. Fire was always a serious hazard in Japan. House fires in the towns were common: the wooden houses were built of light pine and were huddled close together, with their floors of tatami matting and their internal walls of paper, and the fires would spread quickly. Throughout the BCOF area too, accommodation was generally in wooden buildings and there were constant dangers from cigarettes, stoves and faulty electrical installations. There were a number of fires in the Kure area during 1946 and 1947. In May 1947 the station officers' mess and quarters at the BCAIR base at Iwakuni was burnt down, as a result of a careless cigarette, and two RAF officers lost their lives. Many others escaped by sliding down ropes from second storey windows but lost all their possessions. The New Zealanders' area seemed to be particularly affected: a big New Zealand Service Corps supply point building at Chofu was completely destroyed by fire in June of that year, followed by another fire in the garrison stores there in September. This was the seventh major fire in the area and rumours of sabotage began to circulate among the troops but were never substantiated. The faulty construction of flimsy buildings and the difficulty of maintaining complete fire discipline were primarily at fault. When 3,000 Japanese civilians were made homeless by a blaze which destroyed most of Chofu's shopping area in October (nearly 800 were billeted and fed by 2 NZEF), it was clear that the occupation forces were not the only victims.

But the black market and the alleged immorality in BCOF remained the most serious domestic problems during the occupation. They were matters of concern to commanders and, because of sensationalist publicity in Australia, to the public there as well.

12

Fraternisation

Behind those outward manifestations of black marketing and so-called immorality lurked the basic issue of fraternisation and the relationship between the occupiers and the occupied. There was a sharp difference between British and American policy in this respect which characterised their different approach to the occupation more than anything else.

At the time of the surrender in August 1945 Mountbatten had wasted no time in suggesting to MacArthur that it would be the greatest mistake to be soft with the Japanese. '. . . The fact that you have been prevented from inflicting the crushing defeat will, I fear, enable the Japanese to delude their people into thinking they were defeated only by the scientist, and not in battle, unless we can so humble them that the completeness of defeat is brought home to them . . .'.[1]

The British Commonwealth, and more particularly the Australian, attitude reflected this stern approach. Australians had, in MacArthur's words, seen the enemy hordes plunge forward with almost irresistible force to the very threshold of their homeland.[2] Their northernmost city, Darwin, had suffered more than 60 destructive air raids in which several hundreds had died, accompanied by a real fear of invasion: there had been the shock of midget submarine attacks in Sydney, the gateway to Australia; and their soldiers had been engaged in a most bitter struggle against a fanatical enemy under the worst possible physical conditions. They were more sensitive to the Japanese threat in the Pacific than the other Allies and determined to ensure that it would never arise again.

1. An Australian sailor nails up the British Landing Force sign at Yokosuka, 30 August 1945. (*IWM*)

2. Kure, BCOF's principal base. (*Mr E Saxon*)

3. Hiroshima, viewed by ratings of the Royal Indian Navy from HMIS *Sutlej*, February 1946. (*IWM*)

4. Lieutenant General Northcott, C-in-C BCOF with Air Vice Marshal Bouchier, AOC BCAIR arrive at Kuala Lumpur, Malaya, to inspect 11 and 17 Squadrons RAF before their departure for Japan. (*BCAIR*)

5. The Commander-in-Chief BCOF, Lieutenant General Robertson, with his formation commanders. (*IWM*)

L to R.   Brigadier A G Wilson (OC BRITCOM Base), Captain J Brindle RN (NOIC), Air Vice Marshal F M Bladin (COS BCOF), Major General D T Cowan (GOC BRINDIV), Brigadier R N L Hopkins (Comd. 34 Aust. Inf. Bde), Lieutenant General H C H Robertson, Brigadier L S Potter (Comd. 2 NZEF), Air Vice Marshal C A Bouchier (AOC BCAIR), Brigadier G H Clifton (BGS HQ BCOF) and Brigadier Anderson.

6. Japanese repatriates undergoing a customs search supervised by New Zealand troops. (*IWM*)

7. The Pipes and Drums of the Cameron Highlanders showing the flag in Shikoku, 1946. (*IWM*)

8. Shikoku, 1946. A patrol of the Royal Welch Fusiliers. (*IWM*)

9. Japanese children in Hiroshima – curious and friendly. (*Author*)

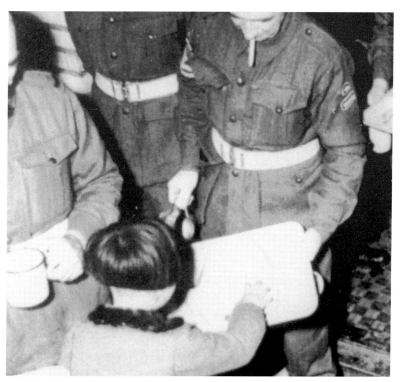

10. Australian soldiers share their rations with a group of Japanese children calling at their camp in Kure, Spring 1946. (*Author*)

11. The Commander-in-Chief, British Pacific Fleet, Vice Admiral Sir Dennis Boyd, during an official visit to HQ BCOF at Etajima. (*IWM*)
L to R. Lieutenant Gibson RN (Flag Lieutenant), Brigadier Clifton (BGS BCOF), Admiral Boyd, Lieutenant General Robertson.

12. The 'torii' at Miyajima, the best-known tourist and holiday resort in the BCOF area. (*Author*)

13. Near Miho. A Spitfire Mk XIV of 11 Squadron RAF passing Mount Daisen. (*BCAIR*)

14. A BCOF Provost Court in session at Iwakuni – a Japanese lawyer is addressing the court. (*IWM*)

15. General Robertson's farewell parade in Kure, 7 November 1951. Inspecting a detachment from the 3rd Battalion, Royal Australian Regiment (then on active service in Korea). (*IWM*)

16. Japanese civilians in Kure watch General Robertson's farewell parade with absorbed but impassive interest. (*IWM*)

Information about wartime atrocities and the agonising revelations by released Allied prisoners of war of their treatment during captivity had sharpened antagonism towards Japan. 'There is universal demand . . . that the Potsdam surrender terms shall be sternly and unwaveringly enforced', said a Sydney newspaper.[3] There were loud and sustained calls for the Emperor to be dethroned and tried as a war criminal. The Chifley government made it clear that it was intent on 'bringing about a radical change in Japanese society by an intensive and prolonged occupation'.[4] Evatt later stressed his own view that 'Australia's very life depends on a just and severe settlement with Japan'.[5]

The difference between this attitude and that adopted by the Americans first emerged at the time of the surrender. MacArthur in his new capacity as Supreme Commander for the Allied Powers had decreed that no swords were to be handed over by the Japanese in the course of their surrender to Allied forces. Slim disregarded this, and ordered that all senior Japanese officers were to surrender their swords to appropriate British commanders in front of parades of their own troops. He, like Mountbatten, was determined to impress on the Japanese that they had been beaten in the field, and to avoid a repetition of the First World War German legend of an undefeated army.

The split between the British and the Americans in their approach to the Japanese characterised by this small but significant episode widened into a substantial difference of opinion about occupation policy. MacArthur's experience in occupied Germany in 1918-19 had caused him to form many positive views about military occupation. He had seen the 'loss of self-respect and self-confidence by the people; . . . the lowering of the spiritual and moral tone of a population controlled by foreign bayonets; the inevitable deterioration in the occupation forces themselves as the disease of power infiltrated their ranks and bred a sort of race superiority',[6] and he was determined to avoid one party becoming slaves and the other masters. In particular, he was opposed to any order forbidding fraternisation, both on principle and because of the difficulty of effective enforcement. In Japan this became his firm policy : 'My father told me never to give an order unless I was certain it would be carried out. I wouldn't issue a non-fraternisation order for all the tea in China.'[7]

This was in fact in line with the official Washington policy, which was that 'association of personnel of the occupation forces with the Japanese population should be controlled only to the extent necessary to further the policies and objectives of occupation'.[8] The intention was that a non-fraternisation order would only be applied if and when SCAP considered it necessary.

At the beginning of the occupation, therefore, the American authorities neither forbade nor encouraged fraternisation. From the initial landings the GIs were not prevented from trying to establish a reasonably friendly relationship with the defeated enemy. It took some while before they were able to reassure the shocked inhabitants of those ruined cities that their fate was not to be murder, rape and plunder. It was the children, drawn from their shattered homes by curiosity and hunger, who formed the first contacts with the troops. The only really strict regulation imposed by SCAP prohibited occupation forces from obtaining food and drink from the Japanese, whose needs were far greater.

MacArthur's self-imposed missionary role also encouraged a warmer relationship with the Japanese. He had undertaken the task of 'democratising' and Christianising a defeated people, in whose eyes he had already become an alternative Emperor. His headquarters contained 5,000 occupationnaires who were dedicated to the transformation of Japan through an ambitious and immense programme of radical reform intended to affect all aspects of public and private life in Japanese society. While MacArthur himself retained the personal aloofness he regarded as proper for his position, the American-Japanese relationship was a vital part of the future, and it was important to him that the Americans should be seen as helpers and protectors, rather than conquerors.

The BCOF policy on fraternisation was far more rigid. Northcott expressed it in a Personal Instruction issued with the approval of JCOSA after reference to Commonwealth Governments.[9] After recognising the impracticability of issuing stringent orders to cover an infinite variety of contingencies, it stated the policy as follows:

'Every member of the BCOF must bear in mind that he is present in Japan in a dual capacity. He is not only a sailor, soldier or airman. He is also a representative of the British Commonwealth of Nations and all that stands for in the world. In dealing with the Japanese he is dealing with a con-

quered enemy who has by making war against us caused
deep suffering and loss in many thousands of homes
throughout the British Empire. Your relation with this
defeated enemy must be guided largely by your own individual good judgement and your sense of discipline. You
must be formal and correct. You must not enter their homes
or take part in their family life. Your unofficial dealings with
the Japanese must be kept to the minimum. You must obey
strictly all instructions regarding establishments or areas
which are placed out of bounds to personnel forming part of
the BCOF. Above all, you must remember the dual capacity
in which you come to Japan and, beyond that, the fact that
the eyes of the Japanese and our Allies and indeed of the
world will be watching you. Much depends on your conduct and on your bearing. Be sure that they remain formal
and that they are in keeping with the dignity and courtesy
which are part of our common heritage and tradition.'

The statement also explicitly prohibited any athletic or sporting
activities with Japanese teams or individuals, and emphasised the
ban on the procurement of food from local sources which the
national shortage of food made so important.

This instruction was included in a handbook called 'Know
Japan' which was issued to every member of BCOF before or on
arrival in Japan.[10] It was generally regarded by all ranks as being
excessively strict and its issue did not, of course, in practice prevent
fraternisation. The Japanese themselves were only too ready to
encourage it in return for the highly desirable supplies of food,
clothing, cigarettes, soap and other necessities they could obtain
from BCOF sources. Similarly, it was naive to suppose that contact
between 36,000 young servicemen and the Japanese female population could be prevented. Nevertheless, the regulations were strict,
they were initially enforced with some consistency, and breaches
were severely punished. 'We still spoke to the Japanese when we
could, but we had to watch where we went – there were MPs around
all the time', recalled an Australian sapper.[11]

British policy on fraternisation in occupied Germany was
much more relaxed. There had been a month of complete non-
fraternisation in the British zone after the surrender to Montgomery
in May 1945, but in June soldiers were allowed to speak and play

with children and a fortnight later permission was given for conversation with Germans in streets and public places, although entry to German houses was still forbidden. In September 1945, only four months after fighting had stopped, the ban on fraternisation was lifted completely, subject only to the restriction that no members of the armed forces were to be billeted with Germans, and marriages were still not allowed.

The contrast of BCOF policy with the easy-going practice of the Americans in Japan was even more pronounced. BCOF personnel on leave or duty in Tokyo were sometimes amused but mainly envious when they saw GIs walking in the street with their arms round their Japanese girl friends. Others noted that in Osaka the US Army had clubs where dozens of Japanese women worked in national dress as barmaids, and there were two American cinemas where three nights of the week were classed as 'date nights' when the American soldier could take along a girl friend, either American or Japanese. This more liberal attitude undoubtedly avoided the furtive sneaking into Japanese houses and the surreptitious meetings in dark lanes which the stricter BCOF policy provoked, as well as the brawls with Japanese which sometimes resulted.

Hunger was probably the most important factor working against the BCOF non-fraternisation ban. The unsupplemented Japanese food ration was insufficient to sustain life. In the first reported case of an American soldier marrying a Japanese girl, the parents stated bluntly that it was a commercial arrangement: 'We can do with some American rations', said the proud father.[12] Most Japanese in the cities were hungry all the time. In Kure the troops were followed nightly by hungry women asking for chocolate, condensed milk, a few ounces of sugar, tins of bully beef or packets of cigarettes. One soldier reported that a young woman had eaten the contents of his five-year-old emergency rations which he had brought from Lae in New Guinea. Many of the women were war widows or their husbands were missing, and relationships which started with the transfer of canteen goods often developed through pity into real friendships.

The difference in national attitudes between BCOF and the Americans had already been detected as early as January 1946 by Japanese newspaper correspondents, who had asked the visiting American Secretary for War why it was necessary to send British and Australian troops to Japan when 'the Japanese were getting on so well with General MacArthur and the American occupation forces'.[13] An evasive answer was given: 'no definite arrangements have yet been made', although in fact the decisions had been taken. The Australian press reported that 'advance guards of the Australian occupation force seem to the Japanese to be frigid and unfriendly in comparison with the withdrawing Americans'.[14] BCOF censorship of Japanese mail later in the year revealed some writers who recalled the days when their district was occupied by American troops, whom they considered 'more kind and attractive' than BCOF troops. It was said of the Australians that there was a tendency for 'even the defeated Japanese to look down on them as grandsons of uncivilised convicts . . . and to see the Australian troops as one level below the Americans even though they were all part of the same army of occupation'.[15]

The stricter BCOF approach also brought some unexpected attention from the Japanese authorities. In March 1946, in the earliest days of the presence of BCOF, the Japanese Foreign Minister, Shigeru Yoshida, publicly commented on the fact that the British and Australians were not fraternising, and described them as 'unresponsive'.[16] It was suggested that bands of geisha girls had been specifically assembled near BCOF camps to entertain the troops, only to be disappointed by this lack of response. Yoshida's comment, although surprising, clearly betrayed the Japanese offical interest in promoting fraternisation, with the beneficial effect it would have for increasing goodwill and shortening the occupation. The more rigid policy of BCOF, and the attitude of the Australians in particular, were regarded as extensions of wartime animosity.

The reaction of the population at large was confused. As a BCOF Intelligence Summary in September 1946 reported, 'while many of the female of the species seem to favour fraternisation, the Japanese male resents it to a marked extent. Many of the reported incidents involving Japanese and occupation troops have as their basis the eternal triangle, as the Japanese male who at first blamed the woman is now inclined to blame the man concerned as well'.[17] BCAIR attempted to sound out Japanese public opinion on the issue in the Iwakuni area and found that many of the people questioned (particularly the men, as might have been expected) said they preferred to keep relations with the occupation troops on a strictly business basis. But there was no doubt that both sexes were amazed and impressed by the normal Western courtesies to women, whom many members of BCOF felt were treated like slaves by their menfolk. It was always noted with surprise when a BCOF soldier got up in public transport to give a seat to an elderly or pregnant woman, or opened a door for a woman to precede him.

BCOF's official policy never changed, and there was still a determination in other unexpected ways to separate BCOF from the life and institutions of the country. In November 1947, for example, the Emperor undertook a royal visit to the Chugoku region as part of a series of tours around the country to develop the new-found popularity which had, with the encouragement of SCAP, replaced his former heavenly status. Chugoku encompassed all the prefectures occupied by BCOF. The military government attitude was that it was an entirely Japanese affair with which they were not concerned, and a BCOF instruction was issued to make it clear that there was no official recognition of the visit, that no BCOF personnel should take part in any official function, and that the Emperor would not visit any BCOF installation.

The imperial route was to start in Tottori and wind its way round the coastal cities, towns and villages of the BCOF area, through Yamaguchi, Hiroshima and Kure, and many smaller places in between. Reports began to come in from Japanese and Korean informers about an alleged plot for the assassination of the Emperor while in Yamaguchi Prefecture. The plotters were said to be Communists who had worked in Korea and Koreans themselves, who were dissatisfied at the strong measures taken by the Japanese authorities to enforce control over Koreans in Japan. It was suggested that there would be an attack by pistol or hand grenade, and that the plotters would escape to Korea by a ship which would be moored near the spot selected for the attempt. Alarm was expressed by the Governor of Yamaguchi Prefecture: his police resources were insufficient, and he asked for assistance from the occupation forces. The Governor of Hiroshima was also worried: there was suspicion of violence on the part of the Mitsubishi employees in Mihara, who were said to be 90 per cent Communist.

This useful opportunity for a closer involvement with local government was rejected out of hand. BCOF Headquarters said that protection of the Emperor was a purely Japanese responsibility: if the Japanese authorities could not cope, the tour should be cancelled. BCOF would not get involved. The final irony was that the tour went ahead without incident, receiving strong popular support.[18]

But as the years passed, the enforcement of the non-fraternisation rules slackened to some extent. Normal social contact with the civilian population was not easy – the language was a considerable barrier – and in many instances undesirable because of the high incidence of VD and tuberculosis among the poorer farming, labouring and artisan classes which were in the majority in the BCOF area. But it was necessary for the troops to mix in the course of their daily lives with the large numbers of men and women of all classes employed by the force as clerical workers, interpreters, kitchen staff, house servants and labourers. At its peak, BCOF employed over 20,000 Japanese workers, and even by the end of the occupation this had only declined to 10,500.

All washing, ironing and cleaning was done by local women employees, which encouraged personal relationships of a close and usually platonic kind. Many friendships were initially established through this employer-employee association and it was natural for them to be continued outside working hours. As the contacts developed and extended to shopkeepers, dealers and officals, an undefined working arrangement was eventually achieved. There were more and more connections through the medium of education, the Japanese schools and the children. In the smaller villages out in the country it was easier for soldiers to meet Japanese of both sexes and different classes: 'human nature and the British soldier being what he is, the barriers were soon down and regular meetings with local families soon started', said a Dorsets sergeant.[19]

As time went on, it was inevitable that the question of marriage between BCOF personnel and Japanese women became a matter of increasing concern, particularly within the Australian contingent who remained the mainstay of BCOF after the departure of the other national contingents. As early as September 1946 a BCOF Administrative Instruction had laid it down that no member of BCOF could marry without the written authority of the Commander-in-Chief and his own commander.[20] If this was disregarded and a marriage was carried out without such an authority by a civilian clergyman or under Japanese civil law, disciplinary action was likely. In no circumstances would approval be given for a marriage between a member of BCOF and a Japanese national. A reminder was also added for the benefit of the Australian contingent that an Asiatic woman of non-Japanese nationality, even if married to an Australian serviceman, would as a general rule be debarred from admission to Australia (the old 'White Australia' policy was still in place).

Cases involving Indian troops, although covered by the blanket BCOF prohibition, needed special care because of the political aspects of the possible relationship in the future between people with common Asian interests. The December 1946 report from BCOF to JCOSA, for example, mentioned that two cases had occurred of Indian personnel desiring to marry Japanese women, but that 'both cases have been avoided without trouble'.[21]

Marriages between men of the BCOF contingents and members of the women's services forming part of the Force, of course, presented no problems, and began to acquire a steady momentum. By December 1946 12 cases had been dealt with and approved by BCOF Headquarters. One of the earliest had an unusual character of its own: at a time when interracial marriages were uncommon and often opposed, an Indian captain on the BRINDIV staff married an English member of the FANYs, and after the military wedding in Okayama the ceremony was solemnised under Islamic ritual in the Muslim mosque in Kobe (the first Service marriage to take place there).

In February 1947 the Australian Cabinet discussed the issue of fraternisation again, in the light of reports that a number of Australian troops had married Japanese girls and were supplying them with money made by selling goods on the black market. The troops concerned were going through a Japanese form of marriage, since they were unable to get their commanding officers' permission because of the ban on fraternisation. It was for consideration whether the ban should be lifted, to conform with the American system.

In the event it was decided that the ban should remain, and a further BCOF instruction in 1948 repeated that no permission would be given to a Japanese or part-Japanese woman to take up permanent residence in Australia, whether married to an Australian or not. On 9 March 1948, Calwell, the Minister for Immigration, in reply to questions in the House of Representatives, gave this a highly-coloured emotional endorsement: '. . . No Australian mother whose devoted son, no Australian wife whose decent Australian husband, lies buried in some Pacific battlefield, will have her feelings outraged by an Australian flaunting a Japanese woman before her . . . While relatives remain of men who suffered at the hands of the

Japanese, it would be the grossest act of public indecency to permit a Japanese of either sex to pollute Australian shores'.[22]

History has since turned this uncompromising statement on its head, but it was popular at the time. The attitude it expressed was reflected in a speech by Robertson in Hiroshima in August 1948, on the third anniversary of the dropping of the bomb. He took the opportunity to remind the Japanese that the fault was theirs, and said 'I hope you will not forget it'.[23] The American press was outraged by the implied criticism by the British and Australians of America's 'soft policy' towards Japan which they felt dominated the ceremony: but Commonwealth public opinion backed Robertson. 'To be tough with Japan is a matter of grim necessity if we wish to save the next generation or the one after that from a similar threat to ourselves'.[24]

There is no doubt that this view also unconsciously demonstrated the continuation of a powerful 'White Australia' school of thought at that time among politicians there and the people they represented. The desire to repel a 'flood of Orientals' and to avoid a 'brindled population' was strongly supported by the electorate in Australia.[25]

A year later something happened to provoke a further review of the BCOF policy on fraternisation. On 23 September 1949, MacArthur issued a new set of regulations designed to lift practically all restrictions on friendly relations between the occupation forces and the Japanese people, with the extraordinary objective, in his words, of 'establishing the same relations between occupation personnel and the Japanese population as exists between troops stationed in the United States and the American people'. Under these new arrangements the troops could now patronise all Japanese hotels, inns and theatres not specifically put out of bounds; they could procure Japanese food and drink provided it was not purchased on the black market; they could compete with or participate in any Japanese sporting team; they could tip domestic servants and give bona fide gifts to Japanese acquaintances; and they could sell or barter personal property provided there was no semblance of black market activities. What was even more important was the approval given for Japanese to visit US service clubs and join in the organised social activities there. Many of these concessions had, of course, been effectively in operation on an unofficial basis for some time, but now official blessing had been given.

This was the subject of immediate comment in the Australian House of Representatives in Canberra, where Dedman, the Minister for Defence, told the House on 30 September that the Commander-in-Chief BCOF had not been instructed to follow the American lead in lifting the fraternisation ban. Robertson had raised the matter and an instruction had been sent to him that 'there was to be no change in the directive previously issued to him on the matter', which forbade fraternisation between Australian forces and the Japanese.[26] Dedman made a further statement on 4 October, repeating that the latitude allowed to troops in a foreign country was entirely one for the commander of the troops but that the Australian Government had made its opposition to fraternisation perfectly clear to Robertson, although it had decided not to protest to the US Government or General MacArthur against his order allowing fraternisation.[27] Public opinion in Australia remained, as always, far more inflexible towards the Japanese than in the United States. There the arguments for rebuilding a friendly Japan under American protection and with American aid as a bulwark against the Communist threat in China and Korea had already outweighed the desire for punishment or retaliation.

Meanwhile, mixed marriages in BCOF continued to take place according to Shinto rites, although they could not be validated by a Christian ceremony within the BCOF environment. Many failed to last because of the difficulties they faced from officialdom, but a number of individual cases received considerable publicity in Australia. The most colourful of these cases, and therefore the one which achieved the widest publicity, concerned a soldier named Frank Loyal Weaver.

Weaver had been returned to Australia from BCOF at the beginning of 1948 as 'mentally unstable'. Although he was only 22, he already possessed a military crime record which included being absent without leave on numerous occasions, theft and arson. Legend had it that he had once set BCOF HQ on fire, and another story tells of him being caught by a senior NCO while driving an enormous low loader out of his vehicle park at 2 am with his Japanese girl friend in the cab beside him. 'I'm just taking the vehicle for a road test', he is reputed to have said.

While in Japan Weaver had gone through a Shinto ceremony of marriage with his girl friend, whom he was also reputed to have set up in a shop stocked with black market goods. After his involuntary return to Australia, he reappeared in Japan on 26 February 1948, having travelled on an American military aircraft with forged American travel documents, and rejoined his wife in Kure. He was arrested and deported, but managed to re-enter Japan again: and this process was repeated a number of times. Weaver's obsessional persistence and ingenuity to some extent endeared him to the Australian soldier, who has always admired the flouting of authority, and he became a minor legend in BCOF.

In January 1952 he entered Japan illegally for the eighth time and was once more arrested. He found that his wife, for whom he had renounced his Australian citizenship in 1950, had remarried. 'The Australian Government will be happy to learn', he said, 'that it has at last succeeded in ending the relationship between my wife and myself . . .' When he was deported for the eighth time, he said 'I won't be back', and returned to life in Australia. He came briefly into public view once again in 1985 as the self-styled founder and secretary of Japan-Australia Pen Friends Association, which was looking for pen friends in New South Wales to write to Japanese high school, college and university students 'in the cause of promoting international understanding, goodwill and lasting friendship on a permanent basis between Japan and Australia'. This was no doubt a vehicle for making money but it was still a touching sign of his desire to maintain links with the country and the people which he had once tried to make his own.

The Weaver case and some others less colourful attracted much press coverage and a mainly sympathetic public response in both Japan and Australia, and led to considerable pressure on the Australian Government, both inside and outside Parliament, to allow entry for Japanese wives of servicemen to Australia. This finally achieved success in March 1952, when the Government formally relaxed the ban on immigration, subject to the authorities being satisfied that the marriage was bone fide and likely to remain unbroken. About 12 cases were pending at that time.

While political change was already beginning to produce a relaxation of the 'White Australia policy', there is no doubt that the BCOF marriages, and the enhanced knowledge of Japan that the occupation had brought to Australia, helped to accelerate that process. No fewer than 868 cases of mixed marriage were handled by Kure city alone,[28] and by the end of the occupation about 200 Japanese wives had settled in Australia.[29]

13

The Sunny Side

BCOF had no formal links with the various civilian Commonwealth missions or the Commonwealth representative and staff on the Allied Council for Japan in Tokyo (the civilian body set up to advise MacArthur on the implementation of occupation directives and largely ignored by him). It had, however, taken on the responsibility of supplying and supporting them through BRICOSAT, its sub-unit in the capital. There were informal visits to BCOF by MacMahon Ball, the Australian representing the Commonwealth on the Council, and by individual members of the Commonwealth missions, but the chain of command remained firmly in the direct line of responsibility from BCOF to SCAP.

However, BCOF was now beginning to sort out its own situation and its own problems by the steady introduction of proper military organisation, with some of the usual faults and all the merits normally to be expected. Increasing bureaucracy was accompanied by a continuing improvement in conditions. Montgomery once said 'the task of influencing an Army which dwells among an alien population is easy: the thinking and way of life of the people is mainly irrelevant'.[1] He was using the phrase in antithesis to his theme of the moment, which was to stress the necessity of the British Army dwelling among its own people in the United Kingdom at the time of the pre-Normandy build-up, to inspire, and be inspired by them. But it is a true reflection of the way in which an army of occupation can cut itself off from its surroundings. The garrison life is self-contained and insulated; contact with the civilian population can be limited and controlled, and lan-

122

guage is a natural obstacle. All these factors influenced BCOF's existence to some degree.

As might have been expected, therefore, most of BCOF's life on and off duty revolved around itself. But when the initial tasks of demilitarisation and supervision of repatriation started to decline in importance as their completion approached, and accommodation started to reach an acceptable standard, units began to concentrate on their patrol responsibilities and the institution of proper training programmes.

The regular soldiers were eager to maintain their fighting capability and hoped that there might be opportunities to utilise it. The operation orders of the Punjabis, for example, made it clear that, while offensive action would only be resorted to in the event of a hostile act against Allied lives or property, it would if resorted to be carried out 'with vigour'. Units would in such a situation employ normal military methods, using their weapons and equipment in the manner they had been trained to use them.[2]

However, the Japanese had no intention of abandoning their attitude of passive compliance. They were far too busy trying to feed themselves and make a living for any violent reaction against the occupation. There were minor incidents – cut telephone lines, stones on railway tracks, thefts, the occasional assault – but they were always carried out by men frustrated by unemployment or jealous of Allied soldiers' attentions to Japanese girls, or by petty criminals. The only real violence came from Communist rioting and disorder in the larger cities to the east, and it was invariably aimed at the civil police rather than occupation troops. The BCOF area remained peaceful, the enemy being boredom rather than hostility.

It was important, therefore, to seek means of developing the traditional ways of keeping the troops occupied and happy. They found some diversion in the new roles which they had to adopt in the course of duty, in particular the water-borne activities which became a permanent feature of life. Since most of the units were located on the coast and many of their duties involved journeying by water, they developed a taste for it and the necessary skills involved. The units on the north and west coasts, charged with preventing illegal immigration, found themselves operating high-speed craft of many kinds and sizes, with the help of Japanese crews and working in conjunction with Commonwealth naval vessels. Troops everywhere sailed boats on and off duty, with varying degrees of danger.

On one occasion a BRINDIV officer and three Royal Army Service Corps private soldiers, with no navigational experience between them and only a one-inch ordnance map for guidance, brought a 50-foot motor vessel on a two-day supply trip for the general from Kure to Okayama. Having survived storms and a leak, they reached their destination as night was falling on the second day, to be told that they had just come through an uncleared minefield.[3]

There was constant travel by ferry and landing barge between the mainland and the islands, especially Etajima, where the Australian hospital and a number of BCOF headquarter units were located, and Shikoku. Troops, vehicles and stores had to be trans-ported on a regular basis. The barge handlers developed a particular skill and flair of their own, and became accustomed to manoeuvring their craft at speed and with precision, although occasionally they would be over-confident and end up on the jetty or with a barge full of sea water.[4]

The colourful pattern of BCOF's own military mixture was another source of diversion. An Australian sapper's contemporary account of a BRINDIV race meeting in Okayama in September 1946 paints a vivid picture.[5] Okayama racecourse had been in use before the war, but had fallen into decay during hostilities, when horse racing had been forbidden by law. The ancient horses were ridden by a variety of jockeys – 'fat turbaned Indian merchants straight out of "One Thousand and One Nights", gaunt long-legged English offi-cers, and some fresh-faced Cockneys'. There was music from the Kumaon band – 'dark-skinned Indians, picturesque in shining white uniforms, with green trappings and turbans' – and most of the races were won (as they should have been) by riders from the 7th Cavalry.

A regular system of sports, recreation and entertainment began to be established. Sporting tournaments at unit and formation level became a regular feature of life. Bands made tours of other units: concert parties from Australia carried out a series of visits which continued throughout the occupation, and in the early days were joined by groups from Britain and India, although the Indian con-cert party was despatched home early, having for unspecified reasons, proved unsatisfactory.[6] The troops even became somewhat blasé: a New Zealand report noted sourly that stage entertainment had to be of exceptional standard to arouse any enthusiasm among the troops – the cinema service remained the most popular form of entertainment.[7]

Radio stations were set up, the principal one broadcasting from Osaka on short wave throughout the BCOF area on a daily basis, with local stations serving the Australian and New Zealand contingents in their own areas. A Force newspaper, *BCON*, was produced by a special BCOF press section in Osaka using the plant and facilities of the Mainichi Press there and grew into a four-page daily, with news from all the participating Commonwealth countries, including an Indian section printed in Urdu.

Meanwhile, substantial progress was being achieved in the provision of the amenities to which Robertson had given priority. Canteens and clubs were gradually set up in all brigade and battalion areas and a chain of leave hostels and holiday homes was developed, both within the BCOF area and in the American zone. By the middle of 1947, there was an impressive network of leave centres, of which the flagship was the Kawana Hotel on the Izu Peninsula just south of Tokyo, a most luxurious Western-style hotel originally built for the 1940 Olympic Games which never took place because of the war. That BCOF should have secured such a prize in the American zone was so unexpected that a strong BCOF rumour suggested that it had been accepted in exchange for the Americans keeping Hyogo Prefecture and Kobe! Other clubs and hotels in the American zone were also established in the leading tourist localities at Beppu, the centre of Japan's best-known hot springs, Kyoto, the former capital, the leading cultural and artistic centre, Nikko, famous for its temples, shrines and mountain scenery, and at Tokyo and Kobe. All BCOF's holiday centres were made available also to British Commonwealth and American civilians in Japan, and the Marunouchi Hotel in central Tokyo became the recognised recreation centre in Tokyo for the British community. 'The rapid transformation which Robertson had effected in the stark conditions which BCOF had experienced in its initial months was one of the more obvious evidences of his flair for organisation', said an ex-service newsletter. 'BCOF enjoyed . . . amenities of a profuseness and quality unparalleled in the history of any of the British Armed Services'.[8]

A notable contribution to the morale of the Force was the participation of the women's services. Each of the hospitals, British, Indian, Australian and New Zealand, had a full complement of nurses who played a busy part in social as well as medical activities, although mainly for the benefit of the officers. Each national contingent also brought with it a team of women welfare workers in various uniforms, some with misleading titles but most with honours deservedly won during the war. BRINDIV and the RAF component of BCAIR were the first to organise themselves carefully in this respect: they were accompanied by the FANYS – the First Aid Nursing Yeomanry – whose role was to drive mobile canteens; the WAS(B), or Wasbees as they were known – the Women's Auxiliary Service (Burma) – who came from the Burma battlefields to run canteens for the troops: and the WVS(UK) and WVS(I) – the Womens' Voluntary Services UK and India – who helped to operate the clubs and leave centres. (The Indians were, unfortunately, worse served than the others: there were only 6 WVS(I) women and repeated requests to GHQ India for more met with a stony silence). Robertson strove hard for similar help from Australia and New Zealand, and the first Australian canteen workers began to arrive in October 1946 and were followed by a steady stream.

All the Commonwealth governments, with the exception of New Zealand, agreed in 1946 that dependents would be allowed to go to Japan. Wives and families of the other three contingents were encouraged to join their menfolk and about 700 families of UK, Australian and Indian servicemen travelled to Japan between 1946 and 1948. This involved the planning and building of special houses, shops, schools and hospitals. Most of the Australian families (over a third of the total) were settled in a new family housing area known as Nijimura (Rainbow Village) at Hiro, where they enjoyed the new sensation of having servants to cope with all the menial tasks of the household. This gave rise to another problem well-known from the days of the Raj: 'there was not enough to occupy the wives, in view of the servant allocation'.[9] But the presence of the families had a double benefit: not only did it raise the morale of the troops, but it also gave many Japanese a novel opportunity to appreciate the way of life of the foreigners and the independence of women in their society.

It was now possible to concentrate on the provision of suitable training areas and the development of proper training programmes. The Force carried out normal training activities on a unit basis throughout 1946, combining them with the demands of their operational duties. Training grounds and firing ranges were established, often some distance from base, and companies would move out to them in rotation. The commanding officer of the Gurkhas noted that a fortnight at a time for each of his rifle companies in camp on the classification range 10 miles from their barracks was most popular, in spite of discomfort and bad weather. 'The reason, I feel, is, he recorded, 'that after an unsettled existence for the first four months . . . preceded by the long wait . . . the men do now feel that they are on the job and that there is a real object in their work'.[10]

Advanced field training began in 1947. 34 Brigade, for example, established training grounds at Haramura, about 20 miles from Kure, where there was already a field firing range over undulating ground used by the Japanese for horsed cavalry training during the war, and at other sites in Okayama and Shimane Prefectures. The one at Nipponbara soon became known as one of the toughest infantry training schools ever run by the Australian Army and exercises carried out there included full-scale manoeuvres with artillery and RAAF support.

These were, however, largely domestic activities. Barriers between the army of occupation and the civilian population remained, established by the official BCOF rules on non-fraternisation, even though a great many unofficial contacts were being developed. The situation was aggravated by the formidable difficulties of the Japanese language. Most of the units had started classes in elementary Japanese even before their arrival in Japan and were now trying to develop them further. There were also simple handbooks which had been written in India and Australia for use in these classes and on an individual basis. But the language did not come easily to the soldiers, who on the whole lacked the persistence required; and in its written form it remained impenetrable except to the most dedicated. Even today, the Western tourist in Japan feels completely at sea in a Japanese city, unable even to read the street signs – how much more foreign must it have seemed to the young soldiers of BCOF in those early post-war years. There was a relatively small cadre of Japanese-speaking intelligence officers and other ranks which had come together, the Australians from Brisbane and the South Pacific, the British from India and Burma, but these were spread thinly and were mainly kept busy in assisting the units in operations. They could do little to encourage the reduction of the language barrier at working level.

There were other strong influences at work. The features of an entirely different civilisation and the resilience and strength of character of the Japanese exerted a strong pull of interest, to many even of fascination. It had been difficult at first to reconcile the apparently pleasant and peaceful nature of the people with the cruel and brutal atrocities of the war. But there was a growing realisation in BCOF that, regardless of the obvious differences and the trials of the past, the people were basically decent, honest, hard-working, fond of children and loyal to those they served. 'What surprised me, and increased my respect for them', said a British officer, 'was their innate kindness to one another in the poor [country] villages, their courtesy and their love and appreciation of beauty for its own sake'.[11] There was also sympathy for the devastation their country had suffered and the hardships they were continuing to bear. Indian troops who had visited Hiroshima had been told that there had been no panic, no crying or cursing at the time of the catastrophe. The Japanese civilians had suffered in patience and silence. It was these qualities of character which were helping them to rise again. The soldiers were especially impressed by the discipline of the Japanese population at large, and, in the words of the official Indian historian, 'many felt that for progress in their own country inculcation of [a similar] discipline was essential'.[12]

Most of the troops lived a restricted life circumscribed by the barrack room and the canteen, with occasional forays to leave centres and to shops and beer halls. 'It was rather like living in cantonments in the days of the colonial empire', noted one British officer.[13] But a surprisingly large number became interested and involved in the life outside, and the opportunities for doing so began to develop. 'Cultural education' enabled the troops to attend tea ceremonies, visit schools for dancing, songs and samisen playing, and even to attend flower-arranging classes. 'Can you imagine a group of rough and ready young Australian soldiers attending flower-arranging classes?' asked one of them.[14] They did, and enjoyed it.

A few individuals with better access than most took the pragmatic view that if any real progress was to be made in the democratisation process which was one of the key objectives of the occupation, it was essential to establish and develop contacts with the civilian population well beyond the notional limits of the BCOF non-fraternisation policy, quite apart from the normal ambition of the young soldier for social contact with the female Japanese.

A senior Australian education officer has described how in their official capacity he and his staff were able to construct a wide variety of links with the local Japanese communities.[15] Exchange concerts were one form of contact which led the way to closer relationships; another was a programme of discussions which the Military Government agencies were prepared to allow him to set up under the label of 'guidance' to local Japanese educationalists.

In the same way an Australian interpreter was able to develop contacts he had acquired in the course of a series of official visits intended to establish whether SCAP directives were being properly observed.[16] Entry into the schools, discussions with pupils and staff, and tours of the classrooms were important avenues of communication with the children, and ultimately their teachers and their parents. Most of the troops concerned themselves with simpler contacts: Christmas parties for the children started in 1946 and became regular features of life in the BCOF area, particularly at battalion level.

Men of all ranks, entranced by the unfamiliar beauty of the villages, the temples and the shrines, became interested in the customs and way of life of this strange people. There were always festivals celebrating traditional holidays or the foundation of particular shrines or holy institutions, with processions, costumes, banners and dancing in the streets. Demonstrations of the martial arts, exhibitions of local art, an understanding of traditional dress, all contributed to the increasing familiarisation with Japanese society in its different facets. Sometimes there were surprising connections. A Dorsets sergeant said 'I enjoyed mostly the Japanese *Kabuki* theatre, the story basic and simple but the actors very good and so colourful'.[17]

Of all the beauty spots which became available within the BCOF area, the most attractive was the island of Miyajima in the Inland Sea, not far from Hiroshima. It was one of the show places of Japan before the war, and its huge wooden *torii* (the gateway to a Shinto shrine) standing 50 feet high in the sea, with the vermilion-lacquered shrine on the shore behind it, became a distinctive landmark throughout BCOF, recalling the pleasure of time spent there. Soldiers remembered Miyajima with special affection – the maple valley with its tame deer, the pagodas, and the thick pine woods where one might stumble on groves of camellias or startle a pheasant into flight.

The luckiest men in BCOF were the officers or NCOs who were able to go off into the countryside in their jeeps on sightseeing trips or on special missions of reconnaissance or supervision. They could stay at small Japanese inns where they would provide their own rations for meals; and they would inevitably find that these would be supplemented by some local delicacy, perhaps a pile of fried oysters landed that day from the sea. They would totter in kimonos on wooden sandals to the local public bath where, mingling with a crowd of naked men and women, they would soap and wash themselves from wooden buckets and then lower themselves gingerly into the painfully hot water of the common pool. There they would soak, exchanging pleasantries in pidgin Japanese with the local community, until it was time to return to their rooms, where the bedding would have been spread on the tatami matting of the floor. In the winter they would be warmed by the little charcoal *hibachi* stove under the bedding quilt.

Thus, in the course of 1947, as the immediate occupation tasks began to diminish, the material conditions of life for BCOF improved substantially. The initial phase of discomfort and improvisation had given way to well-organised programmes of improved housing and amenities. There was a steady resumption of the training, ceremonial and sporting activities which constitute the peacetime military life. The strangeness of the environment had worn off, and the novelty of serving in such a multinational force was beginning to be appreciated, although there were signs that this could cause pain as well as pleasure.

14
Commonwealth Relations

BCOF was unusual in its combination of three Services from four separate countries under the same command: but there was a strong bond of heritage, language and culture tying together the British, Australian and New Zealand components. The Imperial connection was still firm and there was still mention of Empire in official statements and informal conversation in those early post-war years without embarrassment. Empire Day was celebrated by all contingents, and the BCOF Sub Area unit in Tokyo was located in Empire House. Australians and New Zealanders serving in the 1940s had been educated on a British foundation, and 'Home' still meant Britain to many: Sussex by the sea was still more of an emotional influence than Coolangatta or Milford Sound. The national spirit was growing stronger all the time, especially in Australia – one Australian officer said that the first time he really thought of Australia as his native land was when he set sail from Darwin to New Guinea in 1943[1] – but the huge post-war immigration of settlers from continental Europe had not yet taken place and the loosening of the old Imperial ties had yet to occur.

The British admired the enterprise of the Australians but sometimes found their informality and lack of respect for authority difficult to accept. Compton Mackenzie had commented many years before on the Australian soldier's 'mordant humour and egalitarian independence', and his quick intelligence and strong individuality had long been recognised.[2] The New Zealanders, although similar in idiom and attitude to the Australians, were less extravagant in expression. For their part many Australians found the

British aloof and stuffy ('bloody Poms!'), and felt obliged to live up to the image of 'the wild colonial boy'. The British methods of discipline and training were a good deal more than the Australians would tolerate. 'We saw the RSM of the Welch Fusiliers yelling and actually strike some of his squad with his swagger cane', recalled a 66th Battalion officer. 'We watched with amazement – this treatment is unheard of in the Australian Army'.[3]

The relationship between these three contingents sprang from common roots and presented no real problem. However, the Indian contingent, although it constituted over 27 per cent of the Force and provided a major share of the Base and technical troops, could not be assimilated easily because of its differences in religion, culture, language and tradition, and its different political status and future. There were a number of special features involved in the incorporation of an Indian contingent in any mixed formation. Logistics were complicated by the different ration demands of Indian troops: a special team of Viceroy's Commissioned Officers had to be sent to Australia to confirm that the meat supplied was being selected and butchered in accordance with both Hindu and Muslim requirements. Manpower establishments were inflated by the numbers of non-combatants or 'enrolled followers' who were required to carry out the menial tasks which the higher castes were unable to do.

The original directive to the Commander-in-Chief had laid down that the principle of maximum integration of services and personnel of the different national components was to be followed in BCOF Headquarters and in the Force and Base organisations. This was easier said than done. At BCOF HQ the senior staff appointments were in general filled by Australian officers who were familiar with the military organisation in Australia which was responsible for the support of BCOF. This seemed adequate justification for that arrangement. Integration at lower levels, however, which should have been the objective, was difficult to achieve, particularly with respect to the Indian element. There were few qualified Indian staff officers available once the demands of BRINDIV had been met and Australian senior staff officers preferred to appoint subordinates from the other contingents rather than Indians, to whom they found it more difficult to relate.

Integration was more successful in BRITCOM Base and BCOF combined units; indeed the mixture was a rich one. A New Zealand driver posted to the British Commonwealth Army Driving Training School at Matsuyama noted that it was 'a great place. Main staff was Australian, but with Yanks, Indians, Scots, Poms, the RSM was from the Guards, and of course last and least two Kiwis'.[4]

On the whole there was little conflict between the British and the Indian elements of BCOF. The large number of mixed British/Indian administrative and support units in general functioned satisfactorily, in spite of some frictions and jealousies. Care was taken to provide that Indian personnel in an integrated unit would work under their own officers and non-commissioned officers as complete sub-units to reduce the scope for misunderstanding. Within the infantry brigades of BRINDIV there was a healthy mutual liking and respect born of common experience in India and on the battlefield and they were used to serving together. 'The Jocks always got on excellently with the jawans and the Gurkhas', said a Camerons officer.[5] With the Australians it was a different matter. They found the Indians strange and difficult to understand and thought of them as inferior, applying some of the same standards to them as they did at home to their aboriginal underclass.

This did not affect the infantry brigades, who inhabited their various areas in a fair degree of isolation from other national contingents. But it created a substantial problem in those areas where Indians and Australians served side by side – the headquarter and base areas of Kure and Hiro. There was a higher proportion of Indian units here than the Australians expected. One said that the percentage of Indian troops was too great – they were 'so numerous as to give the impression they represent not only India but more than half the Empire'.[6] There was in fact a clear reason for this: Australia and New Zealand could not provide their proper share of base and technical troops, while India could make up the shortfall. Larger demands were therefore placed on GHQ India and the percentage of Indian troops increased as the build-up of the Force progressed. By July 1946 the Indian Army and Royal Indian Air Force was providing nearly 32 per cent of the entire Force.

The base units concerned lacked the discipline of the infantry, and a considerable animosity built up here, based on rivalry over women, the distaste of the Australians for what they saw as the indiscriminate sexual habits of the Indians, and even the envy of the Australians for the sheep being imported for the Indians in comparison with their own inferior diet of tinned meat. There were a number of incidents through 1946 and 1947 leading to confrontations and brawls. One arose from the Australian theft of an Indian sheep; another from an Australian assault by fire hose on Indians whom they had apparently seen through the barrier fence carrying out undesirable sexual operations on young Japanese kitchen boys.[7]

The most serious conflict culminated in a fire fight on 30 August 1947 between men of the Australian 14 Works & Park Squadron and men of the 653 Indian Plant Company, who were located in adjoining camps in Hiro. There had been trouble between these units for some while over Japanese girls in the area. Perhaps emboldened by their move to independence, the Indian attitude became more aggressive in the summer of 1947. On 30 August (as it happened, after Indian independence had been declared) there was an incident on the hillside overlooking the two camps in which an Australian sapper and his girl friend were molested by several Indian sappers. The Australian ran back to his camp and alerted about 50 of his comrades who had been drinking in the barracks canteen and were ready for a 'blue' with the Indians. A full-scale riot developed, with both sides breaking into their armouries and arming themselves for the fray. In the subsequent conflict, rifle fire was opened by the Australians and then became general by both units, lasting for some hours. Before order was finally restored by officers and MPs, an Indian sapper called Mani Ram was dead and three other Indians were wounded. Ironically, none of these casualties had taken an active part in the fight: Mani Ram had in fact been sheltering on the hillside, where he was hit by stray shots from the combat below.

The court of enquiry which followed laid the blame mainly on the Australians.[8] It noted that there had been several cases of ill-treatment of Indians by Australians without any action being taken by their officers, and it was highly critical of their lack of discipline, the inadequate control of the guard and the excessive issue of liquor. The Australian Minister for the Army minuted on the court proceedings 'there is little doubt from the evidence produced that gross laxity exists in this unit and strong steps should be taken to remedy it'. An officer and 15 other ranks were subsequently court-martialled, and an extensive programme of re-training, sport and exercise, coupled with a limitation on the issue of liquor, was instituted to reduce the energy and potential for excitement of the Australians. Perhaps it worked.

The Indian unit did not escape criticism. The state of low morale was blamed on the men's lack of confidence in their British officers, and naturally most of all on the commanding officer, who was reproached for the inadequacy of his arrangements for regular 'durbars' – the informal communication sessions prescribed in Indian Army regulations, at which any man might ask any question or put forward any grievance directly to his commanding officer.

BCOF HQ, reporting the affray with some embarrassment to GHQ India, said that in view of the impending return of 653 Company to India it was not proposed to hold the unit back. Disciplinary action was being taken against the Australian guard commander, the second-in-command and the soldiers known to have discharged firearms in the riot. Charges laid against Australian personnel would not require evidence from Indian witnesses, nor would charges against Indians require evidence from Australians. Copies of the court's proceedings were being sent to India for action there. Meanwhile all leave was stopped in both units until after the departure of the Indian unit, which finally embarked for India on 5 October 1947.

This dramatic example of armed conflict between BCOF contingents was kept secret for many years. It only came to public notice in 1989 when an ex-member of the Australian Army, Neville Rees, appealed to the Administrative Appeals Tribunal against the refusal of a pension, claiming that he had suffered prolonged emotional stress and resulting hypertension as a result of being pinned down under fire by the Indian soldiers in the 'Battle of Hiro'. The *Sun Herald* of Melbourne ran the story in its edition of 9 July 1989 under the headline 'Diggers had troops in "secret" post-war fire fight'. Rees obtained his disability pension and with it the scorn of ex-comrades who felt humiliated by the admission of such un-Digger-like behaviour. Rees did not enlarge on his experience, but one of his contemporaries told the press that 'when you get armies of different nationalities together you will always have trouble. It wasn't an isolated incident – there was many a flare-up between the white BCOF soldiers and the Indians'.[9]

This was usually the result of poor discipline not confined to one side or the other. Thimayya told of another incident of confrontation, when two Australian patients in the Indian military hospital were prevented from bringing girls into the compound by the Indian guard, and summoned their comrades to retaliate.[10] In the ensuing battle, the Indian hospital staff, armed with a variety of improvised weapons, won the day and in their pursuit of the Australians took the opportunity to hurl stones and abuse at the officers' club and the general's house as they passed. The victorious crowd finally returned to the hospital and a court of enquiry in due course dealt with the incident, but the hospital was never quite the same again.

15

The British Brigade

By June 1946 the British infantry brigade, after some initial diversionary movements, had settled down in Shikoku. This, the smallest of the four islands forming the Japanese homeland, was the exemplar of the Japanese rural scene – a spine of rugged hills running up as high as 7,000 feet, with a narrow coastal plain, farming and fishing communities and a few small market towns. The roads were bad but the railways were reasonable; communication with the main island of Honshu was by sporadic ferry.

Targets for demilitarisation were few and minor. Suppression of the black market occasionally provided some diversion. Much effort was required at the beginning to make the various barrack buildings inhabitable. Unfortunately, as the brigade arrived and began to attack the task of refurbishment, SCAP issued a directive controlling the use of wood by occupation troops which made that task even more difficult.

Brigade Headquarters were set up at Kochi on the south coast of the island, together with the Camerons and a troop of 7 Cavalry. The Dorsets were located close by at Gomen, and the Welch Fusiliers were at Tokushima on the east coast. Detachments from the battalions were at the other towns of Takamatsu and Matsuyama. Supporting units (the Indian Field Battery, a field ambulance, and workshop and supply companies) were in other small towns. Regular patrols were made far into the interior on 'showing the flag' expeditions among a surprised but courteous country population: the 'simple kindness and hospitality of the remote mountain folk of northern Shikoku' were especially noted by

the commanding officer of the Dorsets.[1] The extremely correct
behaviour of the local Japanese officials and the absence of any
trouble was noted by many: the commanding officer of the Welch
Fusiliers thought their attitude was 'we will behave correctly and the
sooner these *** go, the better'.[2]

The pattern of life in the battalions depended very much, as
always, on the régime adopted by their commanding officers, but
the experience of the Welch Fusiliers may be taken as typical. The
battalion, once it had made its barracks comfortable with the help
of Japanese labour, had a system under which one company was on
a 6-day patrol through villages, sleeping in the schools; one company was on training; one company was on a 2-day patrol in another
direction; and the remaining company was on guards and duties. All
changed round each week, so that there was a variety of activity
which kept boredom at bay. There was an NCOs cadre, range work,
live firing with 3-inch mortars and Bren guns, and a great deal of
sport.

The social side of life was not neglected. According to the
colonel, 'we had a good canteen in the barracks and a good café in
the town run by four devoted FANYs. We had dances in barracks to
which a lorry load or two of Japanese girls came, and were discreetly taken away at the end of the dance. We were visited by
concert parties, and were lucky enough to have our own band,
which also acted as the divisional band. Japanese waitresses, beau-
tifully attired in national costume, served in the officers' mess.
(They were particularly sad when the battalion left, having benefited considerably from army rations)'.[3] One high spot was a
ceremonial march by the battalion through Tokushima on St
David's Day 1947, with drums beating, bayonets fixed and colours
flying. It was watched by quiet and respectful crowds who were
reported later to have been amazed at the soldiers' silence and discipline in the ranks. The Japanese labourers were courteous to the
point of embarrassment: 'they had to be discouraged from saluting
too frequently'. But there was still sometimes a feeling of slight
unease: 'I think the Japanese kept a good eye on us. I gather', said
the colonel, 'that one labourer in the barracks was really a Japanese
admiral!'

The battalions were widely dispersed and saw little of each
other or of headquarters or other formations, an ideal situation
from the point of view of local commanders. In general, the brigade

led a busy garrison life of drill and ceremonial parades, patrols and sport. The Dorsets' war diary for September 1946 gives another insight into what that life meant for them.[4] On the lst, a party of Royal Engineers arrived to clear the camp area of Japanese bombs and grenades; on the 2nd a reinforcement draft of 6 officers and 130 Other Ranks arrived (at 2 o'clock in the morning!) from Kalyan in India; and on the 6th a party of 3 officers and 65 Other Ranks left the battalion for repatriation and release. Four patrols were mounted during the month, 1 of them at company strength lasting a week. There were concert parties and cinema shows on 9 evenings in the battalion theatre, and an entertainment of a different kind when 2 members of a visiting Parliamentary delegation were flown in to answer troops' questions and stay the night. There were sport meetings, a boxing tournament, football and cricket matches on 5 days. There were even weekly dancing lessons given by ladies of the WVS.

There were also incidents of an unhappier kind. A corporal of the pioneer platoon was drowned at the Takuma holiday camp and buried with full military honours in Kure; and a 15 cwt truck went over the side of the road at Odochi, seriously injuring the driver. He was brought back to Gomen by a rescue party after a laborious journey, and a Dakota landed on the airstrip 10 minutes after their arrival to take the casualty to hospital.

There were, of course, always parades – special church parades, parades to commemorate anniversaries, beatings of retreat and marches through the towns and villages. Throughout BCOF a large part of the troops' time was devoted to them. Commanders have for centuries recognised the disciplinary benefit of organised foot and arms drill as part of the necessary equipment of the trained soldier. Men used to responding smartly and without question to the word of command on the barrack square will, it is reasoned, reproduce that same instant obedience to orders in the more testing conditions of battle. The proper preparation of uniform and equipment for parade becomes a regular routine which enhances the soldier's self-confidence and pride in himself. Slim noted that on the retreat from Burma in 1942 the units who survived the ordeal best were those who maintained their standards of discipline and were able to parade as well at the end of the campaign as at the beginning. But drill parades have a fascination of their own for those taking part. The ability to execute manoeuvres in unison with one's comrades, whether complicated or not, has the excitement and pleasure of playing in an orchestra. The parade commander is the conductor, and a false move or a dropped rifle is the equivalent of hitting the wrong note in a symphony.

Parades in BCOF were a way of life. Because a military band is an important accessory to marching with precision, most of the battalions had their own bands before long. The chores were often a source of complaint – the rehearsals, the long hours spent blancoing webbing to a pristine whiteness – but the results were adequate compensation. Time after time, BCOF soldiers have said that the high spot of the occupation for them was some ceremonial parade – often on the Imperial Plaza in Tokyo. In a sense the parades became a form of street theatre: the kilts and bagpipes of the Camerons always drew a crowd, the women covering their mouths to hide their amusement. There was a sense of occasion, a pride in performing well in front of a big audience. Certainly the Dorsets' high spot had been to troop the colour on the Imperial Plaza during their guard duty there. They were the first British battalion to do so and it was an added excitement to carry it out in front of thousands of spectators, Japanese and American, on the 189th anniversary of the battle of Plassey where they had served under Clive of India as the 54th Regiment of Foot. To the battle honour they had gained there – 'Primus in Indus' – they now felt they could add 'Primus in Tokyo': and their commanding officer sprayed justified messages of pride at the occasion to everybody from MacArthur downwards.

The Dorsets colonel had already been responsible for a special parade in Matsue in celebration of Kohima Day, which commemorated the famous battle at which the Japanese attempt to invade India was halted and turned back. After a ceremonial march through the town with bayonets fixed, led by the colonel on an ex-Japanese cavalry white horse, the battalion formed up in the centre with the Kohima veterans wearing their medals in pride of place. The colonel delivered a rousing speech on the battle and the final defeat of the Japanese, which was translated to a silent crowd of onlookers which included the entire Matsue High School. In it he paid a warm and respectful tribute to the fighting qualities of the Japanese as demonstrated in this great battle, which seemed somewhat at odds with the occupation objective of suppressing militarism in Japanese society and establishing the new constitution

with its 'no war' declaration. There was an added irony in that a
Japanese army division raised in the neighbouring Tottori prefecture
was said to have been effectively wiped out in the unsuccessful 1944
campaign in which the Kohima battle had played such a crucial
part.

The parades in Japan had the added function of 'showing the
flag' to the civilian population in an endeavour to stress the military
strength of the occupation forces. It is perhaps doubtful whether this
was achieved any more than the changing of the guard at
Buckingham Palace gives any real impression of fighting ability:
and the increasing emphasis placed by SCAP on the peaceful development of a new society ran counter to the intention.

Although quiet, Shikoku was, by comparison with conditions
in the Australian brigade area, a reasonably comfortable posting
and the regular British battalions were in any event used to making
the best of their lot. The shortcomings of the overall situation in
BCOF, however, were investigated and reported by many visitors
from Britain and elsewhere, with some attendant publicity. During
the visit of the British Parliamentary delegation in September 1946,
for example, one of its members, the Reverend Gordon Lang, said
that they were 'unfavourably impressed with the conditions under
which British and Australian troops were living . . . the British occupation force is an army of forgotten men'.[5] Lang thought the
situation so unsatisfactory that he sent a telegram direct to Attlee
listing the many complaints made by the troops – delays in mail,
delays in bringing out families, the poor standard of supplies, the
lack of educational facilities and the lack of canteens in outlying
areas. Robertson was already attacking these problems, but an
umcomfortable situation persisted.

Brigadier Fitzroy Maclean, a hero of the European war and
also a member of the delegation, wrote in an article in the
Scotsman[6] of the concentration of the executive authority in
American hands and of the way this American predominance was
illustrated by the relative strengths and disposal of BCOF and the
American occupation forces, 'the latter occupying all the major
industrial and cultural centres, while the British zone is almost
entirely lacking in towns and harbours . . . the lack of adequate supplies and facilities makes it impossible for the Empire contingent to
do themselves justice, especially by comparison with the Americans,
who are as usual magnificently equipped and provided for . . .'

While not decrying American achievements, he regretted that 'both politically and militarily we are . . . taking a back seat in Japan'.

These feelings of discontent at the limited role of BCOF coincided with a fundamental reassessment in London of Britain's various military obligations throughout the world and the means by which her essential overseas commitments might be met. As early as January it had been assessed in London that, to meet the UK's world-wide responsibilities and provide sufficient backing for 'the effective bearing of the commitments of the British Empire', the minimum manpower requirement as at June 1946 would be 2,068,000. Britain would have to maintain substantial armed forces for occupation and internal security duties in Germany, Austria, Italy, Venezia Giulia, Greece, the Middle East, India, South East Asia and the East Indies, Japan and China, with small outlying garrisons in Malta, West Indies, Gibraltar, East and West Africa. As always, the heaviest burden would fall on the Army: in the words of the Chiefs of Staff, 'it is the actual presence of soldiers which is the best insurance against disorder'.[7] It was a mammoth task, and clearly too much for the UK alone. The manpower available was constantly decreasing as a result of demobilisation and the need to redirect the nation's resources to a peacetime economy. Montgomery, the Chief of the Imperial General Staff (CIGS), had already made his view clear that there was no military need for British troops to be in Japan: their presence there was 'on purely political grounds'. The garrison in Japan, he felt, was the least necessary of all the garrisons Britain was supporting around the world.

The Chiefs of Staff gave this view a qualified endorsement. They recognised that political considerations arose in connection with British interests in Japan and with relations with Australia and New Zealand. The only military value lay in the fact that the formation of BCOF had led to the setting up of JCOSA, which was considered to be a considerable step forward in the organisation of Commonwealth defence. But in the face of the urgent requirements elsewhere, they recommended withdrawal of the British brigade as a first step as soon as possible.

The Cabinet Defence Committee accepted this recommendation in October 1946[8], concluding that the possible political advantages of remaining in Japan were small, and agreed that the British brigade should be transferred to join the garrison in Malaya in February 1947. This would enable consequential moves of other formations from Malaya to the Middle East. The RAF and RN contingents and the British army components in BCOF and BRITCOM Base were not then thought likely to be affected.

Under the provisions of the Northcott-MacArthur agreement there was an obligation to give SCAP six months' notice of any reduction in BCOF forces. In November 1946 MacArthur was warned by Washington[9] that the State Department had been informed by the British Embassy that Britain's world manpower commitments might necessitate the withdrawal of the UK Brigade from Japan and that it was likely that the remaining UK and Commonwealth troops would be spread out over the present British zone. Since the British Cabinet had already taken the decision, this was obviously a 'flyer' to establish in advance what the US reaction was likely to be. The State Department had indicated that SCAP would probably be reluctant to agree to any reduction requiring an increase in the number and duties of American troops.

A leak to the American magazine *Newsweek* forced the British Government to admit that reduction of BCOF was under consideration 'in view of the degree of stability already achieved in Japan under Allied occupation'.[10] The Foreign Office was in fact opposing withdrawal on grounds of prestige in the Far East, but recognised that they would have to 'bow to the arguments of the absolute military necessity for retrenchment'.[11]

On 1 December the British Chief of Air Staff, Tedder, who was visiting Japan, reported MacArthur's informal reaction.[12] SCAP said that the British brigade was by far his best land force and he hoped it would not be necessary to remove the whole of it. He spoke of his faith in Anglo-American cooperation and 'the Anglo-Saxon way of life', and his admiration for the high standards set by the UK troops and the educational value of their presence. The Foreign Office's reaction was cynical: they did not doubt MacArthur's sincerity but 'these noble sentiments do not get our businessmen back to Japan, nor restore our trade with that country. The best way to impress the Japanese with our way of life is to resume normal commercial relations with them, and this is precisely what General MacArthur makes so difficult'.[13]

Robertson intervened with an ingenious proposition to retain one of the British infantry battalions as a token of British commitment and to make up the total of 3,500 UK troops required by London to be released by cuts in Divisional and Brigade

Headquarters and the administrative echelons. He still believed that if this were done and the reduction in BCOF limited to 3,500, he could take on Hyogo Prefecture and the prized target of Kobe, although Osaka as well would be too much. MacArthur was reportedly sympathetic to the plan: 'he was not opposed to the withdrawal of UK land forces, but he felt as any other commander would whose best combatant troops were withdrawn'.[14] But although JCOSA were asked to consider this plan, it had no chance of success in the face of the need to keep the British brigade together, which was deemed to be paramount.

Montgomery now lent further urgency to the withdrawal proposal. On 20 December 1946 he pressed the British Chiefs of Staff to take speedy action on the withdrawal of the brigade, and to ensure that it was transferred to Singapore as a self-contained brigade group, including the administrative troops who would be required to give it operational independence, even if there were repercussions on the RAF and other components who relied on them for support. The run-down of British forces in South East Asia was going quickly and 5 Brigade was needed to guard against trouble there.[15]

By the beginning of January 1947 the Chiefs of Staff had formulated the Cabinet decision into a formal proposal to the Americans. This stated that, due to UK commitments throughout the world and the complete lack of any reserve to meet a possible call for British troops for dispatch to Burma or India, it would be necessary to withdraw from Japan not only the UK infantry brigade amounting to some 3500 men (which it had previously been suggested would be the only unit withdrawn), but now also sufficient administrative troops to make the brigade self-contained, and that there might after all have to be some reduction in the RN and RAF components. 'The Governments of India and of the Dominions concerned have been consulted and have agreed in principle to this withdrawal, although the Government of India have stated that they also are considering the withdrawal of their contingent owing to manpower difficulties.' JCOSA had been told to issue movement orders and to ask the Commander-in-Chief BCOF to inform SCAP officially.

Washington was worried that this proposal went a good deal further than the informal advice in November and that it now contained a warning in respect of the Indian contingent as well. MacArthur was reminded that there were no US army troops available to compensate for these withdrawals other than those under his command, and was asked for his comments.[16] The US Chiefs of Staff were surprised and relieved to receive a brief reply: 'Am prepared to accept the British proposal'.[17] MacArthur had already concluded that the occupation was going so well and the Japanese were so acquiescent under his rule that the need for an Allied military presence as an occupation force was diminishing fast, although the need to maintain a US bulwark against Communism in the Far East remained. His Chief of Staff later commented understandingly that the British forces were being reduced 'because of the very extensive demand on British manpower in other parts of the world'.[18] In further discussions MacArthur said that he would not insist on the six months' notice; but with the indication of the likely Indian withdrawal as well in mind, he warned that the total reduction of more than 50 per cent in BCOF strength which this would mean would be a serious embarrassment and he would need to redistribute his forces.

Rumours and speculative newspaper reports had referred to this prospective British withdrawal for some weeks and the junior army minister, John Freeman, on a visit to units in December had mentioned the likely withdrawal of 3000 British troops, partly because the occupation of Japan was more of a success than in Europe.[19] But it was not until January 1947 that orders were issued for 5 Brigade to move from Japan to Malaya, and the transfer was carried out throughout February. Robertson had already said in his usual positive manner that he would make no difficulty about the withdrawal of the brigade and considered that he could still carry out occupation policies with the forces remaining; but in private he was dismayed. According to a British diplomat in Tokyo, he felt that the British 'defection' would result in the whole of BCOF disappearing 'like melting snow', and he did not think the melting would take long. 'He reckons that the governments concerned will get tired of carrying out what is purely a police job 'pour le plaisir des Americains'. If BCOF looked after its own military government and administered the Japanese, he thinks it might be considered worthwhile to keep BCOF in being, but that is not the case'.[20]

During his visit to Japan in December 1946, Chambers, the Australian Minister for the Army, had in fact asked MacArthur whether the Commonwealth could not now take over the military government of their areas of occupation. It was reported that

MacArthur had refused even to discuss the suggestion, and Chambers was impressed by 'the evident determination of the Supreme Commander to retain all the administrative power in American hands'.[21]

If the disappearance of the British brigade was to be borne without a parallel reduction in the area of occupation, the remaining forces and their responsibilities had to be redistributed. It was decided that Shikoku should be added to the responsibilities of 34 Australian Brigade, located in Hiroshima prefecture, but that no major units would be moved to the island: instead, occupation duties would be carried out by frequent patrolling from Honshu.

The reaction in the UK was subdued, although the London *Times* weighed in with an important article and a leader expressing doubt as to the wisdom of the decision to reduce the UK contingent.[22] It was appropriate to recognise the important stake of Australia and New Zealand in the Pacific settlement by selecting Australians to represent the Commonwealth on the Allied Council for Japan and to command BCOF, and by basing JCOSA in Melbourne: but it did not follow that the UK should 'seek to subtract from her proper share in the task of fitting the Japanese people for a peaceful future in the comity of nations'. The British troops were the representatives of Western Europe in the occupation – 'their presence keeps alive among the Japanese the expectation of a renewal of the cultural and commercial relations which have so much to contribute to the recreation of civilised life' There was unfortunately a sizeable gap between the reasoning in London and the realities of life in BCOF, where the ability to influence the Japanese estimation of British prestige and to exploit the 'valuable opportunities of direct contact with the Japanese people' were strictly limited. Even when Fitzroy Maclean entered the debate in support[23], his contention that the retention in Japan of a fully capable UK contingent would materially enhance British prestige and 'might help us to regain the once considerable influence in Far Eastern affairs which we are now so rapidly losing' seemed curiously inflated: his recent visit to Japan with the Parliamentary delegation had apparently left him with a view more rosy than realistic. In general public opinion in the UK was not aroused by the issue.

The Australians, however, took the UK move very seriously. Their Defence Committee had already sounded an alarm to the Cabinet when it heard of the British intention in November.[24] While appreciating the UK's greater burden (it had 1.2 per cent of its manpower overseas, compared with Australia's 0.16 per cent and New Zealand's 0.27 per cent) the Committee considered that the four brigade groups of BCOF provided SCAP with the only operationally experienced formation in Japan and that a reduction would badly affect the operational efficiency of his forces. The proposed withdrawal of the British brigade would reduce the UK Army component from 6,700 to 3,200 and the total UK contribution from 10,000 to 6,500. Any more withdrawals would necessarily bring the whole future of BCOF up for review, because it was clear that 'each of the countries concerned would be glad to be free of this overseas commitment'. There was another quite different fear expressed: US public opinion might demand the similar withdrawal of US forces, leaving Japan open to Russia. But the overall conclusion was firm and faithful to the Imperial concept and to a continuing commitment to the Japanese occupation: 'The retention of BCOF provides the best possible insurance for the safety of the Pacific and Australia, besides fulfilling a national obligation and upholding the prestige of the Empire, in which prestige all countries of the Empire participate'.

The Australian press was seriously concerned when the news became public. A leader in the *Sydney Morning Herald*[25], for example, while acknowledging the pressures of Britain's great manpower shortage, pointed out the adverse effect which this withdrawal would have on her prestige with the Japanese, 'who are little enough conversant as it is with the contribution she made to their defeat . . . The limitation of direct British representation . . . to a few thousand RN and RAF personnel seems particularly surprising at a moment when Britain's principal preoccupation is the expansion of her exports'. It emphasised the fact that ever since the end of the war Empire representation in Japan had been on a highly unsatisfactory basis, with BCOF playing no part in the military government, even in the British zone itself. 'It is astonishing that Britain ever acquiesced in the arrangement, which has made the Japanese look exclusively to the Americans for decisions and help, as well as creating the impression that "while the British parade to impress us, the Americans rebuild our country"'. Fears were also voiced in Australia about the increased burden which a British and Indian withdrawal would throw on the Australian forces and the lack of proper plans for the future of the Australian Services. It was felt that the whole policy governing BCOF needed review.

It was ironic that in the same month that this leader appeared, at a meeting in Tokyo of the United Nations Study Committee (a body consisting of former Japanese diplomats and former representatives on the League of Nations) deep regret was expressed that Britain was playing so small a part in Japan, 'although she had much to offer and had been highly respected in the past'.[26] It was feared that 'Britain was gradually being forgotten in Japan and that for the younger generation she was little more than a name': and she was urged to continue to play her traditional role in the Far East and to exert her undoubted influence for good among all nations in this part of the world.

The reaction of the New Zealand Government to the news of the British withdrawal was cheerful. The Prime Minister, Fraser, had never been convinced of the need for a New Zealand contribution to the occupation and had only agreed to it in the interest of Commonwealth solidarity and a feeling that Australia should not have it all her own way in the Pacific. He had been 'on the lookout for excuses to pull out', according to the UK High Commissioner, especially as the continued maintenance of a contingent in Japan would entail a measure of conscription, which would be politically most undesirable for his government.[27] The British decision confirmed Fraser's own view that New Zealand should also withdraw, since it was 'serving no useful purpose in Japan, which was anyway an entirely American preserve'. It was clear that he would seek his cabinet's approval for withdrawal also. The British considered whether they should encourage New Zealand to remain: but the CIGS recorded his view that 'I am personally against persuading other people to do what we are not prepared to do ourselves'.[28] The British Foreign Office was alarmed by the likelihood that the UK would suffer loss of prestige if they withdrew before the other Commonwealth members, and wondered[29] whether, if the UK proposal to withdraw were to be followed by similar proposals from other Commonwealth members, it might not be better to organise a 33 per cent reduction in each contingent across the board, a somewhat impractical suggestion in view of the time it would take and the military complications it would cause. But the whole future of BCOF was suddenly put under scrutiny by the British decision.

The news of departure came as a surprise and a shock to 5 Brigade. Brigade Headquarters had moved to more comfortable permanent barracks at Zentsuji in the north east corner of Shikoku towards the end of 1946 and the Camerons were preparing to follow them when the movement order was announced. Many of the men of 5 Brigade were disappointed at having to leave Japan. The character of the units had, of course, changed, as the older men left on release and were replaced by fresh reinforcements. The Dorsets, for example, in December 1945 still had over 300 men with campaign experience, of whom 142 had fought with the battalion in Burma: but by June 1946 the Kohima veterans were down to 20. Nevertheless, in the words of one of the commanding officers, they felt they had been '*a corps d'élite* in a picked force for a special role', although they had had doubts about the way BCOF discharged it.[30] 'The American policy of fraternisation was the only real way to put over democracy', said one officer.[31] The British battalions had made themselves comfortable after a great deal of effort and they had a unique opportunity to study the Japanese in their own country. Now they were to be removed in one of the first of those post-war evacuations of British troops which were to become all too familiar. When they left Kure in February 1947 it was snowing hard: three weeks later they were deployed on active service in the tropical heat of Malaya, to combat the Communist threat which later broke out into open insurrection in June 1948.

Just before the British brigade left, probably the most exciting event of BCOF's occupation took place. At 4.20 am on 21 December 1946, in the middle of a freezingly cold night, an earthquake of considerable proportions struck the Japanese islands. It was said to be as powerful as the 1923 earthquake which devastated Tokyo and killed 100,000 people, but on this occasion it caused less damage because the epicentre was further out to sea, the point of origin being south of the Wakayama peninsula, about 200 miles southeast of Kure, and about 100 miles from Shikoku's nearest coast. Nevertheless it was a submarine earthquake of exceptional magnitude, shaking cities from Tokyo to Shimonoseki, and was recorded on seismographs as far away as West Bromwich in England and New Orleans in the USA. The entire Chugoku region was affected, the Inland Sea coast more than most, and the island of Shikoku most of all.

The first signs were the rattling and vibration of doors and windows, 'like a toy in the hands of a mischievous child'. This was quickly followed by the rocking and shaking of entire buildings. The wooden floors began to move and slabs of cement began to fall from the walls. Troops were woken in their barracks by the tremors and, forcing open jammed doors, fled down shaking stairs and out of the swaying buildings into the icy darkness where the ground was trembling under their feet. The major shock lasted for over two minutes and succeeding tremors continued for at least ten minutes and up to twenty minutes in certain areas. The shocks were felt over a wide area of Shikoku and southern Honshu: the Japanese in Kure and Okayama said that they were the greatest ever experienced in those areas. As far as the prefectures in the BCOF zone were concerned, in addition to the severe effect in Shikoku and Okayama, there had been intense tremors in Hiroshima, while Shimane and Tottori had not gone unscathed. Yamaguchi was the only prefecture to escape almost entirely.

The earthquake was followed at 5.30 am by a tidal wave ten feet high which struck the south coast of Shikoku at Kochi and the south east coast at Mugi and Hiwasa, breaking sea walls and causing extensive flooding along the entire coast. Many coastal towns, including Kochi itself, were inundated and hundreds of fishing boats were swept off their moorings or beaches out to sea. In Tokushima all the houses on the sea front were carried away. Everywhere there was considerable damage to both roads and railways. Electrical and water supplies were badly affected.

No casualties were suffered by the British brigade and only a few injuries occurred elsewhere in BCOF: the most serious was probably the Mahratta who was thrown out of a window in the barracks in Hamada and ended up in hospital with a fractured skull. However, there were about 2,500 civilian dead and injured, casualties of the collapse of the flimsy Japanese buildings, and of the fires caused by the damage to electrical lines and by overturned *hibachi*, but most of all of the tidal wave and the flooding. At least 300,000 were rendered homeless. The heaviest damage was suffered in Kochi, where 647 were reported dead, 823 injured and 29 missing. 4168 houses were destroyed, 6798 severely damaged, 6238 flooded and 1960 burned down. Almost as bad, 1868 fishing boats were lost or damaged.

BRINDIV units reported some odd phenomena. The famous Dogo hot springs at Matsuyama were found to have ceased flowing, but new hot springs had emerged between Zentsuji and Tadotsu. Fissures up to 200 yards long and 18 inches wide had appeared in reclaimed land south of Okayama and small springs of hot mud developed temporarily in the same area.

Here was a chance for BCOF to meet an emergency, a challenge always welcomed by a disciplined military force. Northcott had at the outset of the occupation instructed every garrison to prepare disaster plans to cope with natural phenomena such as typhoons or earthquakes, which he said were certain to occur sooner or later. Now these were to come into effect. BCOF units were ordered to give maximum assistance and even before the Japanese could appeal for help, relief was being organised for the injured, the starving and the homeless. A conference took place in Kochi later on the day of the earthquake between the commanding officer of the Camerons, the Prefectural Governor, the Chief of Police and military government staff, and this identified the priority requirements as food, clothing, telecommunications equipment and fishing gear. The loss of so many fishing boats was a serious blow to the economy of the area and Camerons landing craft were immediately assigned to search for and round up boats missing at sea.

A leading part was taken by BCAIR. Their Auster aircraft, operating from rough landing strips, were used to reconnoitre the isolated towns along the flooded coastal plain and later to evacuate seriously injured by air to Honshu. The Dakotas flew in urgently required stores, medicines, clothes and blankets for relief of the stricken areas, operating for long hours day after day, ferrying the supplies to the main centres on Shikoku and often landing on small improvised fields to bring help to places isolated from land, rail or sea communications. In some remote areas food and medical supplies were dropped from the air. The Camerons' and Dorsets' motor transport was intensely busy running stores and supplies from aircraft to distribution centres and operating emergency bus services between Gomen and Kochi.

Four medical teams from the BCOF military hospitals were flown in to give emergency assistance, bringing with them blood plasma, drugs and other medical stores: two were allocated to Kochi, and one each to Takamatsu and Tokushima. Army units patrolled the areas affected, helped to clear debris and to search for survivors in damaged buildings and provided transport when required. HMS *Amethyst*, then temporarily in Kure as part of the British Pacific Fleet's support for BCOF, brought 60,000 sets of blankets and clothing into Kochi, where the destruction of the port's pier made it necessary to unload by tug and tender. The Camerons even found time to give a Christmas party for 300 children on 27 December in what was left of Kochi.

This whole episode offered a welcome opportunity to demonstrate goodwill to the conquered enemy, who applauded it enthusiastically. The civilian governor of Shikoku issued a statement later which acknowledged the vital importance of the assistance given and said 'The Japanese people appreciate the readiness of the BCOF forces to rush aid to them in their hour of need'. While it would have been unthinkable to hope for other disasters to enhance the reputation of BCOF with the Japanese, it is a pity that there were not more opportunities of a similar importance to enable BCOF to demonstrate its efficient organisation in emergency, and to boost its presence from provincial seclusion to national recognition.

16

The Indian Contingent

In contrast to the problems between Indian and Australian base units in Hiro and Kure, the Indian infantry brigade experienced little difficulty with the rest of BCOF. This was largely due to its relative isolation in Shimane and Tottori Prefectures, which were on the northern coast of Honshu. They were under-developed areas dependent on agriculture and fisheries and separated from the busier region of the south by a range of mountains and very poor communications.

BRINDIV Headquarters had already noted a more positive attitude on the part of the Japanese towards Indian troops than towards British troops.[1] Their initial fear of the Indians had been replaced by a desire for closer relations and it seemed likely that this was a legacy of the pan-Asian ideas which had been promoted by wartime Japanese governments.

In this comfortable atmosphere the Mahrattas at Hamada and the Punjabis at Tottori led a quiet, somewhat introverted life. The Gurkhas at Matsue, alongside 268 Brigade Headquarters, seemed to be equally relaxed, but the calm was broken when the battalion was transferred to Hiro to become the permanent guard battalion at BRINDIV Headquarters as Divisional troops. Thimayya wondered why this task was not rotated between battalions rather than being allocated to the Gurkhas permanently.[2] He suspected that the battalion had been detached from 268 Brigade because the British, with Indian independence on the horizon, were anxious to avoid the unsettling influence that the Indian officers might have on the Gurkhas. He thought the British wanted to retain at least one part of the Indian Army on which they could depend and therefore decided to remove the Gurkhas from contact with the Indians as far as possible. This seems an unlikely conclusion: it is more probable that, as an old Gurkha officer himself, Cowan's personal preference for his own troops was the simple explanation.

The move had unexpected results as the Gurkhas came to grips with the unfamiliar conditions of Divisional Headquarters, and a sequence of unhappy events began to unfold. The first sign of trouble came when two Viceroy's Commissioned Officers (VCOs) and a havildar (a sergeant) of the battalion were court-martialled at Division for disobeying orders and sentenced to be dismissed the service. The circumstances are not now known, but for such senior ranks to be charged with so serious a crime was highly unusual.

Meanwhile, another incident developed from the predilection of the Gurkhas for the local women. Gurkhas were popular with Japanese girls: they looked Oriental, and came to terms easily with the Japanese language and customs. But if a Gurkha was caught with a local girl by British or Australian MPs, he was likely to be arrested as an offender against the non-fraternisation rules. This was supposed to be the normal practice with all BCOF personnel, but the Gurkhas saw that it was not being enforced so completely with the Australian troops in the area. They resented this and blamed their different treatment on the much stricter regime of their commanding officer, Lieutenant Colonel Townsend.

One evening a Gurkha was arrested in the house of a Japanese girl by Australian MPs. His comrade escaped to camp and alerted the battalion, a large number of whom thereupon took to the streets in protest. An Indian staff officer serving with Divisional Headquarters, Lieutenant Colonel Virendra Singh, was passing in a jeep at the time. He was surprised to see the crowd, and even more surprised to see that it included the battalion's subedar major, the most senior Gurkha VCO. Virendra Singh stopped to investigate and was told that the men were protesting at their bad treatment by their commanding officer and no longer wished to serve in Japan. He was able to persuade them to return to their lines, on the understanding that the situation would be investigated, and immediately reported the whole matter to Cowan. The General at once went to the lines and spoke to Townsend and to the subedar major and other VCOs, in order to deal with the situation. His fluent com-

mand of Gurkhali and his experience with the Gurkhas undoubtedly enabled him to restore stability.

The battalion's morale suffered from these events. Then, a
week later, the battalion was sent to Tokyo for the month's guard
duty which was performed by the BCOF infantry battalions in turn.
The difficulties with women were worse in Tokyo than in Hiro and
discipline came under severe strain. Townsend was determined to
stop the men bringing women into the camp, and the British officers
were required to do everything possible to prevent this happening.
The Gurkhas reacted bitterly against this treatment and it appears
that some refused to go on parade. This was extremely disconcerting, since the Tokyo guard duty was regarded as an important
display of BCOF efficiency and performance, but the officers were
unable to resolve the situation.

According to Thimayya, he was asked by General Cowan to
intervene, in the hope that the men would listen to a senior Indian
officer. Thimayya therefore went to Tokyo, where he first spoke to
Townsend, and subsequently went on his own to meet and talk to
the subedar major and other VCOs. It was clear that the colonel was
dedicated to his men but that he had little appreciation of the problems set by involvement in the occupation. The battalion had had a
hard war: their three VCs were evidence of that, and Townsend himself had been wounded twice and mentioned in despatches four
times. But now when the other contingents were relaxing in peacetime conditions, he had actually tightened discipline to ensure that
his own high standards were maintained. It showed a lack of that
understanding of human relationships which is essential in all
organisations and had led to uncomfortable rejection by his own
men.

Thimayya's discussions with the battalion's VCOs, at first
awkward and painful, finally cleared the air. The opportunity to
voice their complaints and the understanding that they would be
properly considered put an end to the protest and the battalion
resumed its duties. In the wake of this event, Townsend's position
was a very difficult one and his relations with his VCOs, and particularly the subedar major, were put under great strain.
Nevertheless, he remained in command. (The subedar major left in
February 1947 on early retirement, and his departure was recognised by an excessively eulogistic order of the day from the colonel).

The battalion's troubles, however, were not over. Its war diary up to January 1947 had consistently reported that morale was high and that the men were happy and contented, but a slightly sour note was struck in the commanding officer's January report: 'Welfare and amenities . . . have reached a very high standard.[3] I [Townsend] would in fact suggest that the limit to which welfare should go has been reached since, unless similar strides have been made in other commands, there will be much disappointment and somewhat of an anti-climax when eventually the battalion leaves this country'. The renewal of an emphasis on stricter discipline is noted in the diary for March 1947, when the Colonel commented on the poor condition of clothing, sanitation and standard of cleanliness in the lines, as well as the increasing slackness of the men in various ways, which had led him to institute weekly administrative days and more formal pay parades.

There were other real grounds for concern for the battalion's morale. Half the Gurkha other ranks had had no home leave for 2¾ years, and of these a large number had had none for over 3 years. There was also increasing confusion and bewilderment on strengths and release arrangements. One unfortunate result was that 160 men who had elected to serve for a further year from April 1947 were told in February that they would have to be discharged after all.

In the face of these difficulties, Townsend was glad to depart to the UK on long leave in April 1947. He had been a brave and capable commander in wartime, but found it difficult to cope with the impact on his troops of the conditions prevailing in Japan, and was fortunate to have retained his command there. However, his subsequent career was not handicapped by his troubles in Japan: on the break-up of the Indian Army, he went to the Gurkha component which became part of the British Army, and commanded 1/6 Gurkhas and subsequently a Gurkha brigade with distinction in the more familiar warlike operations of the Malayan emergency, for which he was awarded the DSO and the OBE, later upgraded to CBE.

Some of his contemporaries in Japan may, of course, have been right when they said that the Gurkhas 'had got too big for their boots'. The traditional love affair between the British officers and their Gurkha soldiers was already beginning to wane. The bonds of loyalty and comradeship formed over many years were loosening under the pressures of approaching Indian independence and, for a warlike race, the debilitating circumstances of peacetime.

Auchinleck's report[4] to the British Government on the division of the Indian Army after independence for India and Pakistan noted that the idea held by the British officers that the Gurkhas would always opt to serve Britain rather than India was completely upset by the result of the referendum held in all Gurkha units. Far from a general wish to serve His Majesty's Government, it seemed possible that even the number of volunteers required to fill the eight battalions allotted to Britain might not be forthcoming.

Meanwhile the departure of the British brigade effectively marked the break-up of BRINDIV, and the end of General Cowan's command. It was decided that BRINDIV's armour and artillery were no longer required, and with SCAP's approval 7 Cavalry and 16 Field Battery were withdrawn to India for reorganisation, while the British field battery was transferred to Hong Kong. 7 Cavalry in particular, although the poor state of the roads had limited their effectiveness, had carried out a number of important tactical tasks, including the permanent stationing of a troop at the ferry point at Uno to ensure the maintenance of communication between BRINDIV on Honshu and 5 Brigade on Shikoku.

The BRINDIV units remaining in Japan were to be absorbed into 268 Indian Infantry Brigade, which would then be enhanced to the status of a brigade group. This was to be commanded by Brigadier Shrinagesh, who had taken over from Thimayya in January (Thimayya was in due course to become Commander-in-Chief of the Army of the newly-independent India). There were warm exchanges of farewells between Cowan and Shrinagesh[5], who expressed regret on the breaking up of 'a famous division whose name will always remain in history' and appreciation and gratitude to Cowan for his efforts on its behalf and for his brilliant leadership. 'We have been proud to serve under you', Shrinagesh said, a statement which, while undoubtedly true, carried a poignant meaning only six months before Indian independence and the break-up of the old Indian Army to which they had all belonged.

268 Brigade Headquarters moved from Matsue to Okayama to take over from BRINDIV on 19 March and the Brigade Group came formally into being on 1 May 1947, assuming responsibility for Okayama, Shimane and Tottori Prefectures. But it was already recognised that the Indian contingent would not remain in Japan much longer. Unlike the British brigade, this withdrawal was not governed by manpower shortages and excessive overseas commit-

ments: in the case of the Indian units, the reasons were entirely political.

The Prime Minister of the Indian Interim Government, Pandit Jawaharlal Nehru, had stated in February that in view of the strong feeling in India about the use of Indian troops abroad, they should not be retained in foreign countries unless there were 'imperative reasons' for doing so. His government went further in March by stating that in view of the impending constitutional changes and the consequential reorganisation of the Indian Army they wished to withdraw all Indian troops serving overseas by the end of 1947.[6]

Australia delayed the forwarding to SCAP of India's notice of withdrawal, in the hope of changing the decision. Apart from the desire to maintain a representative force, removal of the Indian base and support units would cause a considerable problem for the contingents remaining, who would be unable to provide replacement easily. Evatt was worried that, as the other BCOF members' contributions declined in strength, pressure would mount in Australia for the withdrawal of the Australian forces as well. He was determined that they should remain until the peace treaty was signed. But in June the Government of India rebuffed his last-ditch request for a token force at least to remain. Its decision had been taken at Cabinet level and any reversal would interfere with the nationalisation of the armed forces. This was becoming a vital issue in the light of the approaching partition of India and the division of its armed forces between the new dominions of India and Pakistan.

The progress of Indianisation in the units in Japan was already well advanced. The reduction in the numbers of British personnel was taking place rapidly: by late 1946, for example, the Mahrattas had over 60 per cent Indian officers. British regular officers were to remain for the time being if they wished to, but all British emergency commissioned officers had to go. Unhappily, the Indian personnel were beginning to become politicised in a way which had always been anathema in the old Indian Army. Congress flags and posters now occasionally appeared, especially at times of festival such as *Divali*, and in some cases were put up at the instance of new Indian officers. The average British officer sympathised with the need to make progress but was concerned at the speed, which meant that inexperienced Indians were having to be promoted fast to fill the gaps. At the same time there was a real fear that the communal strife which was tearing apart the Punjab, the homeland of over half the Indian personnel in Japan, would spread into the army: it was receiving widespread publicity in BCON and the American press. It was largely due to the efforts of the newly responsible Indian commanders that this did not happen.

However, it had not been envisaged in the units that they would return to India so soon. Indian officers' families had been arriving in Japan since December 1946 and continued until May 1947, when an embargo was introduced on further family moves. The ultimate fate of the units and the personnel following partition was still largely unknown. Hindus in a single-class unit like the Mahrattas would naturally go to India; the Gurkha regiments were to be split up between India and Britain (the first and second battalions of the 5th Royal Gurkha Rifles were in fact destined for India), although there would be some degree of option available to individual soldiers; but mixed-class units like the Punjabis and most of the base and support units would be broken up and their personnel distributed between India and Pakistan according to their religion.

Against this difficult background the withdrawal of the Indian contingent suddenly became a matter of some urgency. In spite of earlier warning orders indicating completion of withdrawal by December, it was announced by BCOF Headquarters on 16 July with the concurrence of SCAP that the whole of the Indian contingent would be withdrawn by September, a speed-up reflecting the extraordinary acceleration of the independence process in India. The RIAF squadron had already received warning orders in June for its return.

The planning of this move was complicated by several factors. First, the Indian administrative units were a vital part of the infrastructure for the whole of BCOF and could not be released until replacements were provided from Australia or different arrangements for supply and support were made. They had to remain until the last. Secondly, the supply of shipping required to transport the contingent back to India was outside the control of BCOF, and ships for the transport of stores and vehicles were never available at the right time or in sufficient numbers. Thirdly, arrangements had to be made for the hand-over of occupation duties over the wide area covered by 268 Brigade Group, often with fundamental changes in the way they were to be discharged, because of the lack of adequate resources.

In accordance with the original plan for completion of withdrawal by December, Okayama had been established as the point of concentration for personnel, vehicles and stores, and all units except those already closer to Kure, the port of embarkation, were moved through Okayama. However, on 22 July GHQ (India) ordered that 'for political reasons' all Indian troops were to leave Japan by 15 September, and this, combined with the shortage of shipping, disrupted the careful planning completely. There were unhappy consequences: many support units were broken up to take advantage of shipping space for non-essential personnel, who arrived in India with no parent organisation and no destination. A vast amount of stores had to be abandoned because no shipping was available to transport them before the deadline for the final departure of personnel.

268 Brigade Group closed its headquarters at Okayama on 25 August, surrendering its occupational responsibilities at the same time. These were redistributed by BCOF: 34 Brigade took over Okayama and Shikoku in addition to Hiroshima; the New Zealand brigade took over Shimane in addition to Yamaguchi; and BCAIR assumed responsibility for Tottori from its base at Miho.

Although India would not officially relax the time limit, it was in fact impossible to meet the deadline set for 15 September. The last Indian soldier left Japan on 25 October 1947 in an atmosphere of haste and confusion – a state, it has to be said, to which all soldiers of all nations are well accustomed.

17

The New Zealand Contingent

The area allotted to the New Zealand brigade (2 NZEF) was Yamaguchi Prefecture, which they took over from the 2nd US Marine Division. It was the south west tip of Honshu, on the extreme flank of BCOF, and remote from the seat of power in mainland Japan. Brigade Headquarters were in the town of Chofu, near the sea port of Shimonoseki, but almost half the force was quartered in Yamaguchi itself, an old university town of some historical interest, with the rest of the brigade deployed round the coast of the prefecture. There were main camps at Tokuyama, Ozaki, Mizuba and Bofu, and company posts at Hagi, Otani, Hikari and Kogushi, as well as the repatriation centres at Senzaki and Otake.

The majority of the force at the outset had consisted of non-volunteers who had been promised return to New Zealand after serving six months in Japan. Their diversion to form part of BCOF for an interval on the way home was not welcome and the overriding ambition of a large proportion of the force was to return to New Zealand as quickly as possible. Even General Freyberg, the New Zealand Army commander in Italy, who was confronted with the task of raising the force, had said 'the general desire of everyone to get home and re-established in the new life is most pronounced'. Still, travelling across half the world was a step in the right direction.

But the drab and dreary barracks and camp areas which they had to occupy in this remote corner of Japan were in sharp contrast to the delights of Italy and indeed the enthusiastic advance publicity they had been given before departure. This, combined with the lack of proper amenities and a poor food supply situation, caused a considerable slump in morale. Many of the vehicles and much of the equipment brought from Italy were in poor condition after years of use and caused continual and frustrating problems. One commander reported 'a dogged determination to do as little as possible and to be as troublesome as possible'.[1]

The Maoris were a source of particular excitement. Even the Australians thought they were 'a wild mob', prone to hard drinking and loosing off firearms without fear of the consequences. On one typical occasion reported in Yamaguchi, a Maori sentry awaiting a relief who was overdue returned to barracks, climbed to the second floor and fired his rifle under the bed of his sleeping relief to draw his attention to the time. In addition to their prowess in combat and other qualities, the Maoris had a particular linguistic ability far beyond that of the 'pakehas'. Many of them had become proficient in Italian during their service in Italy, and they picked up Japanese quickly, which may have had some connection with the fact that they had a VD rate eight times higher than that of their 'pakeha' comrades.

The situation changed with the arrival of the reinforcements recruited in New Zealand to relieve the original contingent. These were enthusiastic volunteers who had signed up for a period of 12 to 18 months, with a minimum of six months in Japan, attracted by newspaper advertisements which said 'The Japs never reached New Zealand. But you can go to Japan – here's a chance to do service in unusual conditions in a country few New Zealanders have seen'. In spite of government fears that recruitment would be difficult, there had been a healthy response, although the Minister of Defence at the time commented that 'a good many men who enlisted, such as forestry workers and miners, have had to be rejected because they cannot be spared from their industries. We need timber and we need coal, so these men must stay here'.[2]

In July Brigadier Stewart was replaced by Brigadier Potter who, unlike the rest of 2 NZEF, had seen service in the Pacific, commanding 14 Brigade of 3 NZ Division in the Solomons (New Zealand forces were then part of Admiral Halsey's command and formed one of the spearhead units of 14 US Corps).

By August 1946 the men who had arrived from Italy had all been replaced and sent home, with the exception of a few volunteers wishing to continue. The change-over to a volunteer force had an immediate and beneficial effect. Morale was no longer a problem: a completely different atmosphere prevailed. A major contribution to this was the improved standard of quarters and amenities which had been planned earlier but which the later arrivals were the first to enjoy. Even so, they were ready to say that 'the barracks in two-storeyed wooden buildings, the beds hard and wooden, exposed electric wiring, and latrines between the buildings with honey pots in them, and little land crabs that scuttled everywhere' were not exactly ideal.[3]

But the improvement in conditions made the recruitment in New Zealand of the second relief draft in 1947 an easy task. There were plenty of young men – 19 and 20 year olds – who were not ready to settle down to a routine civilian life and who felt that they had just missed the war and the chance to travel abroad from their isolated country. Service with the occupation force was an obvious choice.

After the completion of repatriation (300,000 returning Japanese soldiers passed through 2 NZEF's centres), the New Zealanders' main duties continued to be the apprehension and repatriation of illegal immigrants to Korea, the disposal of enemy equipment, the search for subversive activities, and the suppression of smuggling. The southern end of Honshu was the Mecca for Korean smugglers, and 2 NZEF's area became known as 'Smugglers' Corner', demanding continuous patrols and countermeasures in cooperation with 81 Wing RAAF.

Although they were the smallest contingent in BCOF, the New Zealanders strenuously maintained an identity of their own. Northcott had noted at the beginning that they were 'somewhat insular in outlook as they were out of touch with progress in the organisation of BCOF until arriving in Japan', and their remote location added to their separateness. For much of the time they kept a direct command link to New Zealand outside the BCOF and JCOSA machinery. This effectively gave the 2 NZEF commander independence on all matters except operational control, which infuriated Northcott and Robertson, and caused some conflict at command levels until it was eventually submerged into the normal channels.

Brigadier Stewart had also established a line of resistance to the concept of 'integration' within BCOF, which was one of its basic tenets, largely because 2 NZEF's limited manpower did not allow for secondment of personnel to integrated units and headquarters.

He preferred to maintain the New Zealand contingent as a national unit, cooperating with the rest of BCOF, rather than integrating with it. There was an eventual accommodation in this area of disagreement, but New Zealand remained largely unrepresented outside 2 NZEF.

Meanwhile the desire for independence persisted. The New Zealanders produced their own 12- to 16-page newspaper, the 'Jayforce Times', with the aim of providing a much wider coverage of New Zealand affairs in all spheres of life, and therefore a closer link with home, than came within the province of BCON, the daily BCOF newspaper. In the field of fraternisation there was an initiative to clarify the BCOF directive in a practical way. The New Zealanders, coming from Italy, and before that the Middle East, had no legacy of bitterness or fear towards the Japanese, and Potter set in motion the relaxation of the non-fraternisation regulations on visits to Japanese homes and theatres. This caused considerable confusion and reaction in New Zealand and elsewhere in BCOF, but it was endorsed within 2 NZEF in March 1947. Japanese homes could be visited 'subject to strict propriety of behaviour'. Yamaguchi was remote enough from the rest of BCOF for this to have no repercussion elsewhere, and there was as a result much more contact with the civilian population. Rugby football was a particular meeting place, and the encouragement, coaching and supply of equipment which New Zealand soldiers gave to the adults, students and schoolboys was remembered long after the occupation.

With most of the restrictions on fraternisation still in force, boredom was a major problem, as it was with the whole of BCOF. The most reliable weapons in the military armoury to cope with boredom have always been intensive training and sporting activities. The Kiwis excelled at both. They were the first to undertake a five day route march in 1947 (later emulated by other contingents), which was carried out by 27 NZ Battalion from Yamaguchi in full battle order for 100 miles over a rough and stony route across mountainous country. The daily march varied between 15 and 25 miles and meals were supplied by mobile field kitchens. Nights were spent either in outlying barracks or in roadside bivouacs. The march was watched in silence by crowds of awed Japanese in the towns and villages through which the men passed and was pronounced a great success, even though a few soldiers finished the march with bare feet.

Sport played a particularly important part in the New Zealanders' life – rugby, of course, but the range was enormous. Athletics, swimming, tennis, cricket, soccer, hockey, basketball, boxing and wrestling all had their followers, and inter-unit and inter-formation competitions and championships provided an important bond with the other parts of BCOF.

As already noted, the New Zealand Government itself was always lukewarm about its occupation commitment, and had been largely influenced by its desire to be seen to support the Commonwealth and the United States as a 'good team member'. The British decision to withdraw their infantry brigade in 1947 encouraged the New Zealand Government to consider following suit and there was anxious debate at Cabinet level on the issue. However, it was considered wiser to relate a New Zealand withdrawal to an appropriate expiry date of the terms of engagement which the different drafts of the volunteer force had accepted. This would enable disbandment to be carried out more easily, and the Americans could be advised that manpower conditions in New Zealand would inhibit any attempt to raise a further replacement force. It was therefore decided to aim for withdrawal in the first half of 1948 and the required notice to SCAP was given.

The situation was complicated by the decision that 2 NZEF should take over responsibility for Shimane Prefecture from the Indian brigade when the latter left Japan in the summer of 1947. By the last quarter of that year the New Zealand battalions were in each case already at least 100 men below strength. In preparation for their evacuation from Japan on completion of the tour of duty, deployment on the northern coast was abandoned and the battalions were concentrated in the new camps then existing at Ozuki and Yamaguchi.

A last-ditch request was made by Robertson to the New Zealand Cabinet in February for the retention of at least one battalion, in order to avoid having to hand back Yamaguchi Prefecture to the Americans.[4] This, Robertson suggested, would be bad for British prestige, which he considered was 'higher than the US in Japan'. But the New Zealand government already had a report from Brigadier Potter giving his view that, compared with the dominating influence of the US, BCOF participation in the occupation was regarded as negligible, and BCOF had no influence on public opinion in Japan except locally, where it was regarded as being of value only as an extension of the police force.[5] Robertson's proposal was therefore rejected as being unrealistic.

With return to New Zealand imminent, the process of disbandment of units began in the second quarter of 1948, and withdrawal of the Army component finally took place over the period July to September 1948. New Zealand's last remaining unit in the occupation, the RNZAF squadron, which had moved from Iwakuni to Bofu, was retained there as part of BCAIR until the end of the year, when it too was withdrawn.

Not everybody wanted to go home, but few were so determined to stay as one soldier (originally from Fiji) who finally gave himself up to American military police in Yokohama in May 1949. He had lived with a Japanese woman since the departure of his contingent, but had had a difficult time and was in rags at the time of his surrender.[6]

18

The British Pull Out

Meanwhile, the effects of the reductions in BCOF were being assessed. Robertson had said as long ago as September 1946 that providing the attitude of the Japanese people did not change and BCOF commitments did not increase 'we could reduce our forces *pari passu* with the Americans, whose strength is already down'.[1] He had not envisaged the reduction being made solely in the non-Australian contingents.

The British Defence White Paper in February 1947 maintained that 'it is the intention of His Majesty's Government to continue to play their part in the occupation of Japan, although some reduction in the size of our contingent is being made'. But a BCOF spokesman said on 16 June 1947 that 'almost the whole burden of the British occupation role in Japan will fall upon the Australians after the departure in the next three months of the Indian contingent and part of the New Zealand army component' [although this was not actually to take place until 1948].[2] This was an exaggeration: on the facts then known, of the remaining Commonwealth force of about 20,000 troops, no more than 11,000 would be Australian. The approximate new strengths would be 11,000 Australian Army and RAAF; 3,000 NZ Army and RNZAF; and 5,000 to 6,000 UK Services. In spite of these hefty cuts, there was to be no alteration of occupation areas or responsibilities.

But now, only six months after the departure of the British brigade for Malaya, consideration was in fact being given to the complete withdrawal of the remaining UK forces. The British Adjutant-General, O'Connor, had visited BCOF in February while the brigade was still in Shikoku and, while satisfying himself on the improvement of living conditions, had clearly concluded that the lack of participation in the military government prevented BCOF from carrying out any useful role in the occupation.

An article in *The Times* of London by its Tokyo correspondent at the time of O'Connor's visit reinforced that view: 'all BCOF units are composed of men of whom their respective countries may well be proud', but the strict non-fraternisation policy and the denial of any part in the administration prevented BCOF from contributing anything to the democratisation of the country. The troops 'are regarded, owing to the nature of their duties, as oppressors, while the Americans are looked upon as liberators'. Many officers believe that 'either the BCOF should have some part under the United States command in the administration of its area, or the force would be better employed elsewhere'.[3]

Even American correspondents were commenting on the strong feeling of the British in Japan that they had been relegated to a position which would jeopardise British prestige and interests in the Far East and that BCOF was playing a secondary role.[4]

Against this background, it was not surprising that the CIGS, Montgomery, was beginning to agitate for the removal of the remaining British component of BCOF. In the course of a recent lecture to the Imperial Defence College in London he had already made it clear that he wished the UK element to be withdrawn entirely from Japan, although he wanted the Australians to stay because he considered it essential that some British Commonwealth troops should continue to represent the Empire in Japan. The Foreign Office learnt about this while preparing a brief for a visit Montgomery planned to make to Japan on his return from a tour of Australia and New Zealand in July and were suitably horrified that the CIGS was meddling in a political issue.[5] What was worse, he was adopting a line directly opposed to Foreign Office policy which favoured a coordinated Commonwealth phased withdrawal, avoiding any need for the UK to take a unilateral initiative. Bevin, the Foreign Secretary, told Montgomery that it would not be appropriate for him to give MacArthur any idea of what the views of the UK might be, since the future of BCOF would be discussed first on an inter-governmental level.[6] As it turned out, Montgomery cancelled the visit to Japan in order to rush home to bolster up the Chiefs of Staff in their efforts to resist cuts in Service strengths being forced on them by Ministers.

However, he pursued his line of thought with a proposal to the Chiefs of Staff in August that unless there were the strongest political objections, application should be made to the Australians to obtain American agreement to the withdrawal of the UK Army component from BCOF.[7] It was perhaps unfortunate that he had not seen BCOF with his own eyes before taking this initiative, but the move seemed sensible in all the circumstances.

The New Zealand Prime Minister, Fraser, had recently reiterated his doubts about BCOF in stronger terms than ever. He emphasised that its existence gave the participating governments no share in the military government or the democratic development of Japan, and questioned whether it provided any real support for the Commonwealth's policy for Japan. Moreover, 'its substantial inferiority to the American forces tends to diminish our prestige in Japanese eyes'.[8]

Fearing that a wholesale withdrawal of the entire BCOF was in the offing, JCOSA registered some fiercely defensive views, with the urgency of the condemned criminal approaching the scaffold (their continued existence went hand in hand with BCOF's). They repeated the well-worn arguments that the presence of BCOF supported the claim of the participants to take part as principals in the formulation of the Japanese peace treaty, and that its withdrawal would damage Commonwealth prestige even more. BCOF's value as a test bed for Commonwealth defence cooperation and in its provision of administrative experience and overseas service to countries who would otherwise lack them was stressed. But some new ideas were put forward which seemed by their unreality to indicate a desperate attempt to build a stronger case: it was suggested, for example, that the presence of BCOF strengthened the position of the Commonwealth representatives on the Far East Commission and the Allied Council for Japan (although the absence of a Soviet share in the occupation had never weakened their vociferous representatives' obstructive activity on these bodies); and that it ensured that 'the Commonwealth's value as an economic and social factor in the development of the Far East was not overlooked or underrated' – hardly a realistic proposition.

The Chiefs of Staff were not impressed and drafted a paper for the Defence Committee which summarised their assessment of the position.[9] 'If we had to consider narrow UK interests only, there would be some military advantages and no disadvantages in the dissolution of BCOF – but in the wider interests of the British Commonwealth, defence and security cooperation with the Americans, the other members of the Commonwealth and ourselves, we should not initiate proposals for the dissolution of BCOF'. They felt that it had been of considerable value as an experiment in Commonwealth cooperation (as Northcott had envisaged it would be) but it was no longer serving any useful operational purpose, and the manpower entailed could not be justified. The UK Army component now only comprised 1650 staff and administrative personnel, but since the administration was integrated, their withdrawal would affect all other units remaining. The RAF contingent of 2340 was also a target for withdrawal, even though it was appreciated that this might mean the break-up of BCAIR, because of its reliance on RAF staff and administrative personnel.

So the Chiefs of Staff recommendation on 13 September 1947 was that the Australian Government should be approached with the object of withdrawing the UK elements of BCOF. The Foreign Office supported this, taking the view that no important political objective was being served by the retention of the UK forces in Japan. They would have desired not to have to take the initiative in such a fundamental move, preferring it to have been part of an agreed general dissolution of BCOF, but saw no alternative 'in the circumstances of our present economic and manpower difficulties'. It was hoped that damage to Commonwealth solidarity could be avoided and that the other Commonwealth countries could be approached 'in such a form as to elicit their sympathetic concurrence' – perhaps a pious hope.[10]

Attlee thereupon signalled Chifley with a request that he approach the Americans for their agreement to the withdrawal of the UK Army Component from Japan as soon as possible and for the withdrawal of the RAF contingent if it was not found possible to make arrangements for their administration.

Before any formal agreement had been received, the Minister for the Army in Canberra announced the impending withdrawal on 4 October, causing a panicky reaction in London, where the Foreign Office was worried that MacArthur might well feel aggrieved at receiving information about the disposal of troops under his command in the first place from the press. British representatives in Tokyo were instructed to smooth over this gaffe as far as possible, but found MacArthur relaxed and sympathetic about the leak. 'No

Australian can be trusted to keep a secret', he said. He would not object to the British withdrawal but deeply regretted their departure and hoped it would not extend to the naval Force 'T'.[11]

The first official advice to MacArthur of the proposed withdrawals came from the American Embassy in London via Washington on 10 October 1947. The signal said,

> '. . . decision has been reached to withdraw UK forces from Japan . . . providing you interpose no objection UK hopes to withdraw UK contingent within next four months . . . Foreign Office also says New Zealand may either reduce or wholly withdraw forces within next few months. Foreign Office says Australian position not entirely clear, but it thinks Australia will retain forces in Japan largely for "representation" purposes . . . while UK Govt regrets necessity for withdrawal UK forces, UK Govt feels that this action will not substantially affect occupation program . . .'[12]

MacArthur's official reply on the following day was as calm and cooperative as the Tokyo talks had indicated. 'While the withdrawal of these troops cannot fail to somewhat lower the efficiency of execution of the occupation mission, the reduction is not of sufficient strength to cause definite abandonment of any phase thereof . . . It is not the purpose of this headquarters to raise any objections to the action of the British Commonwealth in this premise'.[13] MacArthur was not yet ready to admit that troops were no longer required to carry out the occupation mission: but it was already clear, at least to him, that the acquiescence of the Japanese people to the occupation and their subservience to him in his new role of surrogate Emperor had removed the need for a strong military presence. Civil administrators in uniform were all that he required to achieve the objectives he had set for the occupation. The proposed scale of withdrawal was not out of proportion to that which had already been carried out in the US forces: their strength had declined from 120,000 to 80,000 by October.

The Australian staff appreciation[14] of the situation arising from the proposed UK withdrawal noted that the army component of the UK contingent at that time was only 1,400, about 1,000 under strength, and that it comprised engineer, signals and base units, together with staffs in integrated units, all located in BRITCOM

Base and BCOF headquarters. No combat troops were involved. The RAF component of BCAIR comprised 11 and 17 Fighter Squadrons at Miho together with staffs of integrated units at Headquarters BCAIR, with a current total strength of about 2,200. The withdrawal of the squadrons and the consequent closing of the Miho air station would mean, in the view of the Defence Staff, that BCAIR would no longer be able to fulfil its occupational responsibility for Tottori prefecture, which might have to be excluded from BCOF's area of responsibility.

	1 June 1946	31 December 1946	1 April 1948	30 September 1948	1 May 1949
UK	9954	9806	1351	462	16
India	9611	10853	–	–	–
Australia	11446	11918	8203	6224	2503
New Zealand	4425	4444	2455	348	–
TOTAL	35436	37021	12009	7034	2519

Fig. 18.1 BCOF Strengths 1946–49

Nevertheless, formal approval was given for the reduction of the UK component on 2 February 1948 without any change for the time being in area responsibilities, and the contingent embarked on 22 April. A British MP (Teeling), who had visited Japan as a member of a parliamentary delegation, rebuked the Government at the time for its decision to withdraw. He deprecated its 'shelving its responsibilities because of the fear of involvement in any trouble which may arise in that part of the world, and by doing so forfeiting the right to advance proposals in relation to the eventual peace settlement'[15] – the same strange dependence as Evatt's on the need for participation in the occupation to secure governmental influence in the diplomatic field.

A small number of UK personnel still remained in Japan in

integrated units for special duties. BCOF's HQ Signals Regiment, for instance, continued to receive reinforcements for those of its UK personnel being released or repatriated up to September 1948, when the UK element still numbered 62 all ranks out of a combined UK-Australian total of 397. The UK personnel eventually left in November – the final rearguard of the British contingent in BCOF.

The Australian Government had already taken the opportunity of the likely shift in national contributions to reinforce their own control of the remaining force in Japan. At their request the other Commonwealth governments had been reviewing the system for control and administration in the course of 1947. The Australian view was that while JCOSA had been a useful experiment, it was now time for the control of BCOF to come entirely under Australian joint service machinery, with representatives from the contributing countries integrated into it. When a composite force was formed from several Commonwealth countries, it was advisable to place all the contingents under the control of a single country, which should accept responsibility for operations, as had been done when the AIF had been put under the British Commander-in-Chief in the Middle East. There were also more personal objections to the top heavy representation of the UK Services on JCOSA, where the UK representatives all carried the rank of major-general or equivalent, and to the expensively high standard of their housing and support.

Montgomery put his oar in during his visit to Australia in July 1947. 'Australia is not going to be dictated to by anyone . . . we should abolish JCOSA and put BCOF under the Australian Chiefs of Staff', he reported back, and responded eagerly to the other points of argument: '. . . the Australians cannot understand why we maintain extravagant and overloaded staffs in their country and at the same time ask for help because of our manpower and financial difficulties'.[16] JCOSA was certainly top-heavy: a typical meeting chaired by the Australian Chief of the General Staff would include Chiefs of the Naval and Air Staffs, Australia, representatives of the Chief of the Imperial General Staff, the Chief of Naval Staff and the Chief of Air Staff of the UK, a representative of the Chiefs of Staff, New Zealand, and a representative of the Commander-in-Chief, India, all of general officer rank. No wonder they had defended the continued existence of BCOF so strenuously.

Attlee agreed in August that JCOSA should be closed and the Australians should take over the control of BCOF completely, with a single head of a British military liaison mission to be attached to the Australian Chiefs of Staff.[17] The New Zealand Government supported the decision and nominated a joint service representative to the Australian Department of Defence to cover their interests in BCOF. The formal agreement between the Commonwealth governments concerned set the effective date of transfer of control as 1 January 1948 but also made it clear that it was subject to the continued retention by all governments of sovereign control of their own policy and full consultation when their interests were involved.

JCOSA was thereupon dissolved without further ado. It had certainly been a somewhat clumsy and complicated channel of command which had never worked easily. There had been constant friction between the Australian Defence Department, striving to exert its overall authority, and the overseas members representing the other Commonwealth governments, seeking to resist Australian domination. Now these aggravations had been removed and in this season of decline there was no doubt as to who was really in charge.

19

Problems for the Australians

The planned withdrawal represented a drastic reduction of BCOF's forces without any corresponding decrease in their occupational responsibilities and presented serious administrative problems at a time when other confusing factors were beginning to emerge. Newspaper reports had appeared about the likelihood of the withdrawal of the Australian force as well, which brought forth a statement from Canberra to the effect that the troops would not be withdrawn until after the Japanese peace treaty had been signed. On the second anniversary of the surrender in 1947, MacArthur called for an early settlement to ensure that 'this defeated country has the opportunity to become self-sustaining rather than reduced to a condition of mendicancy', but such a settlement then seemed unlikely before the middle of 1948. Australian families would continue to go to Japan up to the end of March 1948.

Against this background and on the assumption that the UK withdrawal would go ahead as requested, Robertson had decided in December 1947 that his remaining forces (together with their families, which were a further complication) would have to be concentrated in the Hiro-Kure-Etajima-Iwakuni areas, and that troops would have to be withdrawn from the prefectures of Okayama and Tottori. It would be desirable to try to retain the small Sub Area base in Tokyo as a token force 'after the peace treaty' and some representation in the Sub Area base in Kobe would be highly desirable as well. 'We have our force at present organised for war, which is a luxury no nation can afford in peace, which means that we must resort to considerable pooling of equipment'.[1] Disposal of surplus stores was going to be a major problem.

These plans were put into operation in BCOF orders issued in April.[2] 34 Brigade was to be concentrated in the Hiro-Kure-Etajima areas by 1 June. The Australian infantry battalions at Fukuyama and Okayama would be withdrawn to Hiro and Etajima respectively, and their occupational responsibilities would be carried out by Field Security personnel (normally including Japanese speakers) remaining in the areas and assisted from time to time by mobile detachments and air force patrols.

This situation was now to provoke further anxious consideration by the Australian Government of their continuing commitment to the occupation. But a surprising and uncomfortable campaign of criticism of the Force was meanwhile building up in Australia. On a visit to Canberra as long ago as August 1947, Robertson had found it necessary to say that BCOF was not getting a tenth of the credit it deserved. 'The troops are setting an example of real democracy to the Japanese', he said. 'They are now well looked after, following a grim time last year. Accommodation is good, and available for all families of servicemen who want to go to Japan. The Australians and New Zealanders, who are new to garrison duties, compare very favourably with the British and Indians, who are experienced in this work'.[3] Complaints by returning soldiers caused General Sturdee, the Chief of General Staff visiting from Australia, to add a rosy contribution: 'The Australians in Japan', he said, 'are as happy as Larry. They will find demobilisation hard'.[4]

But press criticism of the poor state of morale in BCOF, the black marketeering, and above all the high rate of VD, grew louder and louder. A prominent critic was Dorothy Drain, a columnist on the *Women's Weekly*, who is remembered as having waged a bitter campaign against BCOF. In January 1948, a particularly strong attack was launched by B J McDonald, the Federal President of the League of Ex-Servicemen, after a visit to BCOF.[5] 'The Australians in Japan', he said, 'are spiritually leaderless, bewildered and confused', and this was the root cause of their immoral behaviour. He attacked the officers as being guilty of excessive drinking, neglecting the need for training for trades, and having an attitude of contempt for their men. He suggested that there was a campaign to show the men that civilian life was full of restrictions, suffering and shortages, in an endeavour to retain them in the service. This provoked the Minister for the Army, Chambers, into calling in March for a full report into the allegations.[6]

Robertson and his senior officers sprang to the defence of BCOF. 'The Australians are undoubtedly the best troops in Japan . . . our units are probably the finest in the world', said Robertson in understandable hyperbole.[7] A senior surgeon in BCOF, Lieutenant Colonel Jones, was quoted on return to Australia as saying that the discipline in BCOF was superb, and that charges that morale had broken down were ridiculous. 'The worst features of the occupation of Japan are the shocking laxity of some young American soldiers and the atrocious condition of Japanese hospitals'.[8] The Chaplain General said that the press reports grossly defamed Australian troops: 'I never saw a drunken soldier in Japan, and the troops were the best dressed and behaved I have ever seen', he reported.[9] Perhaps this was as much a tribute to his escorting officers as to the troops themselves.

Chambers' enquiry, carried out by his legal adviser and subsequently confirmed by a visiting team of chaplains, reported that the black market was negligible, amounting to little more than the barter of canteen goods and other supplies coming mainly from the crews of visiting ships. VD was a problem but not particularly high. The charges that the men were neglected by their drunken officers were utterly unfounded. All ranks who were interviewed were indignant and distressed at the charges: they were a splendid well-behaved body of men.

Even MacArthur was persuaded to add his endorsement to the rebuttal of the criticisms, and duly responded: 'In my long military career, which includes five occupations, I have never seen better troops', he said. 'They were magnificent in the field and they are magnificent in occupation. I would like the Australian people to know these men are tops.'[10]

Nevertheless the VD situation was extremely serious. By March 1948 over 13,000 cases had been reported in BCOF, although many of them were re-infections of the same men. The New Zealanders had already noted that 'regardless of the efforts of the occupation forces and military government, VD is the greatest menace to occupation force troops in Japan'.[11] As the statistics of cases mounted, urgent conferences at Commander-in-Chief level formulated a vigorous anti-VD drive in the spring of 1948. This was directed primarily at separating infected Japanese women from the troops. Prostitutes who could not be fully treated in hospital were to be evacuated from BCOF troop areas and BCOF medical services were to supervise treatment of VD in Japanese hospitals as much as possible. Provost anti-vice squads were to be strengthened and, in cooperation with the civil police, were to arrest Japanese women infected with VD who were engaged in prostitution or were in contact with BCOF troops. Dependents were only to employ Japanese labour who were prepared to volunteer for VD examination.

The fact that prostitution was highly organised to the point of being a social institution in Japan did not help. Each town and village had its 'house of entertainment', and its inmates were licensed and bound under legal contract to their employers. The contracts were usually established between the parents of the girls and the brothel-keepers. An early SCAP directive had required the Japanese Government to annul the laws authorising or permitting licensed prostitution, as contravening democracy and individual freedom. The Government had duly complied, but it was difficult to demolish such an integral part of social life and, in the absence of proper policing, abolition was largely ignored or concealed from their staffs by the brothel-keepers.

BCOF left monitoring of the legal situation to the Japanese police, but all brothels were put out of bounds and military police carried out regular checks to try to enforce this, with only limited success. A proper system of authorised brothels with regular medical screening would have undoubtedly reduced the incidence of disease to a reasonable level. An attempt was made to promote this idea in BRITCOM Base, as John describes, but was frustrated by commanders apprehensive of the effect on their reputations at home.[12]

The persistently adverse publicity in Australia had a damaging effect on morale in Japan. Some BCOF men were so ashamed by the reports that they removed their colour patches and badges on return to Australia to hide their identity.[13] In May the VD issue became a matter of debate at Cabinet level, where a more balanced view prevailed. It was recognised that VD was a world-wide phenomenon following the war, especially in occupied countries. BCOF rates of VD among both British and Australian troops were much below the rates in Germany, and the British classification of the disease was much wider and stricter than in other countries, including the US. The problem was serious, but it would be quite wrong to suggest that VD was invented by Australian troops or that it was peculiar to Japan.

An Australian parliamentary delegation which visited Japan in August 1948 had a good deal to say about the erroneous reports about the troops' morality and their general behaviour, which were strongly resented by the members of BCOF. It seemed to be a malicious campaign mounted by a sensation-seeking press. 'The morality of the troops left nothing to be desired', they said. 'We are proud to be Australian and proud of our country's representatives in the occupation troops.'[14] They wanted to ensure that the reputation of the troops was cleared.

Meanwhile, BCOF was trying to carry through its concentration and reorganisation of the reduced occupation force. On 1 June HQ BCOF and HQ BRITCOM Base were amalgamated and part of BCOF headquarters moved from Etajima to Kure. The disposal of surplus stores and equipment following the rundown represented a major task. Hundreds of tons of serviceable stores – clothing, tents, beds, bedding, accommodation stores – were shipped back to Commonwealth countries; items not required by them and not included in the category of warlike stores were offered for sale to the Japanese Government through SCAP; and stores not wanted by the Japanese were sold as scrap or destroyed.

The fate of the remaining Australian forces in Japan was now the subject of vigorous discussion against the background of the progress of the occupation. By early 1948 the process of demilitarisation and demobilisation was practically complete. All arms factories and arsenals had been dismantled, with the exception of a few remaining under US Army control. The armed forces had been demobilised except for the large number of surrendered personnel still held by the USSR, which were estimated to total about 700,000 and remained a source of continual friction between SCAP and the Russians. The surrender of arms and ammunition was almost wholly completed, although some small caches of ancient flintlocks and swords were still being unearthed.

The process of demobilisation had been achieved speedily and effectively without launching large bodies of insecure and restless soldiers upon the civil population, and the vast majority of ex-servicemen were now trying hard to readjust to civilian life either in industry, agriculture or fishery, in conditions of some hardship. They had no regret that the war was over, and they hoped they would never be called upon to serve again. Although there were many ex-service associations and clubs, they existed primarily for mutual assistance and social purposes, and there was no sign of any revival of militarism, for which the occupation authorities (principally the US Counter-Intelligence Corps) kept a careful watch.

The military objectives of the occupation had clearly been achieved, and the Australian Defence Committee was asked by its Ministers in April 1948 to consider allowing the strength of the Australian contingent to dwindle by administrative action to 5,000, following the final withdrawal of the UK and New Zealand components.[15] The Committee first considered the value of BCOF from a military point of view, noting that after June 1948 BCOF's strength would be reduced to about 6,850, of whom 6,250 would be Australian, compared with the peak Australian strength in 1946 of 11,918, and that it would be accompanied by a proportionate reduction in effectiveness. From the purely Australian Service point of view, they concluded that continued participation in the occupation would still be of value for two reasons: first, in the strengthening of the goodwill established during the war with the US and in the gaining of useful experience in American methods which would result from continued cooperation with US forces in Japan; and secondly, 'because it is essential, in order to prevent the resurgence of Japan, that the occupation should continue until a peace treaty has been concluded' which would guarantee the future security of the whole Pacific area.

It was perhaps naive to assume that a continued Australian contribution, however small, to the occupation forces would automatically earn a seat of influence at the peace treaty negotiations: but this assumption ran like a continuous thread from the earliest days of Evatt's loud claims for a presence in Japan and continued to be an important factor in discussions on Australian policy throughout the occupation.

The minimum useful Australian military contribution to the occupation was considered to be a self-contained brigade group with air and naval support totalling some 7,000: but it was also realised that owing to manpower difficulties it would in fact not be possible to envisage an Australian component of more than 3,700 by the end of 1948. The Defence Committee's final conclusion was that, if for political reasons it was necessary to participate in BCOF after that date, only a token force could be provided, consisting of

one infantry battalion, one RAAF squadron and one ship with supporting units, in all totalling 2,750 service personnel. Far from
allowing the strength of BCOF on a solely Australian basis to dwindle to 5,000 as suggested by Ministers, it was going to shrink to less
than 3,000.

This debate was well aired in public. There were strong influences at work in the interests of reducing BCOF to a token force for
ceremonial guard duties only. It now seemed unlikely that the peace
treaty, which had been the main justification for Commonwealth
involvement in the occupation, would materialise soon. In spite of
the British and Australian desire for an early peace settlement, the
Communist threat in the Far East from both the Soviet Union and
China had persuaded the US that a peace treaty would leave Japan
unoccupied and incapable of defence against such a threat and that
delay was preferable. At the same time there was a pressing need to
put every able-bodied Australian into national production. Public
opinion towards BCOF had become unfavourable as a result of the
recent unofficial reports of lowered standards of morale. The Evatt
arguments for an 'equal voice' seemed to lose their force the longer
it took to get to the treaty negotiations. The press was urging governments to end what they saw as the morale-sapping role of the
troops in Japan. But Australians and New Zealanders were still
vividly conscious of the heavy sacrifices in the war against Japan
and remained solidly behind the determination to secure a protec-
tive peace treaty.

The Australian Government finally took the plunge and put
their proposal formally to the Americans at the end of May for the
progressive reduction of their contingent to the single battalion, the
single squadron and the single ship, to be completed around 31
December 1948.[16] They gave as their justification the convenient
excuse that demilitarisation tasks in the BCOF area were completed
and conditions in the area were now settled, which was certainly
correct.

MacArthur accepted the decision without comment: his view
was that such decisions were for the governments concerned to take.
But he was quick to point out the repercussions to Washington.
The token force of 2,750 to which BCOF's original strength of
38,000 was now to be reduced would be 'completely inadequate' for
the occupation of the BCOF area: and he insisted (in case others
used the same argument to reduce his force's strength) that physical

demilitarisation had only been an incidental occupation task and its completion did not justify a reduction in occupation forces.[17] MacArthur's minimum strength requirements had been based originally on the presence of a substantial Commonwealth force (at the outset estimated as 43,600) and on relatively favourable conditions in the Far East. Now the Commonwealth force was disappearing: and in the light of developments in China and Korea the favourable conditions no longer existed. 'At this critical juncture the military capabilities of the Occupation Force may have a decisive effect on Japan and in the Far East as a whole'. MacArthur called on Washington to provide additional anti-aircraft artillery forces and an additional infantry division to take over the BCOF area.[18]

Meanwhile, the planned reduction of BCOF began to go ahead. The scattered BCOF installations outside Hiro, Kure and Iwakuni were vacated progressively and turned over to US Eighth Army detachments. Action was put in hand to dispose of stores and equipment. Families were concentrated in the dependents' housing estates at Hiro and Iwakuni. Empire House in Tokyo was retained for the use of the Commonwealth Missions, and the Marunouchi Hotel was kept as the sole surviving leave centre. Following the withdrawal of the New Zealand contingent, SCAP decided that, with the location and reduced strengths of BCOF's remaining tactical troops, it would not be possible to continue BCOF's operational responsibility for Yamaguchi and Shimane prefectures, and the Force was relieved of them. The area of BCOF's responsibility was now reduced to Hiroshima Prefecture and the police district of Iwakuni (Yamaguchi Prefecture) only.

Robertson's position as Commander-in-Chief naturally came under pressure as the run-down progressed and his determination to maintain his status intensified accordingly. One major threat, as he saw it, was personified by General Gairdner, the British Prime Minister's personal military representative to MacArthur. Gairdner had built up a close relationship with MacArthur and his senior staff, as well as with Gascoigne, the senior British diplomat in Tokyo. Robertson was resentful that his own position was made unnecessarily delicate by the presence at MacArthur's elbow of this British general without any troops under his command. In June 1948 Robertson raised the issue with the Foreign Office in London while on a visit to the UK: Gairdner was 'undermining his position and intriguing against him'[19], and the last straw was that he had

handed out British honorary decorations to American officers at a
parade in Tokyo, 'when this was the proper function of the British
C-in-C'. (It is worth noting that this was Robertson's description of
his own appointment). The fact that Gairdner had been awarded a
knighthood (an honour which Robertson coveted) on the very day of
his call at the Foreign Office added fuel to the flames. Whitehall considered that the continuing friction was largely Robertson's fault,
since he was 'of a jealous disposition and rather vain'[20], but
Gairdner's post was an anomaly so long after the end of the war,
and it was decided that it would be best to terminate the appointment since, as Bevin minuted to Alexander, the Minister of Defence,
'his continued presence is the source of continual irritation to the
Australian C-in-C'.[21] Robertson's forceful persistence and egotism
had achieved his objective.

In a further endeavour to shore up the weakening position of
BCOF (and his own), Robertson came up with a new proposition
for its deployment. Since he would be down to around 3,000 men by
the end of 1948, he suggested to MacArthur that BCOF should be
transferred to Tokyo, with the surviving air force squadron going to
an airfield near the capital. It would undoubtedly be better for publicity purposes to have the Commonwealth contingent in Tokyo
rather than hidden away in the wilds of south west Japan.
MacArthur did not reject the idea immediately, and Gascoigne
thought it a good one.[22] It would show the flag and, more in his own
interest, it would improve the supply and support of the UK Liaison
Mission. But Canberra did not approve: they thought that BCOF
would disappear into the mass of the US Eighth Army, losing its
identity, and there would be no publicity advantage to be had. It
seemed a surprising conclusion which ignored Robertson's flair for
assertiveness and independence.

During the last months of 1948, the State Department tried
hard to get the Australians to retain a BCOF of division strength in
Japan until it was generally agreed that a substantial reduction
could be made in all occupation forces, but the attempt failed.[23]
Robertson had already advised SCAP[24] that 34 Brigade less the one
battalion and 81 Wing RAAF less the one squadron would have left
for Australia by 8 December. Perhaps making a virtue of necessity,
the State Department now appeared to think that complete removal
of BCOF forces from Japan might now be desirable and asked
MacArthur for his comments on this 'including [the] military as

well as political implications *vis-à-vis* Japanese people and Allied representatives in Japan'.

MacArthur's response was harsh but to the point. From the military aspect, BCOF was now so small as to be negligible. From the Japanese point of view, withdrawal or retention 'can be regarded as a matter of indifference'. But for the US to initiate a movement for complete withdrawal would, he considered, harm relationships with Australia and the Commonwealth: 'it is doubtful that any advantage which might accrue from the withdrawal would warrant the scars which might result . . .'.[25] MacArthur was as anxious to avoid hurting Commonwealth feelings as London had been at the time of final British withdrawal.

So MacArthur put on one side the continued existence of BCOF. He concentrated his efforts on continuing to stress the problems which its reduction had caused. From the SCAP point of view, the established organisational structure of five divisional areas, of which BCOF had been responsible for one, was the minimum requirement for a balanced administration. Although Eighth Army was temporarily taking over BCOF's area and functions, any attempt to reallocate them permanently to his remaining four divisions would result in such a dilution of forces as to 'make questionable either the purpose or the capability of the occupying power'.[27] Because of the complete dependence on the rail and tunnel system for inter-communication in Japan, it was essential to have local forces properly distributed throughout the country and capable of coping with disorder without reinforcement. Relatively small numbers of dissidents, he warned, could seriously jeopardise the prestige and authority of the occupation. (The fact that neither disorder nor dissidents ever existed during the occupation was not allowed to diminish the argument).

But it was the external situation which worried MacArthur and the US Government most. The Communist successes in China combined with the Soviet build-up in Asia constituted, MacArthur believed, an increasing threat of direct military action against Japan. It was vital that the US should maintain an adequate force in Japan not only to meet this threat, but to be seen by the Japanese to do so. In the American view an early peace treaty was no longer desirable, because it would leave Japan powerless to resist Soviet infiltration. It might be better for the occupation to be prolonged indefinitely to retain a strategic position in Japan and build up the Japanese economy on a capitalistic basis. Although some of their experts had advocated a long occupation, this attitude was now disputed by the British, and indeed by the Japanese, who had often suggested that 'GHQ' should stand for 'Go Home Quickly'; but progress towards a peace settlement slowed down to a halt. MacArthur believed that Japan's faith in the leadership of the US and its determination to guarantee Japan's security had to be maintained if Communist pressures were to be resisted, both inside and outside the country. It was not only the successful accomplishment of the occupation which was at stake, he considered, but also the future support of the Japanese nation for the US in the event of war.

MacArthur deployed these arguments in a renewed impassioned appeal to Washington for the extra division to replace BCOF and to remedy what he described as the critical shortage resulting from its reduction.[28] Even if BCOF were authorised to participate in the defence of Japan (and special agreement was required before Commonwealth forces could be committed to assist US resistance to an external attack), the remnants of BCOF would be of little help. The tactical requirement for at least five divisions remained. The need for troops to replace BCOF had been evident since May 1948 and was not a new or unexpected demand on US resources. MacArthur was fully aware of the budgetary problems, but pressed his case with customary hyperbole: 'in view of the disaster to the US position and objectives in the Far East which can result from a failure to meet this vital requirement . . . arbitrary budget limitations should not operate to incur such grave national risk without further policy consideration at the highest governmental levels'.

Washington was sympathetic to the problems caused by the BCOF reduction, but did not accept that it posed a grave risk to the security of the US and, while appreciating the new circumstances prevailing in the Far East, was not prepared to be helpful: there was no possibility of allocating MacArthur any greater share of the 677,000 troop strength available world-wide than his present allocation. He would, in the manner of commanders throughout history, have to do the best he could with what was already at his disposal. There was no evidence, they added, that any increase in British Commonwealth Forces would result from the inter-governmental negotiations which had taken place so far.[29] This was an accurate reading of the Australian Government's attitude. MacArthur had already labelled the negotiations as 'academic'.

The reducing Australian commitment to BCOF took place against the background of the development of a whole new post-war defence policy for Australia. Traditionally, the country's military needs had been met by a small regular cadre (the Permanent Military Forces, or PMF) supported by a large volunteer reserve (the Citizen Military Forces, or CMF). Neither of these forces could be compelled to serve overseas, although most of them did. However, in the event of war, it had been the practice to raise an expeditionary force specifically for service overseas. In the First World War this was entitled the AIF (Australian Imperial Force), and in the Second World War the force raised in 1939 became the 2nd AIF.

At the end of the war, Australia had an Army of nearly 400,000 men, mostly overseas, made up of pre-war PMF, the CMF and the AIF, known together as the AMF (Australian Military Forces). There was an urgent need to proceed with early demobilisation, to enable the nation to redirect itself towards a peacetime economy. At the same time, plans for future defence policy and the forces which would be needed were still in the melting pot. It was generally agreed, after the alarms of the war and its impact on Australia, that strong defence forces were vital for the country's security, no matter how much reliance could be placed on the elimination of Japan as a future military threat. While the debate on the nature of the post-war forces continued, it was essential to make some provision to meet the BCOF and other commitments. A decision was therefore taken to establish a temporary organisation known as the Interim Army: this included all those still serving in the Australian Military Forces on 1 October 1945 plus all those who joined after that date. Recruitment for enlistment in the Interim Army on a two-year engagement started in earnest in February 1946.

In June 1947 the government decided to form the post-war defence forces on the basis of a regular army of one independent brigade group (PMF) and a reserve of two divisions, with supporting formations (CMF), a total of nearly 70,000 men. The PMF was renamed the Australian Regular Army, or ARA, and recruitment started immediately to bring it up to the intended strength of 19,000, of which the brigade with BCOF would form the field force.

The brigade then in Japan therefore became in effect the heart of Australia's post-war regular army. However, recruiting for it had a poor response, and it proved impossible even to keep pace with wastage. The result was that 34 Brigade's strength declined in an alarming way: by the middle of 1948 the battalions were down to a third of their establishment strengths. While occupation duties were now far less demanding, it was humiliating for 67 Battalion to have to engage Japanese to guard their barracks as they did when they went to Tokyo for duty in late 1948.

In accordance with the Government's decision to reduce the Army element of BCOF to a single battalion, two of 34 Brigade's three battalions – 65 and 66 Battalions – were withdrawn to Australia in December 1948, while the third, 67 Battalion, remained in Japan as the core unit of BCOF. In March 1949 the battalions were redesignated as 1st, 2nd and 3rd Battalions of the new Royal Australian Regiment (RAR), the first regular Australian regiment of infantry.

The veterans returning to Australia in 1948–49 were not treated as conquering heroes. Many of them were shunned when they got home. The adverse publicity they had received had turned the civilian population against them. One infantryman recalled how, when his girl-friend's mother found that he had been with BCOF, 'I was shown the door straightaway!'[30] There was also a public fear that the servicemen might be contaminated with radioactivity, which was just beginning to be understood. 'Nobody wanted to know us', said a 67 Battalion NCO.[31] It was just like the reception given in later years to Vietnam veterans. There was much bitterness and disillusionment on the return home. It took time for the BCOF people to recover a reasonable reputation in Australia.

The responsibility of all BCOF's occupation duties, such as they were, now fell on the 3rd Battalion (3 RAR) and 77 Squadron RAAF, together with a small intelligence unit for field security and interpreting duties. The battalion's capability was seriously affected by its weak manning situation: reinforcements were irregular but wastage on account of discharge remained painfully regular. At about half strength and with a grave shortage of junior officers, it was difficult for the battalion to carry out a sensible programme of training as well as the formal duties of occupation. But these were now at a minimum level. There were guards to be provided in Kure and Hiro, and one company was permanently on guard duties in Tokyo in accordance with Robertson's proclaimed intention to retain the commitment 'because I consider this representation essential for the prestige and continued recognition of the BCOF in

Japan'.[32] Plans were drawn up for deployment throughout the prefecture in the event of disorder, but no need for them ever arose.

In fact the last occupation force guard took place at the Imperial Palace in May 1949, its place being taken thereafter by Japanese police. This reduced the guard responsibilities in Tokyo considerably and an active training programme was now more feasible. The effort and enthusiasm put into the building up of a new *esprit de corps* for the battalion were beginning to show real results.

SCAP's famous instruction of September 1949, effectively abolishing any barriers between the Japanese and the Americans, further modified the role of the occupation. In view of the completion of demilitarisation and the advances of social and economic reform, the Japanese Government could now be permitted greater responsibilities. There was no longer any need for strict surveillance by the occupation force, which would now assume the nature of a friendly protector. BCOF's Intelligence and Detailed Interrogation Unit (CSDIC) was disbanded in December, and all field intelligence operations in the BCOF area were handed over to the US Counter Intelligence Corps.

In early 1950 persistent rumours began to circulate in Japan that the remaining Australian troops would be withdrawn before the end of the year. Japanese newspaper reports claimed that the Empire Day parade on 24 May and the King's Birthday parade on 12 June in Tokyo would be the Australians' swan-song and that withdrawal would follow soon after. The Minister for the Army (Francis) took it upon himself to deny these rumours, saying that no decision had been made. This was typical government deception: in fact an official note from Canberra had already been presented in April to the US Government through the Australian Ambassador in Washington asking for agreement to the complete withdrawal of BCOF from Japan.

This decision had been taken for a number of practical reasons. It was an expensive and tiresome task to maintain a small force of under 3,000 over the long supply line from Australia. About one-third of the strength were Interim Army personnel who had exceeded their term of engagement and could in theory go at any time, while the period of engagement of a proportion of the regulars would begin to expire early in 1951. New recruitment of volunteers for the maintenance of the Force would, on the experience to date, be extremely difficult.

At the same time, the Australian Government had decided on the introduction of national service, which traditionally requires the dedication of considerable regular resources to the training of temporary soldiers. It was estimated that 3,720 additional permanent personnel would be required for the training and administration of the annual national service intake. The maintenance of BCOF in Japan was a significant drain on the limited manpower of the Australian regular forces, while its return to Australia would be an important factor in the success of the national service scheme.

It had at last been admitted that the continuation of a share in the occupation at the present reduced level did nothing to ensure Australia's security or her status in the Pacific scene. The stalemate between the major powers over a Japanese peace treaty seemed likely to continue indefinitely and Canberra had realised that the future safety of Australia depended far more on a mutual security pact with the United States than on a punitive settlement with Japan. There was no further point in staying in Japan.

MacArthur accepted the position and merely confirmed that his command was prepared to assume responsibility for the functions and areas assigned to BCOF when it was withdrawn. Washington, however, was anxious to ensure that when the Australians announced BCOF's withdrawal, they did so in a way which did not imply that the action had been taken by the Commonwealth through any dissatisfaction with the continuation of the occupation. When Menzies made the announcement in Canberra on 26 May 1950, therefore, he did so with emphasis on the need to have additional forces in Australia around which would be built a stronger armed force in the future. He added that discussions were in progress on the timing and method of withdrawal, but it was expected that some time would elapse before the actual movement of men and stores began. The whole operation would extend over a considerable period. 'Since its inception the whole of the Force had worthily represented the British Commonwealth and had carried out its duties of the military control and demilitarisation of its area with great efficiency and credit'.[33]

The men of BCOF were happy to be relieved of the uncertainty and indecision about their future. As 3 RAR started to prepare for its return to new barracks in Enoggera in Queensland and the task of sorting out BCOF's equipment and stores began, there was a flurry of valedictory messages. MacArthur's to Menzies was typically lavish

> 'the BCOF has been tops . . . in deepest sincerity I shall greatly regret the severing of my contacts with your troops. Their discipline, conduct and bearing have on all occasions and in all circumstances been exemplary. Australia can well be proud of what they have done here . . . I shall ever look back with pride and affection to my association with your magnificent fighting men'.[34]

Attlee was a little slower and less flowery but no less generous with his message: 'Now that the decision has been taken to withdraw the BCOF from Japan, I should like to express the thanks of the United Kingdom Government to the Australian Government for the admirable way in which the representatives of the Australian armed forces have carried out their task in Japan on behalf of the Commonwealth. They have played a major part in the BCOF from its landing in Japan in 1946, and for nearly two years they alone have maintained the force. I join you in your tribute to the efficiency with which they have carried out their duties throughout this period'.[35] The air and naval components of BCOF were, of course, inextricably involved in these proposed arrangements for rundown and withdrawal. But they had each led a different existence from the army component and had accumulated quite different experiences over the previous four years.

20

The Commonwealth Air Force

BCOF's air force (BCAIR), although an integral part of the Force, had had a special identity and character of its own. One in every six men in BCOF was a member of BCAIR, and yet the air component was concentrated in only three locations – the bases at Iwakuni, Bofu and Miho. This had made it possible to achieve a high standard of facilities for the airmen much sooner than for the army units, whose movement and dispersal made it difficult to marshal resources efficiently.[1]

In addition to its facilities for flying, Iwakuni possessed accommodation for over 4,000 men. The runway and hangars had suffered much bomb damage and required urgent attention, but the majority of the other buildings were intact, although badly in need of repair, and there were potentially good arrangements for recreation, including an Olympic-sized open air swimming pool, a cinema and canteens. The New Zealand squadron and 1315 Communications Flight were fortunate in many ways to be stationed there, together with the RAF hospital, although, as is normal, somewhat inhibited by their uncomfortable nearness to BCAIR Headquarters. But Iwakuni was a good place for BCAIR HQ, and it was able to provide the transit facilities necessary to discharge its role as BCOF's principal airport. Most BCOF personnel and their visitors travelling by air passed through Iwakuni, and a great deal of effort was invested in bringing it up to a standard which the rest of BCOF found difficult to emulate.

Conditions at Bofu for the RAAF wing were to start with even better than at Iwakuni: there was excellent accommodation, com-

191

plete with steam-heated rooms, although this was somewhat depleted three days after the Wing moved in by a fire which quickly destroyed four two-storey barrack blocks.

The base occupied by the RAF and RIAF squadrons at Miho, set on the north coast about 120 miles to the north east of Iwakuni and surrounded by pretty countryside, was another first-class station. There were good runways, plenty of concrete parking space, and three useful hangars which were soon made serviceable.

Miho completed the 'strategic triangle' of BCOF air bases, which now housed a total of 150 high performance single engine fighter aircraft, as well as BCAIR's Dakota and Auster communications aircraft. The RAAF Airfield Construction Squadron was responsible for repairing and maintaining the bases and earned a high degree of respect throughout BCAIR for its efficiency and its effective use of Japanese labour: at the outset at Miho, for example, a force of hundreds of Japanese women plucked the overgrown grass from the airfield by hand.

BCAIR now assumed an important role in the policing of the occupation. From the beginning, squadrons carried out a daily air surveillance of the whole BCOF area. Much of the country over which the patrols extended was extremely rugged: one pilot said 'we wouldn't have dug them out till kingdom come if they had decided to fight'. Timings and areas patrolled were varied so that all pilots became familiar with all parts of the BCOF area and because in the early days it was considered desirable that the Japanese should not know when to anticipate a reconnaissance. Pilots were to report on any concentrations of personnel and on the serviceability of towns, bridges, and railway systems. They complied enthusiastically. One pilot reported that he had spotted a group of Japanese being trained in visual signalling and ground patrols rushed to the scene, only to find an open-air class from the local girls' high school in progress! but from time to time the air patrols revealed valuable discoveries. 14 Squadron RNZAF, for example, were successful in locating a number of 40 mm. anti-aircraft batteries whose existence had not been disclosed to the occupation forces.

In July 1946, the Miho-based squadrons flew as a wing for the first time, and it became apparent that the short range of the Spitfire was a real disadvantage when used in this way for cross-country 'wing shows' – the air force equivalent of 'showing the flag' – since, after allowing 25 minutes for the forming up and for the landing of three squadrons, only about 60 minutes' actual flying time was left. Patrolling was best undertaken on a single squadron basis, and was rotated between them.

Special attention was devoted to surveillance of the Tsushima Strait between Japan and Korea, monitoring ship movements as part of the efforts to prevent illegal immigration. In good weather the coast swarmed with small, often unseaworthy, vessels crowded with illegal immigrants and smugglers of black market goods from Korea. The immigrants were a particular hazard because of the fear that they could cause serious epidemics in Japan by spreading the cholera which was raging in Korea. BCAIR pilots flew constant operations to spot suspicious vessels, working in conjunction with BCOF boarding parties using high speed launches, who intercepted the vessels or alerted ground patrols to those who managed to avoid interception and land on the coast.

Flying, of course, has an intrinsic attraction of its own, and this offered a challenge to BCAIR pilots, quite apart from their occupation duties. Handling a modern fighter aircraft, carrying out surveillance, flying training, air-to-air combat and ground attack exercises, had an excitement which was denied to the troops on the ground on their routine patrols and parades. And there was plenty to do. 17 Squadron's operations record book for June 1946, for example, showed that the squadron flew 210 hours in the month, more flying than they had done in any month since the war.[2] A typical day would comprise four sorties on patrol over Shimane Perfecture, four sorties on practising formation flying and quarter-attacks, two on aerobatics and dog-fighting, and an aircraft flight test. Often the squadron would have 12 aircraft airborne on different missions at the same time.

Moreover, these flying activities involved a degree of cooperation between the different national components of BCAIR and with the US occupation forces which was never available to the ground forces. On 14 November 1946, for instance, a special BCAIR fire power demonstration was mounted in which a composite force of 36 RAAF Mustangs, 12 RNZAF Corsairs and 12 RAF Spitfires carried out a joint attack on a very large stockpile of Japanese armaments which had been collected on the small island of Onasamishima, north of Etajima in the Inland Sea. The target was attacked by bombs, cannon fire and rockets, with outstanding success, resulting in its complete destruction. The exercise was particularly pleasing for BCAIR, because it was witnessed at close quarters from the Royal Indian Navy sloop *Narbada* with acclamation by Eichelberger, the commanding general of the US 8th Army, under whose operational command the land component of BCOF fell. Bouchier, who had accompanied Eichelberger, sent the squadrons a fulsome message of congratulations, with an undertone of relief that things had gone so well. When the Spitfire wing from Miho carried out a similar fire power demonstration in September 1947, their instructions were to ensure that the bombs fell on land and not in the sea, for maximum effect, and not to worry about the targets![3]

In July 1947, a mass Allied formation flypast was organised over Tokyo to mark American Independence Day celebrations, when one RAAF Mustang squadron and two RAF Spitfire squadrons flew in formation with 300 American aircraft from the US zone. Relations with the US air force were warm – flying is a special bond. When BCAIR put together a composite squadron for a flypast over Tokyo to mark the wedding of Princess Elizabeth and Prince Philip in November1947, the squadron was based at the American base at Johnson Field, and 17 Squadron's diary noted that 'the pilots were amazed at the tremendous reception and overwhelming hospitality of the American forces, the like of which is rarely met'.[4]

But it was not easy to maintain an adequate level of efficiency in the face of the difficulties which built up through 1946 and 1947. In the early drafts from the UK there was a large number of former aircrew made redundant by the war's ending and remustered into different non-flying trades at lower ranks. Even so, there always seemed to be a shortage of pilots and skilled ground staff, with the regular departure of personnel on release and repatriation. Reinforcements arrived only intermittently and usually lacked operational experience. In August 1946, for example, 11 Squadron had only six riggers available for duty against an establishment of 22. This, combined with a perennial shortage of spares, led to a high percentage of the aircraft becoming unserviceable, particularly in the RAF and RIAF squadrons, whose old Mk XIV Spitfires had 'naturally been pretty well hammered in the Far East war'.[5] In 17 Squadron it was difficult to get as many as 12 aircraft airborne out of a complement of 18. When the aircraft were ready for flying, and there were enough pilots on hand, there was frequent grounding because of faulty petrol or a shortage of fire-fighting foam: and when these faults were rectified, the unreliable Japanese weather would often intervene, even in summer.

Bad weather conditions had been a hazard ever since they had claimed three aircraft trying to get into Bofu on the original ferry flight of 81 Wing from Labuan. Weather forecasting was uncertain, and the lack of navigational and landing aids made flying over the mountainous countryside even more difficult. There was a fairly regular series of accidents during BCAIR's time in Japan, some due to weather, others due to engine failure or the habitual 'pilot error'. Several fatalities took place when aircraft engines failed and the pilots bailed out but parachutes failed to open or opened too late. The most bizarre incident concerned a Spitfire which overran its runway and overturned in a paddy field: the pilot drowned in the flooded paddy before the rescue team could reach him. But flying high-performance aircraft is a potentially dangerous business and BCAIR's accident rate was probably no worse than that of any other formation.

When the Indian brigade left Matsue for home in the summer of 1947, together with the RIAF squadron, the New Zealand brigade took over responsibility for the discharge of occupation duties for Shimane Prefecture, while BCAIR found itself allocated the responsibility for Tottori Prefecture, by virtue of its remaining presence in Miho. This may have been the first time since the RAF's activities in Iraq between the wars and the establishment of the base at Habbaniya, that a Commonwealth air force had assumed duties of this kind.

The Indian squadron had had a happy occupational tour. It had made full use of the sports facilities and amenities at Miho, and its men had enjoyed guard duty in Tokyo, local sightseeing tours and leave at the various BCOF centres. It was a completely 'national' unit: in common with the rest of the Indian Air Force, it had never carried British officers on its strength, although RAF officers had been attached in the early years. And it was a 'non-class' unit – that is to say, unlike most Indian Army units it was not manned or divided on Hindu or Muslim lines, and it achieved an admirable integration of interests. All ranks celebrated both Hindu and Muslim holidays together without conflict, setting an example which the nation and its politicians were unable or unwilling to follow. Operational efficiency was reasonably high, and the squadron played its part in BCAIR's programmes for operations, flight and ground training. The pilots were enthusiastic, although there was some lack of regard for their skill amongst the more experienced aircrew of other contingents: 'they did not impress us as pilots', said a New Zealander, 'and were forever getting lost and almost running out of fuel'.[6] It was particularly bad luck that in the same month (June 1947) when orders were received to prepare for the squadron's return to India, there occurred the worst accident they had experienced. Two Spitfires collided in cloud after a sudden deterioration in the weather while patrolling over the Miho–Hiroshima area, and both pilots were killed. While flying can never be separated from risk, it was an unhappy leave-taking.

Although they were never officially part of BCAIR, the various Commonwealth air forces ran regular courier and supply flights from the different home countries and other overseas bases, and became an important contributor to the occupation. Perhaps the most impressive was the service run by 41 Transport Squadron RNZAF between New Zealand and Iwakuni, primarily in support of the RNZAF fighter squadron but also providing a facility for the whole of the New Zealand contingent. This service was carried out by crews flying old Dakotas over what was at that time the longest and most difficult route in the world. It ran from Whenupai in New Zealand, via Norfolk Island, Brisbane, Cloncurry, Darwin, Morotai, Tacloban, Manila, Laoag and Okinawa to Iwakuni, and each Dakota covered 12,452 miles on the round trip.

The decision to withdraw the majority of RAF units in 1948 with the rest of the UK component meant the end of 11 and 17 Squadrons at Miho. In January, the squadrons ceased flying. Since it was uneconomic to transport the aircraft back to the UK where there were many hundreds of Spitfires available in good condition, guns, radio equipment and instrument panels were stripped from the aircraft in preparation for their destruction. On 23 February both squadrons were disbanded, the remaining personnel transferred temporarily into the Station staff, and the aircraft were destroyed. It was a sad and empty feeling for the ground staff who had laboured so hard to keep the aircraft flying, and for the pilots who had flown them.

34 Brigade took over responsibility for Tottori prefecture, and the airfield at Miho was handed back to the USAF in May. Following the rundown of RAF units at Iwakuni, it was decided that 81 Wing RAAF would return from Bofu to Iwakuni to take their place, and that the New Zealand squadron would move to Bofu instead, a form of mildly amusing musical chairs.

Further complicated exercises came thick and fast for 81 Wing in 1948. In March an exercise was carried out in conjunction with the 315th Composite Wing of the USAF, whose aircraft were unexpectedly intercepted by RAAF Mustangs and RNZAF Corsairs during a simulated attack on the Tokuyama oil refinery. In April a series of mock attacks were launched on two US warships; and in July Operation Platypus was carried out in conjunction with the Americans, involving 81 Wing and the New Zealand squadron in covering a simulated landing from the sea followed by operation from an advanced landing ground, which was then put under air-to-ground attack.

In September 1948 it was decided, as part of the decision to cut back the Australian commitment to the occupation, to disband the whole of 81 Wing with the exception of 77 Squadron, which would then become the single RAAF occupation squadron which the Australian Government wished to retain in Japan as part of the reduced contingent which had been accepted by MacArthur. And so on 2 October 1948 76 and 82 Squadrons RAAF were disbanded, and their Mustang aircraft were shipped back to Australia in the new year. In the face of these reductions it was agreed with the 5th US Air Force, BCAIR's superior formation for operational purposes, that daily surveillance patrols over the BCOF area could be discontinued.

The New Zealand squadron was also withdrawn at the end of 1948, a few months after the New Zealand Army contingent. There was a special frustration about their withdrawal: they had spent many weeks of work on upgrading the Corsair aircraft for the return journey, and were surprised and shocked when it was finally decided that it would be uneconomic to take them back to New Zealand after all, and that they should be destroyed by fire on the departure of the squadron, together with spares and other equipment. It was said that the commanding officer Squadron Leader St George, took a last flight, landed, parked, said 'Burn the bastards', and walked away.

So, by the end of the year, 77 Squadron RAAF was the sole survivor of BCAIR's once substantial force, and its operational area was confined to the Iwakuni police district. Nevertheless, it was still the largest flying unit in the RAAF, operating 40 Mustangs, two Dakotas, three Wirraways and two Austers with a complement of nearly 300 personnel.

One result of these changes was that the squadron found itself involved in ground activities in its occupation area which it would have normally left to the Army, over and beyond its normal flight patrols and training. In January 1949 the squadron provided six teams of observers for surveillance of the national elections in the area and its Auster aircraft had the unusual task of dropping leaflets on the towns and villages encouraging the people to vote. During that spring the squadron's intelligence section became involved in surveillance of Communist activity in the Iwakuni area at a time when it was feared that Communist infiltration, supported from North Korea, was beginning to threaten factories in the district through the channel of the labour unions.

Life at Iwakuni was now that of an established garrison station. There was regular flying, a great deal of sport, well-organised leave and holiday facilities, and a large number of families in comfortable married quarters with Japanese servants in attendance. But there were dramatic changes in store in 1950.

21

The Naval Involvement

It was the British Pacific Fleet which had put the first armed men from the Commonwealth ashore in Japan at the time of the surrender: and it was the same Fleet whose contribution to BCOF had arrived first on the scene in 1946.

By the end of the war, the British Pacific Fleet was a substantial force, even by American standards. It comprised a fleet of 142 warships, including 4 battleships, 5 fleet aircraft carriers, 12 other carriers, 10 cruisers and a swarm of destroyers, sloops and frigates. The Fleet carried 612 aircraft, of which about 250 could be launched operationally at any one time, and there were nearly 900 more naval aircraft in reserve in the theatre. There were 33 minesweepers and a host of smaller vessels. There were also 29 submarines under command, although these operated mainly out of Fremantle in Western Australia.

The Fleet was supported by a remarkable Fleet Train of 94 ships whose task it was to supply whatever was needed, wherever and whenever it was required to maintain the Fleet proper at sea. The Fleet Train was a motley collection of shipping, formed from whatever ships could be found, manned with such personnel as were available and sent out to the Pacific in varying states of capability, efficiency and morale. It was described as 'an international fleet, including Norwegian masters, Chinese deckhands, Dutch mates, Lascar firemen, Captains RN and Papuan winchmen'.[1] There was an extraordinary variety of vessels: colliers, oilers, tankers, ammunition ships, floating repair ships, floating docks, net layers, aircraft ferry ships, aircraft maintenance ships and victualling storage and supply ships.

Operations had not been easy. The Fleet and its Train operated 4,000 miles from its base in Sydney and 16,000 miles from its home ports and its ultimate source of supply of weaponry and manpower. At its peak it embodied 125,000 men ashore and afloat, most of whom came from the UK – 'the largest group of Britons ever to come south of the equator since the Boer War'.[2] (A permanent link resulted – 3,000 of them took their discharge in Australia).

At the time of the surrender, the Fleet was engaged as Task Force 37 in continual air strikes and bombardment on the Japanese mainland as part of Halsey's US Third Fleet. A large part of the Fleet had withdrawn to Australia on 10 August for logistic reasons, having been at sea continuously for 55 days, or more in some cases: but 22 ships, headed by the battleships *Duke of York* and *King George V*, entered Tokyo Bay and were present at the surrender ceremony, having already put ashore the first British landing parties.

By the third week of September, the bulk of the Fleet was on its way home, but a number of ships remained in Japanese waters and the Commonwealth navies continued to be represented there until the peace treaty in 1952. There was some competition to be involved: Auchinleck had been quick to ask for the Indian Navy sloops *Godavari* and *Cauvery* to be included in the naval occupation force, since it had already been decided that British Indian troops would form part of the Allied land forces of occupation, and for the ships to be given 'the opportunity to enter Japanese ports and their sailors to place their feet on Japanese soil'.[3] The Admiralty welcomed the idea, although the size and composition of the occupation force was still under discussion with Washington at that time.

The proposals made in Washington in October 1945 by the Australian Government on behalf of the Commonwealth envisaged that in addition to land and air forces, British Commonwealth naval forces would also participate in the occupation, but that this would not form part of the Australian discussions and would be pursued directly between the UK and the US Governments. They subsequently agreed that a squadron of the British Pacific Fleet, which would include ships of the RN, the RAN and the RIN, would be stationed in Japanese waters under the operational control of the American Admiral commanding the detachment of the US Fleet.

This squadron became known as Force 'T' and was commanded initially by Vice Admiral E J P Brind RN, and from 24 December 1845 by Rear Admiral E R Archer RN.

Meanwhile the question arose of the formation of a naval shore component for BCOF. It had been established that BCOF had to be self-sufficient, and, whether the Force was to have its own port or share an American-controlled port, there was a need for a port party to supervise the operations involved ashore. It was decided that the personnel would be provided by the British Pacific Fleet or the East Indies Fleet, but the Admiralty stressed the need for the port party to be a particularly efficient one.

The party eventually formed up in Hong Kong under the aegis of the Pacific Fleet and moved on the landing ship HMS *Glenearn* to Kure, which had been allocated to BCOF for its sole use. The party, consisting of 350 men and 75 vehicles, arrived in Kure on 1 February 1946, in advance of the arrival of all other BCOF units, and officially took over the operation of the port from the US Navy on 18 February to prepare for their reception.

In their regular task of organising the receipt, loading and unloading, provisioning and despatch of vessels, the port party had the assistance of two Docks Operating Companies, one Australian and one Indian. The Australian unit had been recruited from dockers in Darwin, and arrived after a particularly circuitous and frustrating journey by air via Sydney, Brisbane, Morotai, the Philippines and Okinawa, to coincide with the arrival of the first troops from Morotai. But the port party found itself faced with several unusual assignments. There was the clearance of wrecks and jetties; inspection and report was required for all Japanese naval vessels sunk, beached or damaged in BCOF area ports; and destruction of 24 submarines had to be arranged. It was a varied menu. In June 1946 the port party was recommissioned as HMS *Commonwealth*, in the naval habit of treating shore establishments as ships (normally known as 'stone frigates'); and the first port director, Captain J Grindle RN, became HMS *Commonwealth*'s captain.

Force 'T' had a kaleidoscopic existence as vessels regularly changed station between Japan and other Far Eastern waters according to the dispositions of the Pacific Fleet. Usually a ship would spend no more than a few months at a time as part of Force 'T' before being relieved and returning to the China station. But when on duty in Japanese waters the ships had an active time. They were often called upon to dispose of Japanese naval vessels by gunfire or depth charges: the destroyer HMAS *Quiberon* and the sloop HMIS *Sutlej* between them sank 17 submarines from Kure in this way by the middle of May 1946. The Force was heavily involved in patrols to prevent smuggling and illegal immigration, especially in the Korea Strait, and coordinated frequent inter-service operations with BCAIR and land force units to round up interlopers. There were unexpected assignments: HMIS *Narbada* served as an observation platform for US and BCOF commanders to witness bombing attacks by BCAIR on arms dumps; and in January 1947 HMAS *Arunta* made a mercy dash to intercept a US transport sailing from Seattle to Sasebo with a dangerously ill army wife aboard.

The ships' crews also had the advantage denied to the army and air force occupation forces of regular visits to Japanese ports in the US areas of occupation, particularly Yokohama and Atami on Honshu, and Nagasaki, Kagoshima and Sasebo on Kyushu, with the close contacts and the unexpected comforts which resulted. HMAS *Arunta*, for example, spent Christmas 1946 tied up in Sasebo harbour alongside a US army rifle regiment, with which the classic exchange of liquor from the Australians for food from the Americans cemented a friendly relationship. There were the same surprises which the soldiers encountered on their brief visits to Tokyo: 'we didn't need side arms to control our men, as did the Yanks', said a sailor from HMAS *Quickmatch*. The US Navy did not bother to inspect their recreation parties before going ashore, and some carried their caps and wore unpressed uniforms: 'if we had tried the same thing we would soon have been in the rattle'.[4]

In April 1947 JCOSA raised the desirability of including Force 'T' in the naval component of BCOF, which hitherto consisted only of the port party. As it still expected to take full advantage of all BCOF's shore facilities and amenities, Force 'T''s independence was a little irksome, and JCOSA saw an opportunity to enlarge its sphere of command. The Navy stood firm, however, and after some months of wrangling JCOSA dropped its proposal.

When the last British personnel were withdrawn from BCOF in 1948, Force 'T' ceased to exist, and subsequent naval representation became the sole responsibility of Australia. The RAN took over the task of working the port of Kure, and raised a port party to relieve the RN. HMS *Commonwealth* was appropriately renamed HMAS

Commonwealth and continued to function, but with a much lower work load. The Australian Government's decision in mid-1948 to reduce the strength of BCOF to a nominal level by the end of that year included the retention of a single ship alongside the single battalion and single air force squadron. Throughout 1949 and the first half of 1950 the RAN maintained by rotation one of its ships constantly in Japanese waters to meet that commitment, and by that stage no less than 15 RAN vessels had served on BCOF duty at one time or another.

In mid-1950, as part of the disbandment of BCOF then planned, HMAS *Commonwealth* was closed down, and its equipment, vehicles and boats were returned to the RN or the RAN. But the process was to be reversed soon afterwards by the outbreak of the Korean war: the Commonwealth navies were galvanised into action once more, and the port of Kure was again to become a centre of intense and important activity.

22
Korea and the Revival of BCOF

The start of the Korean war and the subsequent United Nations' resolution of 27 June 1950 to furnish such assistance to South Korea 'as may be necessary to repel the armed attack' sounded alarm bells throughout the Pacific. MacArthur was appointed commander of the United Nations forces and directed to undertake the military intervention in defence of Korea on behalf of the United Nations from his base in Japan. For this desperate task he had 'four woefully under-strength occupation divisions scattered from Kyushu to Hokkaido and one battalion of Australians',[1] although, of course, there could be no question of deploying the Australians without Canberra's approval.

Washington authorised the provision of American naval and air cover for South Korean forces on 29 June, and soon afterwards asked for a clear indication from Australia of the support it would be prepared to provide for Korea.[2] The British Government had already taken the decision to place its naval forces in Japanese waters at the disposal of the US and the Australian Government decided to follow suit, although the only ships available were a destroyer and a sloop.

However, it was in the air that the Americans needed BCOF assistance most and they now began to bring pressure to bear for the use of 77 Squadron in Korea. Their Mustang aircraft were ideal for long-range ground attack, the Americans had no Mustangs any nearer than the continental United States and 77 Squadron had achieved a reputation as the best fighter squadron in Japan.[3] A formal request was made by MacArthur to Robertson and provoked much anxious discussion in Canberra. There was a reluctance to alter the previous decision to withdraw the RAAF component of BCOF, but it was clear that support for the US would win Australia credit in the future security arrangements in the Pacific, which was such an important objective for them. Robertson had warned the squadron to stand by for operational duties on the receipt of MacArthur's request, and was advised on 30 June that the Australian Government had given its agreement for the commitment of the squadron to operations over Korea.[4]

At that time it was still intended to proceed with the withdrawal of the occupation force. But the British Government suggested that if this went ahead at such a critical stage it might be misunderstood in the US. Menzies agreed and announced on 1 July that the withdrawal would be deferred. This naturally gave rise to much speculation in Australia and Japan about the possible commitment of BCOF's ground forces to Korea. A BCOF spokesman poured cold water on these rumours: '. . . there were not enough infantrymen in Japan now for that type of operation'.[5] But it was confirmed that reinforcements would be sent to 77 Squadron, which was now in action over Korea.

The Australian Government was anxious to avoid any involvement of ground forces. The Army component in BCOF was now down to a strength of 2069. Of this the only combat troops were in 3 RAR, which had a strength of less than 600, compared with its war establishment of 950. The battalion had been intended for occupation duties and was not equipped with the heavier weapons such as anti-tank guns and bren-gun carriers which would be necessary for warlike operations. Its personnel would have to be re-engaged as volunteers for Korea, since their present terms of enlistment limited their liability to service in Japan. Furthermore, there would be great administrative difficulty in operating such a small force alongside the much larger forces of the US in Korea. Robertson was asked to do whatever he could to avoid a request being made by SCAP for use of the army component.[6] He advised Canberra that MacArthur had no intention of asking for it unless a disaster situation arose in Korea, and that in any case a formation of brigade strength was the smallest which could be considered of any value.[7]

77 Squadron meanwhile had become heavily engaged in operations over Korea, where its aircraft were being used for ground attack on North Korean tanks and trucks and for escorting

American bombers on raids on North Korean lines of communication. The USAF commander, Stratemeyer, was keen that the squadron should move from Iwakuni to Korean airfields as soon as they could be made available, so that the aircraft could spend more time over their targets. Robertson resisted this on the grounds that the squadron was dependent on the BRITCOM Base at Kure, and that Iwakuni was a more secure base while the fluid situation in Korea continued. The squadron accordingly continued for another three months to fly from Iwakuni, which had now become an operational airfield which it shared with an American bomber group. Troops of 3 RAR, newly trained in the use of anti-aircraft guns, manned the airfield defences against possible North Korean air attack with a feeling of excitement and some envy of the battle-worn air crews.

By late July the situation in Korea had become desperate. The whole of the US Eighth Army in Japan had now been committed to the battle, with the exception of the 7th Infantry Division, which remained in Japan as the only US formation left for the maintenance of the occupation. Nevertheless MacArthur reassured Robertson that he would not ask for 3 RAR.

However, on 25 July, there was a sudden grave deterioration in the Korean battlefront situation and SCAP requested the immediate use of the battalion.[8] The practical usefulness of a few hundred Australian troops lacking appropriate arms and equipment for a major land battle was highly questionable; and it was ironic that this tiny vestige of BCOF which MacArthur had dismissed scornfully in 1948 as being of negligible value should now become an object of great worth in the context of the Korean war. Robertson himself believed that the battalion should not be used: it would be far more useful in relieving American troops in Japan who could then be deployed in Korea without the equipment and logistic difficulties which would attend an Australian involvement.

But the issue had now assumed important political proportions. The US was desperately anxious to obtain material support from other nations, and an immediate Australian commitment, however small, would be far more important than a larger one later. For Australia here was a unique opportunity 'to cement friendship with the US which may not easily present itself again', in the words of Spender, the Minister for External Affairs[9], and to guarantee American support for further arrangements for mutual security in the Pacific, which was always the principal Australian objective. It was now also known that the British Government, having so far abstained, was on the point of announcing its own intention to commit ground forces, and Australian Ministers considered it highly desirable to precede that announcement with their own, to show that they had an independent policy and were not merely following on slavishly behind the United Kingdom.

The Australian Chiefs of Staff had already decided that the urgency of the Korean battle situation outweighed Robertson's concerns. Refusal to commit the battalion could have a serious effect on US-Australian relations and indeed cause problems between American and Australian troops in Japan. The Chiefs accordingly recommended that 3 RAR 'after being armed as adequately as possible' should be put at SCAP's disposal, provided that sufficient personnel volunteered for service in Korea.[10]

On 26 July, therefore, the Australian Government announced that it had decided to provide ground troops for use in Korea, the composition and size of such forces to be sorted out later.[11] Robertson was advised and he ordered 3 RAR to prepare for active service.

But it took time to get the battalion ready. Of the 550 men in Japan only 26 did not volunteer for Korea; but some of the volunteers were judged to be over age for active service and were posted to BRITCOM Sub Area Base in Tokyo, whose personnel now took over BCOF's guard duties there.[12] Reinforcements to bring the battalion up to its total war establishment of 1010 had to come from Australia, where volunteers from 1 and 2 RAR were supplemented by men specially recruited for service in Korea. As the RAR historian has noted ruefully, it took the resources of all three battalions as well as special enlistments to maintain one battalion in the field.[13] Although some weapons and transport were made available from US Army stores in Japan, most of the newly strengthened battalion's equipment had also to come from Australia and the month of August was one of hectic training and preparation for its arrival.

Meanwhile the New Zealand Government, itself eager to show its support for the US-led United Nations cause, had made a commitment of an army contingent. At the same time it had proposed that this should form part of a joint British Commonwealth force, in which a New Zealand field artillery regiment could serve. This was a proposal welcomed by the Americans, who hoped that the

Australian and New Zealand contingents might form the nucleus of a British Commonwealth Light Division.

By early August the Commonwealth plans were beginning to take a more positive shape. Britain and New Zealand confirmed that their governments were making firm arrangements to commit ground forces. In the case of Britain these would consist of an infantry brigade group and an armoured regiment. New Zealand would contribute its field artillery regiment and a small force headquarters. Australia's contribution would be the single infantry battalion from Japan. It was agreed that the whole force should form an expanded brigade group under the command of the senior British officer and that it should be supported from the BCOF base in Kure, with a smaller forward base in Korea. The Australian Government took the view that, while operational control of the force would be vested in SCAP, non-operational control and administration should be Robertson's responsibility. Robertson would report to the Australian Chiefs of Staff, supported by their British and New Zealand liaison missions, along the lines of the earlier BCOF arrangements. The recent experience of Commonwealth cooperation in the occupation had led to a general agreement that BCOF should be adopted as a model for the new force.

In response to yet more urgent appeals from the battle front, the British Government decided to send forward without further delay the two infantry battalions of 27 Brigade stationed in Hong Kong (lst Battalion The Middlesex Regiment and 1st Battalion The Argyll & Sutherland Highlanders) as an interim measure, pending the arrival of 29 Brigade from the UK. The Australian Government then decided that 3 RAR should be joined with these two battalions to form the initial component of the British Commonwealth force; and the Australians arrived at Pusan in Korea on 28 September 1950 to become part of 27 Brigade, now retitled 27 Commonwealth Infantry Brigade. The official British historian noted that 3 RAR was 'a force of volunteers . . . eager for action. Its officers and men had a professional look about them'.[14]

BCOF now found itself without any combat capability in Japan. Its single fighter squadron had been detached to operate under the USAF, initially from its home base at Iwakuni and subsequently from October 1950 onwards from bases in Korea itself. Its single infantry battalion had been detached to join the Commonwealth ground force in Korea. The naval ships which intermittently became part of the occupation when they entered Japanese waters had been collected into a new British Pacific Fleet under US operational control and initially based at Sasebo in Kyushu. But BCOF now found a new role as the main support base for the Commonwealth effort in Korea. Robertson had at an early stage foreseen that when a Commonwealth force was mounted in Korea there would be a need for a base in Japan with a chain of supply forward to the front line, including some kind of advanced base in Korea. This support activity, into which he threw his tremendous energy and organising ability, became his own key role in the Korean campaign and that of the remaining elements of BCOF in Japan. But before this sensible arrangement came into being, there was one significant organisational obstacle to be surmounted.

This had arisen from the appointment in August 1950 of Air Vice Marshal Bouchier as the British Chiefs of Staff's liaison officer with MacArthur in his capacity as Commander-in-Chief of the United Nations forces in Korea. Whitehall had advised Gascoigne in Tokyo in July[15] that Ministers and the Chiefs of Staff in the UK decided they needed a senior military representative at MacArthur's headquarters, in the same way that Gairdner had operated during the war and afterwards. They felt they needed a source to provide them with first-hand reports of MacArthur's plans and periodic appreciations of how the situation in Korea was likely to develop, in view of the possible repercussions for British interests elsewhere in the Far East and South East Asia. If the US Chiefs of Staff agreed, it was intended to appoint Bouchier to the post.

Bouchier had been Air Officer Commanding BCAIR in Japan in 1946–48, and was well known to MacArthur and the SCAP staff, and, of course, to Robertson himself. He had become a great personal favourite with the American air force generals, who were said to have admired his professional knowledge and war record: but in his own way he was as egotistical as Robertson, with whom his relations had sometimes been strained.

Gascoigne's reply to London showed that he was unhappy about the proposal.[16] He considered that Gairdner himself would be the better choice: he was of very senior rank, of the same service as MacArthur, and had always got on very well with him. 'General Robertson will in any event be likely to resent an appointment of this nature and it might be unwise to send out Bouchier who has recently served under him'.

Attlee's private secretary suggested that it would be a good idea to have a word to Menzies about what was being suggested, since 'it is indeed possible that General Robertson . . . may resent the appointment . . . he is a particularly touchy individual and we have had a good many difficulties with him in the past . . .'.[17] Attlee accordingly spoke to Menzies, who agreed with the need of an officer at MacArthur's headquarters and said that there would be no cause for Robertson to be offended. He would see that 'this was made all right'.[18] This was in the belief that Gairdner was the appointee – Attlee had said to Menzies that he was sure Gairdner was the right man to send. But while these exchanges were taking place, the Ministry of Defence in London had already sought and obtained the US Chiefs of Staff agreement to the appointment of Bouchier! While Attlee was considerably put out by their mistake, it was decided to let the Bouchier nomination stand rather than go back to the Americans again.

So Bouchier, appointed through a failure of inter-departmental communication, took up the post, which made him the channel for direct contact between SCAP and the Chiefs of Staff in the UK, cutting across Robertson's own responsibility for all Commonwealth military activities in Japan. Robertson, an intensely proud and capable commander, reacted with vigour against this apparent diminution of his own standing and influence with SCAP: he was not going to allow Bouchier (his former subordinate) to intervene in a situation which he saw as his own preserve, or use to be made of BCOF facilities at will without any acknowledgement of its independent command. 'I feel that we are just being made use of on the one hand and being insulted and slighted on the other', he signalled to Canberra.[19]

This prompted the Australian Chief of the General Staff, General Rowell, to take the matter up directly with Slim, the Chief of the Imperial General Staff. 'The more or less complete sidetracking of BCOF', he said, ran entirely counter to the concept of Commonwealth cooperation. 'As things stand today, C-in-C BCOF is under no obligation whatever to afford British troops any facilities. In actual fact your people are compelled to use our signals and cipher staff . . . No doubt . . . Bouchier and Coad [commander 27 Infantry Brigade in Korea] will be wanting hospital accommodation and the like'.[20] The facilities would, of course, be forthcoming, but the command arrangements had to be sorted out.

With the intervention of Slim, this new affront to Commonwealth sensitivities was eventually put right. While operational control remained with SCAP, Robertson in his capacity as Commander-in-Chief BCOF was appointed in November 1950 as non-operational Commander-in-Chief British Commonwealth Forces in both Japan and Korea, with responsibility for their administration and control. He was to report to the Australian Chiefs of Staff, along with their British and New Zealand liaison missions, on the lines already well established for BCOF. It was made clear that Bouchier was to remain solely a channel of communication and information for the UK, and would have no responsibility for the troops in the field or in the base areas: and he was told to maintain a close liaison with Robertson and given a firm reminder of the latter's overall responsibilities. Robertson had seen off Bouchier as effectively as he had disposed of Gairdner.

While it retained the nominal occupation responsibility for Hiroshima Prefecture and the Iwakuni police district, BCOF's activities now became almost entirely orientated towards the support of the Korean campaign. BCOF was formally charged with the supply and maintenance of the 'Kure element of the British Commonwealth Forces Korea Base' and with the provision of administrative facilities for the Naval Officer in Charge, Kure. The port at Kure was now busy with movements of ships – warships from the Commonwealth fleet undergoing repair or maintenance, troopships with reinforcements *en route* to Korea. In the first quarter of 1951, 44 major vessels were worked in the port, including four troopships. In the following quarter this went up to 55 major vessels, including five troopships. When the British admiral in charge of the Far East station visited Kure in the summer, there were three aircraft carriers, six destroyers and two frigates present.

The movement of personnel in and out of the BCOF area increased dramatically. Additional accommodation was procured to cope with troops in transit or on leave. BCOF's hospitals were full with casualties evacuated from Korea. Base workshops were enhanced to provide 3rd and 4th line support facilities for the Australian and New Zealand vehicles in Korea, and to deal with the repair of equipment and weapons for all British units in Korea.

In July 1951 the provision of an additional brigade by the Canadian Government allowed the formation of a British Commonwealth Division, consisting of 25 Canadian Brigade, 29

British Brigade and 28 British Commonwealth Brigade. 3 RAR was now part of the latter. The formation of the Division gave BCOF an additional and unusual responsibility, since its General Officer Commanding was given the right of appeal to the Commander-in-Chief BCOF if he disagreed with any order given him by an American commander, and through Robertson to the Australian Chiefs of Staff in the manner already laid down for BCOF procedures.

The intensification of Commonwealth traffic through the BCOF area produced the usual complications. There was an increase in VD, especially among troops from Korea: but BCOF was now better able to cope. In addition to the appearance of oral pencillin as a valuable prophylactic, energetic measures taken with the cooperation of the Japanese police managed to control soliciting and prostitution far more successfully than in previous years. There were, of course, the other disciplinary problems always to be expected with troops back from the excitements and stresses of hattle and not particularly enamoured of their allies. The BCOF military police detachment in Tokyo reported in early 1951, perhaps with a secret smile, that the discipline of British Commonwealth troops, principally those from Australia and New Zealand, had deteriorated. 'The behaviour of these servicemen towards Americans in general and American military police in particular has created a bad effect.'[21] Additional BCOF military police had been sent to reinforce the detachment.

The second half of 1951 saw the emergence at last of the final draft of the peace treaty with Japan. Australia's doubts and fears about the lenient treaty which the United States had wanted had been removed by the new security agreement reached between Australia, New Zealand and the United States (ANZUS), and both treaties were signed in San Francisco in September 1951. One of the principal clauses of the treaty with Japan provided for the withdrawal of all occupation forces; and this threw doubt on the future position of BCOF, which was still providing the base facilities for the British Commonwealth forces in Korea. When the peace treaty came into effect, BCOF would no longer have any legal status in Japan and alternative arrangements would have to be made to meet the continuing need for support to the forces in Korea.

Consideration was initially given to transferring all the support facilities from Japan to Korea, but it was soon realised that they were too extensive to make this a practical proposition,even if the security situation in Korea were to allow it. The Australian Government decided instead that when the treaty came into force BCOF would be disbanded and replaced by the 'British Commonwealth Forces, Korea' (BCFK), whose continued use of base facilities in Japan in what had been the BCOF area would have to be the subject of a new agreement to be negotiated with the Japanese Government, on the lines already being organised for the United States' continued use of its bases there.

It was a pity that Robertson did not stay to see the end of the occupation. He had been an inspiring leader who had won the respect of the Americans as well as the admiration of his own force. But the Australian Government decided that it wanted Robertson back in Australia as 'a prominent leader with strong public appeal'[22] to take over as director-general of the recruiting campaign to build up the regular and reserve forces to their required strengths as soon as possible. The British Chiefs of Staff suggested that it might not be sensible to appoint a new Commander-in-Chief to Japan when the occupation was due to end shortly, but this view was disregarded and Robertson was recalled.On his death in 1960 the *Sydney Morning Herald* described him as 'one of Australia's most loved, at times most hated, and at all times most spectacular soldiers'.[23] He was undoubtedly guilty of arrogance, ambition and lack of tact:[24] but these and his 'undisguised egotism [and] self-assertion'[25] have often been typical of the qualities of many successful generals – Montgomery and MacArthur himself were two cases in point and they were important factors in establishing and maintaining BCOF's self-confidence and pride.

The British diplomats in Tokyo were sorry to see Robertson go. They had their conflicts with him in the past. Back in 1947, Gascoigne had drawn attention to the difficulties he had experienced from the Commander-in-Chief's marked antipathy towards civilians, 'whose presence I know he deeply resents during a time of military occupation'.[26] There had been further trouble when Robertson's resentment of Gascoigne and objections to Gairdner had become embarrassing. 'Robertson should . . . confine himself to ruling over his military zone in western Japan', said Gascoigne, 'and not try to usurp the authority which Gairdner and I wielded in Tokyo'.[27] But there had been grudging but genuine praise as well. 'Although Robbie and I have not always seen eye to eye', he said years before, 'I do admire the way he has kept BCOF going'.[28] When the time came for him to depart, Gascoigne praised the way Robertson had carried out his liaison duties with the Americans. Clutton, Gascoigne's colleague in the UK Mission in Tokyo, was especially congratulatory: while Robertson's undoubted administrative abilities might be of more value in Australia, 'he has done a first-rate job here and his loss, particularly at this juncture, will be considerably felt . . . Gascoigne feels he should stay'.[29] Robertson himself did not want to leave,and solicited the support of the British mission for an approach from London to Canberra, but to no avail.

There was a splendid farewell parade on 7 November on the Imperial Plaza in Tokyo in which British, American, Australian, Canadian and New Zealand troops took part and a US howitzer battery fired a 15-gun salute. MacArthur delivered a complicated but friendly tribute: '. . . General Robertson has performed his duty here in a consciously and uniformly superior manner. His soldierly qualities have been devoted to the attainment of our common objectives in a cooperative spirit of the highest order'.[30] This convoluted prose was typical of MacArthur's style, which on another occasion had drawn a smug Foreign Office comment: 'The Supreme Commander is a great man, but his prose style is very unendearing. It is pompous, theatrical and obfusc'.[31]

There was argument between the Commonwealth partners on the rank and name of his replacement. Some felt that the appointment should be downgraded, but it was finally agreed that the post should remain at lieutenant-general level, in order that it should be senior to that of the divisional commander in Korea, who was still subordinate to the Commander-in-Chief BCOF in respect of all non-operational matters. An Australian, Lieutenant-General Bridgeford, was approved as replacement and took over from Robertson in November 1951. He almost immediately got into trouble by saying that BCOF would cease to exist on 15 December 1951, which was the date it had set for the hand-over of its responsibilities in Japan to Administrative Headquarters BCFK. Following a reproof from Canberra he had to warn all concerned that 'pending the ultimate decision to withdraw BCOF it is most important that nothing be done or said to create the impression that the present reorganisation in any way amounts to a withdrawal of BCOF from Japan'.[32] While the reorganisation had in fact disbanded all BCOF units and had mustered the personnel into BCFK units, BCOF continued a nominally separate existence.

This only lasted a few more months. The peace treaty became effective on 28 April 1952 and BCOF formally ceased to exist on that date. Theoretically, occupation forces should have been withdrawn within 90 days, but negotiations with the newly-independent Japanese Government for an agreement on the continued use of Japan as a base for British Commonwealth forces in Korea did not start until the beginning of July. Such arrangements should, of course, have been made before the ratification of the treaty. When the British Minister of State, Selwyn Lloyd, made a statement in the House of Commons on 1 July[33] which envisaged the retention of most, if not all, of the important Commonwealth installations at Kure, it was attacked by the Japanese press[34] as an infringement of sovereignty. But Kure provided facilities for the docking and repair of naval units, the transport and storage of stores and equipment, and the major repair and refitting of vehicles, guns and equipment – all facilities essential for the support of the Commonwealth operations in Korea and not available anywhere else. It was, of course, expected that continuation arrangements would be made, but the Commonwealth powers were now in a weak negotiating position, and agreement was still required on costs and jurisdiction, on which some dispute persisted.

It seemed a strange coincidence ('no accident', said the *Sydney Morning Herald*[35]) that this negotiation to determine the status of the Commonwealth in Japan and the conditions of use for the Kure base opened against a background of Japanese press attacks[36] on what was described as a 'reign of terror' by Commonwealth troops in the Kure area in the months following independence. These were largely based on claims by the Mayor of Kure that 83 crimes had been committed by foreign soldiers between April 28 and June 25, 58 of them by Canadians and 9 by Australians. The Japanese Government itself found that the accusations were grossly exaggerated, and was somewhat embarrassed by the result of a BCOF analysis of the complaints which showed their triviality.[37] One alleged instance of 'assault' it was found related to 'the forcible rejection of professional amorous advances'. The 'slanderous and unfounded' accusations were noted in Australia, where it was firmly believed that there were 'many elements in Japan which wanted to see the Commonwealth forces pushed out of Kure'. They were believed to include 'naval and shipbuilding interests anxious to get their hands on the Kure installations, and nationalists who regard the presence of foreign troops as incompatible with Japan's sovereignty and a distasteful reminder of enemy occupation'.[38]

The Japanese Government rightly ignored the clamour about sovereignty, recognising the political and economic advantages of accepting the continued presence of Commonwealth forces. The Korean war had in fact, through its vast local purchases and use of facilities in Japan, saved the country from an economic slump and had set it firmly on the course of future success and prosperity.

Pending a later contract to give all UN forces in Korea legal status and rights to facilities in Japan, an interim agreement was reached in August. This limited British Commonwealth ground forces in Southern Japan 'as much as possible' to Hiro, while naval forces would limit themselves to 'the minimum facilities' at Kure. It seemed an acceptable compromise, saving face on both sides.

23

Post-Mortem on BCOF

So finally it was all over. For its first two years BCOF had been a truly cosmopolitan and powerful formation, with some specified tasks of significance. Never before in modern British military history had such a variety of tradition, costume and colour been incorporated in one integrated formation. But as the Commonwealth partners' differing priorities asserted themselves, the tasks of occupation diminished, and its area of responsibility reduced, so BCOF went into slow decline. It was a natural reduction which was only to be expected as the occupation progressed.

By 1950, BCOF had tailed away into a tiny token force, barely capable of maintaining itself, much less taking any active part in the occupation. The military need had long since disappeared. The occupation which some had said would last a generation, even a hundred years, was in military terms effectively at an end after only three years, even though the peace treaty which formally terminated it was delayed for another four. A passive Japanese people had offered no resistance, and SCAP's reforms of Japanese society needed no heavy military presence once the initial tasks of repatriation and demilitarisation had been completed. The outbreak of the Korean war had for a time given BCOF a new life and its last two years were a time of drama and excitement, but its original purpose had evaporated.

Scholars and diplomats, particularly in Britain, have declared almost without exception that the whole BCOF exercise was a waste of time. A former British ambassador to Japan who had also served in BCOF, Hugh Cortazzi, has said,

'from a national and Commonwealth point of view it is hard
to see what practical purpose was served by the British
Commonwealth Occupation Force . . . our presence was useless in defence terms . . . we had no role in military
government . . . as a result our security role was really mean-
ingless'.[1]

It is true that the lack of participation in the military government
machinery automatically relegated BCOF to a supporting role.
Once the repatriation and the demilitarisation were completed,
BCOF troops found themselves engaged in police duties of a peaceful and undemanding nature hardly suited to a highly trained
military force. The Americans were determined to retain unitary
control: as early as 1944 they had decided that nothing should be
allowed to 'prejudice the dominantly American character' of the
occupation which will eventually take place.[2] From their point of
view and indeed that of Japan itself, this sensibly ensured that policies and programmes could be pursued in a single-minded fashion
without distraction or dispute (whether they were 'good' or not).
The Allied Council for Japan and the Far East Commission in
Washington proved to be no more than superficial devices for inef-
fective consultation between the Allies without managing to
interfere with SCAP's progress along the course he had set.

However, the original policy paper written by the SWNCC in
Washington, while making it clear that the US would insist on being
'the controlling voice in the occupation authority' in Japan, had
talked about the Allies participating in 'the military control of
Japan' and in 'the occupation authority'. It should have been entirely
feasible for Britain to have achieved a position, albeit in support of
the US, which gave BCOF some opportunity to appear, to the
Japanese as well as the Americans, as partners in the business of
administration. For example, provided that they followed SCAP's
directives and chain of command correctly, there was no good reason why the military government teams in the BCOF zone should
not have had a strong BCOF flavour. At the very least, even if they
could not be manned entirely by BCOF, they could have been established as integrated units combining BCOF and US personnel.

The time for this to have been negotiated was in the autumn of
1945, when the US was desperate to start repatriating its own troops
from Japan and needed the extra manpower from BCOF to meet

what it then regarded as the occupation commitment. But the British Foreign Office had effectively already sold the pass on this issue. In its first proposals to the State Department in August, the Foreign Office had conceded that civil administration should be an American responsibility: and from then onward there was no further discussion or consideration of this being shared, even on a limited and local basis. When Robertson tried to engineer some involvement in 1946, which with his good relationship with MacArthur he might have been able to achieve, he was, as we have seen, told by JCOSA to forget it.

For BCOF personnel to have been seen in strength in the military government teams in the BCOF zone would have undoubtedly been beneficial for the reputation of the British Commonwealth. As it was, the small three-man groups which Robertson had managed to insert into the US organisation had no visibility and little effect. A general Japanese reaction was to view the Commonwealth troops, with their bands and parades, as playing soldiers, while it was the Americans who were helping them to build their new country. Indeed, a press correspondent reported that 'the Japanese outside the Kure area look upon Empire troops as camp followers or paid mercenaries of the Americans'.

Even if some substantial involvement in local military government teams had been obtained, its impact would still have been limited. The teams were after all no more than surveillance units intended to ensure that SCAP's directives, as diffused through Japanese local government channels, were being properly implemented. The heart of the military government lay with MacArthur in Tokyo, where the vast reforms were generated. BCOF could never have any influence on their formulation – the Commonwealth representatives on the Far East Commission and the Allied Council for Japan were the only hope in this respect – nor on their implementation. By the same token it could not carry blame for any failures, although these did not become apparent until after the end of the occupation.[3]

The limitations imposed by the fact that BCOF occupied a relatively remote and thinly populated part of the country might have been eased by an extension of its zone to include an area of greater importance. Here there seems little doubt that Northcott could have obtained the Osaka-Kobe area for BCOF in his initial negotiations with SCAP in December 1945. His reluctance to go for it and to settle for Hiroshima instead looks now to have been faint-hearted and lacking in resolve: but it must be said that at the end of 1945 the completely passive acceptance of the occupation by the Japanese was still not fully appreciated; and Northcott's unwillingness to take on very highly populated areas was from a purely military standpoint understandable. However, in doing so, he relinquished the key opportunity to acquire a really worthwhile platform for BCOF, which might have brought with it those attendant political and commercial advantages for which the British in particular had once hoped. Perhaps Robertson, if he had taken command at the beginning, would have achieved a more satisfactory outcome.

Another major factor in limiting the value of the Commonwealth occupation was, of course, the hard line taken by BCOF on fraternisation, principally reflecting the strict attitude of the Australian government and people. There is no doubt that this prevented the establishment of links and friendly relationships on the lines of the association between the US and Japan, and a good many potentially valuable connections were lost. Although the troops were generally well regarded, it has to be admitted that the impact of BCOF on the Japanese civilian population was, with only a few exceptions, insignificant.

Apart from the inhibitions of the non-fraternisation policy, it was also felt by many that a clearer communication to the troops on the objectives of the occupation could have led to them making a significant contribution to the democratisation process and to the development of Japanese society along Western democratic lines. Only troops with a defined operational role, such as the bomb disposal squads, had a sense of mission. The supervision of elections, in particular, seemed to be a rewarding and worthwhile contribution to democracy, in which contact with the Japanese was essential and beneficial. But the bulk of the occupation force had little sense of mission and tended to turn inward upon itself. Perhaps a real opportunity for a period of influence was missed, limited though it might have been.

On the purely military side, there were real achievements for the professional soldiers. The organisation and maintenance of a supply line stretching for 6,000 miles over two hemispheres, giving complete logistic support to the whole of BCOF as well as to all official Commonwealth nationals in Japan, was itself a feat of considerable proportions. To put together and set to work a combined and fully integrated force of so many different arms and nationalities was a task of unusual difficulty. In Northcott's words, BCOF 'was a great experience in the integration of Empire forces and Empire cooperation', and, as he had forecast, provided 'most valuable experience in the joint higher direction of British Commonwealth forces'[4] which was to serve the Commonwealth well in the Korean War and later in the smaller actions in Malaya and Borneo. The ability and necessity to cope with BCOF's complicated command structure, involving responsibilities to both SCAP and JCOSA, and through the latter, the national governments, made any future staff assignment simple by comparison.

From the American point of view, BCOF was a useful contribution to the military presence in occupied Japan. It assumed responsibility for one of the five divisional administrative areas into which SCAP had divided the country, saving US manpower and expense. The energetic efforts MacArthur made in 1948 to secure an additional division in replacement of BCOF, and his dire prophecies of the future when he failed to do so, were proof enough that BCOF played an important part in SCAP's strategic and tactical planning.

In terms of the Commonwealth, BCOF had some political significance. On the purely historical plane, it is worthy of note that this was the last time that an Indian armed force, representing all three services, served under the British flag alongside other members of the old Empire. Even in those last few months before independence for India and, as it turned out, for the new nation of Pakistan, the words 'Empire' and 'Imperial' were freely used in official and unofficial documents and speeches, without resentment on the part of the Indians. The Indian brigadier, on his departure from Japan three days after independence, was still able to say that the Indian contingent had 'represented worthily the British Commonwealth in the eyes of her Allies, and consolidated and enlarged..the fellowship and unity of effort which were forged in war'.[5] Although the excitement of independence was on the horizon, they still felt they were part of the family.

For Australia and her relationship with Britain, BCOF was a watershed, the sign in some ways of coming of age, a recognition of Australia's military independence. The UK's handling of Commonwealth relationships was never sensitive enough. Successive British governments seemed to assume that consultation with Commonwealth governments on issues affecting all was desirable but not essential, and that the mother country knew best. This was the cause of constant irritation and often angry reaction. Throughout the BCOF story, it had been a recurring problem: the original assumption that the Canadians would join in, the conflict about the separate Australian command, even the activities of Gairdner and the appointment of Bouchier, left a trail of uncomfortable disputes. Nevertheless the Australian determination to lead in BCOF secured for her from the beginning the command of the force both in Japan and through JCOSA in Australia, and therefore the prime position *vis-à-vis* SCAP and the American command. Her resolve to continue the BCOF presence in Japan until the peace treaty, after the departure of all the other contingents, left her with full administrative control after the dissolution of JCOSA and sole remaining representation on behalf of the Commonwealth. The Australian position in Japan enabled her to be the first ally into Korea in support of the United States.

Evatt's mission to establish Australia as a Pacific power in her own right seemed therefore to have been to some degree accomplished. It had been matched by Britain's early departure from BCOF, a hasty retirement which underlined her inability to find the resources for a continued presence in the Far East under the economic and manpower pressures of other more important commitments closer to home. To many in those days it was another sad stage in the steady retreat from her once-great Imperial presence overseas. In effect, Australia had picked up and carried the Pacific flag which Britain had dropped, and public opinion in Australia appreciated this and applauded it.

The Foreign Office in London understood the importance of this change of roles. In discussing an Australian proposal to allot Malaya and Indonesia to Australia's areas of strategic responsibility, an official minuted '. . . we have already had the experience of surrendering our position to Australia in Japan, and unfortunately it is a fact that politically this has not been a success [for the UK] . . .'. Any further surrender of responsibility to Australia in a wider field 'would be likely to lead to the final extinction of UK influence in the area involved'.[6]

In the development of Australian post-war defence policy, BCOF played a catalytic role. For the first time Australia had a continuing overseas military commitment in peace-time and had to create a permanent military force to support it, in place of the pre-war organisation which depended on a small regular cadre and a much larger part-time resource. BCOF was in effect the seed-bed of the new Australian regular Army.

The shift of responsibility from Britain to Australia through the BCOF experience at the same time strengthened the US connection with Australia. From 1948 onward Australia was the one foreign supporter of the US in the occupation of Japan, and she looked to the US for that same protection in the future which she had received in the war and which Britain had been unable to give. New Zealand too, although her involvement was more limited, had by her participation in BCOF stressed her new commitment to the Pacific in the field of defence, in contrast to the traditional role in the Middle East allotted to her in pre-war Imperial defence policy. The stronger links between the US, Australia and New Zealand manifested themselves later in 1951 in the ANZUS mutual defence pact between the three nations, which the Australian Government had been pursuing for years as a major objective in its post-war foreign policy. There was a reminder of this close alliance and combination of interests later when Australian and New Zealand units went to Vietnam to support the American cause, from whcih Britain was wisely absent.

But it is at ground level perhaps that one should look for the real significance of the British Commonwealth occupation. As Enoch Powell has said, 'the historian chronically ignores the emotional factor – understandably, because it is unquantifiable . . . and difficult to handle'.[7] But the emotional factor was an overriding influence in the self-justification of BCOF. Taking into account the replacements and reinforcements over the years in question, it is estimated that a total of over 80,000 men and women served in BCOF. With few exceptions they (and not just those who had fought in the war) felt that it was right to be in Japan and that it was absolutely necessary for the Commonwealth to be present in the occupation in recognition of what had gone before: and today's survivors still do. 'We had to make our presence felt there', said one BCOF veteran.[8] It seemed to be a proper acknowledgement of their countries' important part in an arduous and unpleasant war. 'With eleven fighter squadrons plus bomber, anti-submarine and torpedo squadrons fighting the Japanese north of New Zealand', said a New Zealand pilot, 'we were obliged to take part in the occupation'.[9] In those years immediately following the war, there was still a feeling of Empire, a common bond which made the joint endeavour in Japan exciting and worthwhile. King George VI's Empire Day message in 1946 (to be read out by Northcott at a special parade in Tokyo) seemed to hit the target: 'The British Commonwealth Occupation Force in Japan symbolises that unity of purpose which has inspired my peoples in the perilous years through which we have passed'.

From the point of view of the British contingent, the involvement was all too brief, especially for the infantry brigade. It was an episode which, if nothing more, satisfied the ambition to be in at the death, as one officer put it.[10] Once there, the regular units concerned took Japan in their stride as they might have any other station: but it was regarded as a worthwhile operation which according to another officer erased any doubts as to who had won the war and broke the myth of Japanese invincibility.[11] Perhaps it helped to open the eyes of the country to the nature and power of the West. Further than that, on a personal level it was a memorable experience which built up many close and friendly relationships within the contingent and with the Australians and New Zealanders, to the extent that even after such a relatively short period of service together, a strong BCOF Veterans Association and a BCAIR Japan Association still flourish in the UK, with firm links with their many counterparts in Australia and New Zealand. Behind all this there was a vague but hopeful feeling that 'we laid the groundwork for a better understanding between East and West'.[12]

The New Zealanders, too, recognised the importance of the experience. It was the first time they had served as occupation troops in a country they had helped to defeat in war (Italy did not count because she had changed sides), the first time they had been incorporated into a British Commonwealth force, the first time they had been under the overall command in peacetime of a wartime ally. Whether it was disturbing or memorable, there was a lasting effect on the participants, suggested one of the Kiwis.[13] Most found it a unique opportunity to visit a strange country before returning to their Antipodean isolation.

The Indian contingent's experience in Japan was more confused. The infantry brigade derived confidence and prestige from its existence as an independent formation established under Indian command and on an equal footing with the other brigades. As the Indianisation of the battalions progressed, the incoming Indian officers found a new professional future opening up for them. On the other hand, while the personnel in the Indian base and support units on which BCOF was so dependent often matured from integration or working with the other nationalities, they sometimes suffered from racial hostility and aggravation. As Indian independence approached, the Indians became less and less prepared to occupy the inferior position to which they had become used. A new self-confidence grew from the important role they realised they were playing in the Commonwealth team. They benefited perhaps more than the other national contingents from their contact with Japanese life. It was easier for them to acquire some facility in the language and to reach an understanding of Japanese customs and manners. They found another Asian nation which even in defeat demonstrated remarkable characteristics: a high standard of education and universal literacy; a relatively advanced stage of technical development; and a general discipline of a level unknown in India. They were able to identify the need to emulate all these in their own country for its future progress. It was tragic that when they went home it was to a land running with blood and to the traumatic split of the armed forces between India and Pakistan. But they remembered the lessons of Japan.

It was, however, the Australian involvement in BCOF which had the most effect, both on those directly concerned and the country from which they came. About 45,000 Australians served in BCOF from its beginning to its end, and for two thirds of the time of the Commonwealth occupation it was represented solely by Australians. BCOF veterans in Australia are strongly bonded together and their Associations are very active, not only in comradeship but also in self-interest.

The Australian Government was eager enough to capitalise on its BCOF activity on the political front and to realise whatever benefit could be achieved. It did not, however, treat its veterans kindly, and they had some specific causes on which they fought the government. These were principally related to the refusal of the government to accept that service in BCOF should be considered as active service. The most important effect of this was that the service pension normally available at the age of 60 to personnel who had been on active service anywhere in the world was withheld (although disability pensions for disablements received in service were provided).

Another consequence of this attitude, which was of a less material nature but important to all involved, was the refusal of the government to issue service ribbons or even a 'Returned from Active Service' badge for service in BCOF. The Americans issued medals for occupation service in Japan and also in Germany Indeed Australia issued medals for service in the UN peace-keeping forces in the Sinai and Zimbabwe. It seemed odd to BCOF veterans that a 'Returned from Active Service' badge was awarded to conscript troops for service during Japanese air raids on Darwin and to garrison troops for service at the Japanese prisoner-of-war breakout from the camp at Cowra in New South Wales, but was denied to BCOF volunteers while a state of war still officially existed between Australia and Japan. Without a 'Returned from Active Service' badge a BCOF veteran could not join the Returned and Services League of Australia (the RSL) and was denied until 1979 the right to march with them on Anzac Day, that great demonstration of national pride and tribal ritual.

The first inkling of this policy in fact emerged in 1946, when MacArthur put forward a citation for a Medal of Freedom with Silver Palm for Northcott on the occasion of his leaving Japan. The citation mentioned his 'exceptional understanding of occupational objectives' and his 'most distinguished contribution to the Allied war effort as well as to the success of the occupation of Japan'. The Australian Prime Minister refused to approve this, however, because no further British awards would be made in respect of non-operational services and therefore similar awards could not be allowed in the opposite direction.

The frustration and emotion engendered by this governmental attitude, particularly on the part of the volunteers for Japan of the 2nd AIF (which technically came to an end in July 1947 and was succeeded by the Interim Army) found a small outlet in the striking and issue of its own medal by the BCOF Association of Queensland. This was enthusiastically taken up by other BCOF associations in Australia, New Zealand and Britain, and over 5,000 had been issued by 1989. Such pride and comradeship among and between the veterans of the old Commonwealth must rate as a special bonus in the assessment of the accomplishments of the BCOF experience.

In recent years attention has increasingly been given to a much more worrying aspect of service in the occupation. According to normal actuarial calculations, if the 45,000 Australians who served in BCOF had lived their lives in Australia without joining the armed forces or ever serving in Japan, between 33,000 and 36,000 would have been expected to be still alive in 1991. In fact, less than 18,000 were left, which indicated a very high mortality rate among Australian BCOF personnel. The cause of this was increasingly suggested by BCOF veterans associations from the incomplete evidence available to be cancers and related diseases arising from the radiation in the Hiroshima area. Many Australian troops were stationed there for several years, whereas the Americans only required a period of 30 days service in Hiroshima or Nagasaki before July 1946 to qualify for compensation. There is consequently growing pressure from veteran groups in Australia for eligibility for pensions where cases can be established. BCOF associations in the UK and New Zealand have also been working to establish the same links between service in Japan and causes of death with a view to proper recognition along the same lines. It may never be established as a common cause but remains an issue of real concern.

So the overall picture is a patchwork. The occupation can be presented as a scene of great expectation and unforeseen decline. History, in the words of Barbara Tuchman, is the unfolding of miscalculations. There was a major miscalculation by the Commonwealth governments, especially the Australian, of the benefits to be derived from taking part in the occupation, in shaping the peace settlement in the Far East and in establishing a position of influence in Japan for the future. There was a particular miscalculation by the British, who had a special interest in trying to restore the prestige which they had lost on the collapse of their Far Eastern empire in 1942, and who mistakenly believed that participation in the occupation would assist in some unquantifiable way ('prestige' was the word most commonly used in British official documents supporting the occupation). But the occupation was a unique experience, both for governments, for their armed forces and for individuals. It was a coming together of an extraordinary mixture of people and nationalities in what they saw as a shared and justifiable enterprise: English, Scots, Welsh, Australians, New Zealander 'pakehas' and Maoris, Mahrattas, Gurkhas, Sikhs, Punjabi Mussulmans, Rajputs, Hazarawals, Jats, Madrassis and Bengalis, serving together under the same flag in the last gasp of an Empire which would never be seen again.

There were special ironies: BCOF was the best equipped and best trained force in the occupation but was never allotted a significant role. Its progressive withdrawal began just as its installations, barracks and amenities were reaching a proper standard, after a dreadful start, and after overcoming a severe campaign of press criticism, especially in Australia. Its commander saw his command decline from an army corps to a single battalion, but was still able to keep the flag flying high.

As far as the real value of the Commonwealth participation in the occupation is concerned, let the last simple word rest with an Australian corporal who said: 'We all thought the occupation was a worthwhile exercise, and from the ordinary soldier's point of view, we did a good job for the Commonwealth, but of course history and the commanders will be the judges'.[14] It was a modest epitaph for a unique adventure.

Bibliography

Unpublished Official Documents
Official papers held by Public Record Office, Kew
– PREM series, especially PREM 8
– CAB series, especially CAB 79 and 80
– FO series, especially FO 371
– WO series, ecpecially WO 106, 172 and 268

Records held by the Australian War Memorial, Canberra, especially the AWM 113 and 114 series

Records held by the Australian Archives, Canberra

Records held by the MacArthur Memorial, Norfolk, Virginia

Published Official Documents
Current Notes on International Affairs, Canberra, 1945–52.

Documents on New Zealand External Relations, Vol.II: The Surrender and Occupation of Japan, Wellington, 1982.

Foreign Relations of the United States, 1945, Vol.VI, Washington, 1969.

Press
The Daily Express (London)
The Scotsman (Edinburgh)

The Sun Herald (Melbourne)
The Sydney Morning Herald
The Times (London)

Unpublished papers
Chida Takeshi, Kure City Historical Section – 'The Occupation of
Japan by the BCOF, with the focus on changes in the fraternisation
policy', article written c.1991.

Waters, CWP – 'Anglo-Australian Diplomacy 1945-1949: Labour
Governments in conflict', Ph.D.thesis,University of New South
Wales, 1990.

**Interviews and correspondence with individuals (with former affil-
iation shown)**

In the UK: Terence Altham (2 RGR)
            Peter Arthur (1 Mahratta)
            Desmond Ashe (RAF Iwakuni)
            Paul Bates (HQ BCOF)
            Field Marshal Lord Bramall (HQ BRINDIV)
            Tom Cattle (2 Dorsets)
            Group Captain D D Christie (RAF Miho)
            Commander E A J Collard (HMS Commonwealth)
            Lieutenant Colonel L J Egan (2 RWF)
            Lieutenant Colonel Patric Emerson (HQ BRINDIV)
            R D Farthing (HQ BCOF attd 2 Dorsets)
            George F Gair (2 NZEF)
            Alan Grieve (2/5 RGR)
            W R Hancock (HQ BRINDIV)
            M Killick (1 Mahratta)
            Major-General I H Lyall Grant (HQ BRINDIV)
            Lieutenant Colonel D J S Murray (1 Camerons)
            Professor T B Millar (67 Aust Inf Bn)
            C R Pitcher (2 Dorsets)
            Peter Pounsford (5/1 Punjab)
            Brigadier ap Rhys Pryce (CO 2 RWF)
            Viscount Slim (HQ BRINDIV)
            C Smyth (BCAIR)
            Major-General Virendra Singh (HQ BRINDIV)

Arthur Williams (2 RWF)
Air Commodore Sir A L Winskill (CO 17 SQn RAF)
Lieutenant Colonel L H Yates (2 RWF)

In France: J-P Boillot (French Navy)

In Australia: Bob Aird (1 Aust Armored Car Sqn)
            Bob Bell (130 Aust Gen Hosp)
            P Coles (140 Bde Wksps)
            Arthur W John (AAEC,Britcom Base)
            J Kayrooz (81 Fighter Wing RAAF)
            Major-General B McDonald (67 Aust Inf Bn)
            S Margetts (65 Aust Inf Bn)
            D E Murphy (67 Aust Inf Bn)
            P T Murry (65 Aust Inf Bn)
            T Passfield (113 Aust Cipher Section)
            J J Roche (67 Aust Inf BnBn)
            L S Roach (67 Aust Inf Bn)
            E Saxon (HQ BCOF,attd 2 NZEF)
            H S Seaburn (AEME,Britcom Base)
            R Waddy (65 Aust Inf Bn)
            J Wallace (67 Aust Inf Bn)

In New Zealand: Air Commodore M Gunton (14 Sqn RNZAF)

In the United States: General F J Sackton(SCAP)

Books

van Aduard, E.J. *Japan-from surrender to peace*,The Hague, Martians Nijhoff, 1953.
Allen, L. *Sittang – the last battle*, London, Macdonald, 1973.
Allen, L. *The End of the War in Asia*, London, Hart-Davis, MacGibbon, 1976.
Attlee, C.R. *As it happened*, London, Heinemann, 1954.
Barber, L.B. *War Memorial*, Auckland, Heinemann Reid, 1989.
Buckley, R. *Occupation Diplomacy-Britain, the United States and Japan 1945–1952*, Cambridge, Cambridge University Press, 1952.
Clifton, A.S. *Time of Fallen Blossoms*, London, Cassell, 1950.
Clune, F. *Ashes of Hiroshima*, Sydney, Angus & Robertson, 1950.
Connell, J. *Auchinleck*, London, Cassell, 1959.

Ehrman, J. *History of the Second World War – Grand Strategy*, Vol.VI, London, HMSO, 1956.

Eichelberger, R.L. with McKaye, M. *Our Jungle Road to Tokyo*, New York, The Viking Press,1950.

Evatt, H.V. *Australia in World Affairs*, Sydney, Angus & Robertson, 1946.

Evans, H. *Thimayya of India – A Soldier's Life*, New York, Harcourt Brace, 1960.

Farrar-Hockley, A. *The British Part in the Korean War, Vol.1 – A Distant Obligation*, London, HMSO, 1990.

Gatacre, G.G.O. *A Naval Career – Reports of Proceedings – 1921–1964*, Manly, NSW, Nautical Press & Publishers, 1982.

Gilbert, M. *Never Despair – Winston S.Churchill, 1945–1965*, London, Heinemann, 1988.

Gray, E. *Operation Pacific*, London, Leo Cooper, 1990.

Green, P.M. *Memories of Occupied Japan*, Blackheath, NSW,1987.

Grey, J. *The Commonwealth Armies and the Korean War*, Manchester, Manchester University Press, 1988.

Harries, M. and S. *Sheathing the Sword – The Demilitarisation of Japan*, London, Hamish Hamilton, 1987.

Havers, N. *March on!*, Worcester, Square One Publications, 1992.

Horner, D.(ed) *Duty First – the Royal Australian Regiment in war and peace*, Sydney, Allen & Unwin, 1990.

James, D.H. *The Rise and Fall of the Japanese Empire*, London, Allen & Unwin,1951.

John, A.W. *Uneasy lies the head that wears a crown*, Cheltenham, Victoria, Gen Publishers,1987.

Kawai, K. *Japan's American Interlude*, Chicago, University of Chicago Press, 1960.

Kenrick, V. *Tokyo Days*, Tokyo, Kinokuniya, 1956.

Kirby, S.W. *History of the Second World War – The War against Japan*, Vol.5, London, HMSO, 1969.

Lockwood, D. *Australia's Pearl Harbour – Darwin 1942*, Melbourne, Cassell, 1966.

MacArthur, D. *Reminiscences*, London, Heinemann, 1964.

Manchester, W. *American Caesar*, Boston, Little, Brown, 1978.

Mark, E.M. *The Allied Occupation of Japan*, Westport, Connecticut, Greenwood Press, 1948.

Matsuoka, Y. *Daughter of the Pacific*, London, Heinemanne, 1953.

Montgomery, B.L. *Memoirs*, London, Collins, 1958.

O'Neill, R. *Australia in the Korean War 1950–53 – Vol.I, Strategy and Diplomacy*, Canberra, The Australian War Memorial & the Australian Government Publishing Service, 1981.

Pacific War Research Society, *Japan's Longest Day*, Souvenir Press, Tokyo, 1968.

Schaller, M. *The American Occupation of Japan*, New York, Oxford University Press,1985.

Singh, R. *Official History of the Indian armed forces in the Second World War, 1939–45: post-war occupation forces: Japan and south-east Asia*, Kanpur, Orient Longmans, 1958.

Slim, W. *Defeat into Victory*, London, Cassell, 1956.

Souter, G. *Lion and Kangaroo – The Initiation of Australia*, Sydney, Collins,1976.

Stargardt, A.W.(ed) *Things worth fighting for – the speeches of J.B.Chifley*, Melbourne, Melbourne University Press, 1952.

Tennant, K. *Evatt – Politics and Justice*, Sydney, Angus & Robertson, 1970.

Trotter, A. *New Zealand and Japan 1945–1952*, London, The Athlone Press, 1990.

Tuchman, B.W. *Sand against the Wind*, New York, Macmillan, 1970.

Ward, R.E. and Sakamoto, Y. *Democratising Japan: the Allied occupation*, Honolulu, University of Hawaii Press, 1987.

Whan, V.E.(ed) *A Soldier Speaks: Public Papers and Speeches of General of the Army Douglas MacArthur*, New York, 1965.

White, N. *How Bluey and friends occupied Japan 1946–1947*, Wentworth Falls, NSW, TWJ Associates, 1991.

White, O.G.W. *Straight on for Tokyo – the War History of 2 Dorset 1939–48*, Aldershot, Gale & Polden, 1948.

Wildes, H.E. *Typhoon in Tokyo – The Occupation and its Aftermath*, London, Allen & Unwin, 1954.

Willoughby, C.A. and Chamberlain, J. *MacArthur: 1941-1951 – Victory in the Pacific*, London, Heinemann, 1956.

Articles

(1) Appearing in *The British Commonwealth and the Occupation of Japan* ed.I.Nish, London, Suntory-Toyota International Centre for Economics & Related Disciplines, London School of Economics,1983:

234   Japan and the British Commonwealth Occupation Force

Bolton, G. 'Australia and the Occupation of Japan'.
Daniels, G. 'New Zealand and the Occupation of Japan'.
Goodman, G. 'MacArthurian Japan: Remembered and Revised'.
Ion, H. 'Canada and the Occupation of Japan'.
Nish, I. 'India and the Occupation of Japan'.

(2) *Appearing in Aspects of the Allied Occupation of Japan*, ed.I.Nish, London, Suntory-Toyota International Centre for Economics & Related Disciplines, London School of Economics, 1986:

Buckley, R. 'Working with MacArthur: Sir Alvary Gascoigne, UKLIM, and British Policy towards Occupied Japan 1945–52'.

(3) Appearing in *The Occupation of Japan 1945–52*, ed. I. Nish, London, Suntory-Toyota International Centre for Economics & Related Disciplines, London School of Economics, 1991:

Iokibe, M. 'The Occupation: The Second American-Japanese Encounter'.
Miller, W. 'Some British Reflections on the Occupation of Japan'.

(4) Appearing in *East Asia in the Postwar Period 1945–55*, ed. I. Nish, London, Suntory-Toyota International Centre for Economics & Related Disciplines, London School of Economics, 1991:

Kibata, Y. 'Britain and the Far East during the first Cold War 1947–1955: Cooperation and Rivalry in the Commonwealth'.
Trotter, A.'New Zealand and East and Southeast Asia, 1945–55'.

(5) Appearing in *The British Commonwealth and its Contribution to the Occupation of Japan 1945–8*, ed. I. Nish, London, Suntory-Toyota International Centre for Economics & Related Disciplines, London School of Economics,1991:

Beasley, W.G. 'Personal Reminiscences of the Early Months of

the Occupation: Yokosuka and Tokyo, September 1945–
March 1946'.
Cortazzi, H. 'Britain and the Occupation of Japan: A person-
al experience and some comments'.
Millar, T.B. 'An Australian's Experiences in BCOF: Kataichi
and Hiroshima, 1946–7'.

(6)   Appearing in the Proceedings of the MacArthur Foundation
      Symposium on *The Occupation of Japan: The International
      Context* 1982, ed. Burkman, Norfolk, 1984:

      Buckley, R. 'Competitor and Ally: British Perceptions of
      Occupied Japan'.
      Dingman, R. 'The View from Down Under: Australia and
      Japan 1945–1952'.
      Sackton, F.J. 'The Occupation of Japan in International
      Perspective: An Overview'.

(7)   Appearing in the British *Army Quarterly*, London:

      Piggott, F.J.C. 'Occupying Japan', April 1947.
      Walsh, J.'British Participation in the Occupation of Japan',
      October 1948.

(8)   Appearing in the Proceedings of the Seventh Biennial
      Conference. Japanese Studies Association of Australia,
      Canberra, 1991:

      Simmonson, O. 'Exotic equal or problem child? Allied forces
      and Japanese people during the occupation', Canberra, 1991.

Notes

Abbreviations used in the Notes

ADM	Admiralty papers, Public Record Office
AIR	Air Ministry papers, Public Record Office
AWM	Australian War Memorial, Canberra
CAB	Cabinet papers, Public Record Office
DEFE	Defence Department papers, Public Record Office
FO	Foreign Office papers, Public Record Office
FRUS	Foreign Relations of the United States
MA	MacArthur Archives
PREM	Prime Minister's papers, Public Record Office
SMH	*Sydney Morning Herald*
WO	War Office papers, Public Record Office

Prologue
1   SMH, 31 August 1945.

1. The End of the War
1   MacArthur to Marshall, 19 June 1945 – C19848, MA
2   Prime Minister to Dominion Prime Ministers, 31 July 1945 – PREM 8/29.
3   *Ibid.*
4   Kirby, *History of the Second World War: The War against Japan*, Vol. V, p.225.
5   Joint Planning Staff paper, 7 August 1945 – CAB 79/35-37.
6   Chiefs of Staff paper, 7 August 1945 – PREM 8/29.

7 Foreign Secretary to Cabinet Defence Committee, 8 August
   1945 – PREM 8/29.
8 Cabinet Defence Committee minute, 8 August 1945 – PREM
   8/29.
9 Slim, *Defeat into Victory*, p.529.
10 Kirby, *op.cit.*, p.134.
11 Roach to author.
12 Murray to author.
13 Gunton to author.
14 Slim, *op.cit.*, p.528.
15 FRUS, 1945. Vol. VI, p.559.
16 Allen, *The End of the War in Asia*, p.75.
17 McDermot to Bevin, 14 December 1945 – FO 371/54088.

2. The Occupation Proposals
1 CIGS to Cabinet Defence Committee, 10 August 1945 – PREM
   8/34.
2 Chiefs of Staff to Cabinet Defence Committee, 13 August 1945
   – PREM 8/34.
3 Prime Minister to Dominion Prime Ministers, 13 August 1945 –
   PREM 8/27.
4 Kirby, *op.cit.*, p. 228–229.
5 Mackenzie King to Attlee, 13 August 1945 – PREM 8/27.
6 Kay, *Documents on New Zealand External Relations, Vol.II*,
   No.542, p.1287.
7 Australian Government to Dominions Office, 17 August 1945 –
   PREM 8/192.
8 Department of State Policy Paper, 22 June 1945.
9 Evatt to Secretary of State, Washington, 22 August 1945.
10 Attlee to Chifley, 25 August 1945 – PREM 8/192.
11 Chiefs of Staff to Prime Minister, 30 August 1945 – PREM
   8/192.
12 Chifley to Attlee, 10 September 1945 – PREM 8/192.
13 Chiefs of Staff to Prime Minister, 12 September 1945 – CAB
   79/39, COS(45)221.
14 Chifley to Attlee, 21 September 1945 – PREM 8/192.
15 Australian Defence Committee Minute No.357/1945 of 23
   August 1945 – Australian Archives Series A 2031.
16 Attlee to Evatt, 25 September 1945 – PREM 8/192.
17 Evatt to Attlee, 30 September 1945 – PREM 8/192.

18 SWNCC 70/5, quoted in FRUS, 1945, Vol.VI, p.613 *et seq*. The full text is given in Appendix A.

19 FRUS, 1945, Vol.VI, p.668 *et seq*.

20 *Ibid*. p.670.

21 *Ibid*. British Foreign Office to State Department, 18 August 1945.

22 Marshall (Washington) to MacArthur (CINCAFPAC), 15 September 1945 – WX 64221, MA.

23 SMH, 15 September 1945.

24 FRUS, 1945, Vol.VI, pp.717–718.

25 SMH, 12 October 1945.

26 CINCAFPAC to WARCOS, 19 September 1945, MA.

27 Chifley to MacArthur, 22 September 1945 – quoted in CR 52878 from CINCAFPAC to WARCOS,MA.

28 CINCAFPAC to WARCOS, 23 September 1945 – CA 52230,MA.

29 Washington (Marshall) to CINCAFPAC (MacArthur), 3 October 1945 – WX 72310,MA.

30 CINCAFPAC to WARCOS, 4 October 1945 – CA 52719(WD 1307),MA.

31 Marshall to MacArthur, 9 March 1947 – W 93582,MA, and MacArthur's reply of same date.

32 MacArthur to Marshall, 27 September 1945 – WD 1287,MA.

33 FRUS, 1945, Vol. VI, pp.744–747.

34 FRUS, 1945, Vol. VI, pp.818–819.

35 FRUS, 1945, Vol. VI, pp.853–854.

36 FRUS, 1945, Vol. VI, pp.860–861.

37 Marshall to MacArthur, 20 November1945 – W 84062,MA.

38 Wedemeyer to MacArthur, 2 September 1945 – CFBS 6792,MA. Wedemeyer had succeeded Stilwell as chief of staff to Chiang Kai-shek and commander of US forces in China in October 1944.

39 Wedemeyer to Marshall, 10 November 1945 – CWX 558,MA.

40 *Keesing's Contemporary Archives*.

3. Preparing the Force for Japan

1 White, *Straight on for Tokyo*, p.306.

4. Negotiating with the Americans

1 FRUS, 1945, Vol. VI, pp.762–763.

2 FRUS, 1945, Vol. VI, pp.744–747.
3 FRUS, 1945, Vol. VI, pp.763 *et seq.*
4 As was common in the Services, the initials of the title BCOF became a two-syllable word, pronounced BEE-KOFF (in the same way that SACSEA became Sack-see), and although it sounded rather like a minor ailment the Force was known as such thenceforward.
5 Quoted by Gilbert, *Never Despair*, p.166.
6 MacArthur to Marshall, 20 November 1945 – WD 1398,MA.
7 FRUS, 1945, Vol. VI, p.875
8 Evatt to Addison, 4 December 1945 – PREM 8/192.
9 SCAP (MacArthur) to Joint Chiefs of Staff, Washington – CAX 56193,MA.
10 CAB 80/103,COS(46)270(0).
11 FRUS,1945,Vol.VI,Appendix 17. This is quoted in full at Appendix B.
12 Sackton to author.
13 *Ibid.*
14 CAB 80/103,COS(40)270(0).

5. The Long Wait

1 Murray to author.
2 Pitcher to author. The pre-war Lee-Enfield rifles were issued to enable the use of the old-fashioned long bayonet for ceremonial duties.
3 Auchinleck to Viceroy, 26 November 1945 – quoted by Connell, *Auchinleck*, p.806.
4 CAB 80/677.
5 Wildes, *Typhoon in Tokyo*, pp.193 and 300.
6 McDonald to author.
7 *Ibid.*
8 CAB 80/103,COS(46)270(0).
9 'The History of 2 NZEF' J Force Newsletter.
10 Quoted by Rajendra Singh, Official History of the Indian Armed Forces in the Second World War 1939–45, p.22.
11 SMH, 16 January 1946.

6. On Japanese Soil

1 See Front End Paper. The mobilisation of the Force from the three continents – Europe, Asia and Australia – was a major

logistic achievement, having regard to the tremendous demand for shipping in the immediate post-war period.

2   Cattle to author.

3   John, *Uneasy lies the head*, p.4.

4   Roach to author.

5   CAB 80/103,COS(46)270(0).

6   *Ibid.*

7   Northcott to JCOSA, 8 March 1946 – FO 371/54088.

8   Murray to author.

9   Australian Associated Press report, 3 August 1946.

10   Address to United Services Institute, Sydney, 14 November 1946.

11   This was recollected by the Ministry of Defence, London, when responding on 16 September 1946 to an enquiry from Attlee on possible extension of the BCOF area – PREM 8/167.

12   CAB 80/103,COS(46)270(0).

13   Cattle to author.

14   See Back End Paper.

7. The Task

1   See Appendix C. This was a practical summary of the much more detailed provisions of the US 'Initial Post-Defeat Policy' paper SWNCC 150/2 of 12 August 1945 – FRUS, 1945, Vol. VI, p.609 *et seq.*

2   Ward, *Democratising Japan*, p.17.

3   Rajendra Singh, *op.cit.*, p.86.

4   White, *op.cit.*, p.316.

5   Waddy to author.

6   SMH, 29 May 1960.

7   *Ibid.*

8   CAB 80/103,COS(46)270(0).

9   Wallace to author.

10   SMH, 12 July 1946.

11   SMH, 13 July 1946.

12   SMH, 24 July 1946.

13   SMH, 26 July 1946.

14   John, *op.cit.*, p.25.

15   AWM 114/130/1/10.

16   Williams to author.

17   Arthur papers.

18   Roach to author.

[19] UKLIM Periodical Report No.3 to Foreign Office, London, for March 1946 – FO 371/54144.

[20] CAB 80/103,COS(46)270(0).

[21] Egan to author.

[22] CAB 80/103,COS(46)270(0).

[23] SMH, 24 September 1946.

[24] SMH, 22 November 1946.

[25] SMH, 14 December 1946.

8. Relations with the Americans

[1] Gregory Pemberton, article in *Weekend Australian Review*, 28/29 March 1992.

[2] Manchester, *American Caesar*, p.360.

[3] Statement from MacArthur accompanying the official announcement of the Northcott–MacArthur agreement of 30 January 1946 published as Appendix 17 to FRUS,1945,Vol.VI.

[4] MacArthur, 'Too Late', 16 September 1940, in *A Soldier Speaks* (ed.Whan).

[5] MacArthur, *Reminiscences*, p.332.

[6] Willoughby expresses a rather wild view that it was the British who influenced Truman to dismiss MacArthur, in resentment at their failure to get MacArthur to agree to the inclusion of Japan in the sterling area.

[7] Stilwell, J W, *The Stilwell Papers*, 1 January to 25 August 1944.

[8] Article by Anthony Whitlock, SMH, 1 August 1947.

[9] John, *op.cit.*, p.5.

[10] T B Millar, LSE Symposium, 5 July 1991.

[11] Note from Ismay to Churchill, 27 July 1945 – PREM 8/31.

[12] Manchester, *op.cit.*, p.473.

[13] These are reproduced in Willoughby and Chamberlain, *MacArthur – Victory in the Pacific*.

[14] UKLIM Periodical Report No.3 to Foreign Office, London, March 1946 – FO 371/54144.

[15] Capt. F C Hutley, quoted in BCOF Veterans Association of NSW Newsletter Issue 32 of August 1992.

[16] Statement by SCAP of 13 February 1947.

[17] Murray to author.

[18] Saxon to author.

[19] Coles to author.

[20] Williams to author.

21 Pitcher to author.
22 Margetts, Cattle, Dear (with variations), and others too numerous to mention.

9. A Wider Responsibility?
1 Gairdner to Attlee, 23 August 1946 – PREM 8/167.
2 JCOSA to Cabinet Offices, 11 September 1946 – PREM 8/167.
3 Minutes of conference between JCOSA and Robertson, 24 September 1946 – AWM 114/130/1/29.
4 Gascoigne to Foreign Office, London, 23 October 1946 – FO 371/54109.
5 *The Times* carried a story on these lines on 20 October 1946.

10. Reactions to Japan
1 Waddy to author.
2 Arthur papers.
3 Clifton, *Time of Fallen Blossoms*, p.56.
4 Boillot papers.
5 Smyth to author.
6 BCOF Instruction No.4 of 26 March 1946.
7 Gair to author.
8 Coles to author.
9 Gunton to author.
10 Hancock to author.
11 Arthur papers.
12 Pitcher to author.
13 Cattle to author.
14 Arthur papers.
15 See Appendix D for an account of one such occasion contained in the Arthur papers.
16 Clifton, *op.cit.*, p.56.
17 Caiger, article in SMH of 4 April 1946.
18 BCOF Intelligence Review 1946 – AWM 114/130/1/13.
19 Noted in the 2 NZEF Quarterly Report for the quarter ended 31 December 1946 – AWM 114/130/1/17.
20 BCOF Intelligence Review 1946 – AWM 114/130/1/13.
21 Article by John Deane Potter in London Daily Express, 12 August 1946.
22 Leslie Hoffman, quoted in article The Fall of Singapore, *Weekend Australian*, 15/16 February 1992.

[23] Quoted in Royal Navy Monthly Intelligence Report for April 1946 – ADM 223/223.

[24] Virendra Singh to author.

11. The Seamy Side
[1] T B Millar, LSE Symposium, 5 July 1991.
[2] 2 NZEF Quarterly Report for the quarter ended 31 December 1946 – AWM 114/130/1/17.
[3] Margetts to author.
[4] JCOSA Progress Report No.2 on BCOF – AWM 114/130/1/10.
[5] John, *op.cit.*, p.26.
[6] Murray to author.
[7] CAB 80/103,COS(46)270(0).
[8] Letter to SMH, 9 February 1946.
[9] White, *How Bluey and friends . . .*, p.79.
[10] Clifton, *op.cit.*, p.148.
[11] White tells in *How Bluey and friends . . .* (pp.55–59) of a clash in an Osaka beer hall between a group of Australians and New Zealanders on the one hand and American military policemen on the other, in the course of which one of the MPs wildly loosed off an entire magazine from his sub-machine gun. Luckily no one was hurt.
[12] BCOF Provost Court proceedings reported in AWM 114/233/3/2.

12. Fraternisation
[1] Letter from Mountbatten to MacArthur – BA C169, Broadlands Archives.
[2] MacArthur, *op.cit.*, p.262.
[3] SMH, 10 September 1945.
[4] Australian Government to Dominions Office, London, 11 August 1945 – CRS A 3317 102/45, Australian Archives.
[5] SMH, 23 October 1945.
[6] MacArthur, *op.cit.*, p.282.
[7] Manchester, *op.cit.*, p.469.
[8] Washington to CINCAFPAC, 2 September 1945 – WX 56906,MA.
[9] JCOSA Plan Minute No.102 of 20 February 1946 – A 5954/1, Box 1890, Australian Archives.
[10] *Know Japan* was prepared under Northcott's auspices, in line

with the view he expressed in the foreword that 'although we may not like the Japanese people, we must learn something of their history and customs, so that we can help them to make themselves fit to take their place alongside the other peoples of the civilised world'. The booklet made a valiant attempt to provide the basis for an elementary understanding of Japan and its people: and it sought also to explain the different influences and pressures which had produced the extraordinary contrasts in the race which the occupation troops found so puzzling.

[11] Coles to author.
[12] Caiger, article in SMH, 4 April 1946.
[13] SMH, 12 January 1946.
[14] *Melbourne Sun*, 14 February 1946.
[15] Chida, 'The Occupation of Japan by the BCOF'.
[16] Caiger, article in SMH, 4 April 1946.
[17] BCOF Intelligence Review 1946 – AWM 113/130/1/13.
[18] See AWM 431/2/1 for this account.
[19] Pitcher to author.
[20] AWM 114/475/2/1.
[21] AWM 114/130/1/11.
[22] SMH, 10 March 1948.
[23] SMH, 8 August 1948.
[24] A selection of views of this kind was contained in an ABC radio programme broadcast on 25 August 1948, under the title 'Should we be tough with Japan?'
[25] According to L C Haylen, a Member of the Australian House of Representatives, quoted by John, *op.cit.*, p.83.
[26] SMH, 1 October 1949.
[27] SMH, 5 October 1949.
[28] Chida, *op.cit.*
[29] *Australian Encyclopaedia*, quoted by John, *op.cit.*, p.83.

13. The Sunny Side
[1] Montgomery, *Memoirs*, pp.228–229.
[2] 5/1 Punjabi War Diary, January-August 1946 – WO 172/10229.
[3] Hancock to author.
[4] White, *op.cit.*, p.99.
[5] SMH, 21 September 1946.
[6] Rajendra Singh, *op.cit.*, p.148.

[7] 2 NZEF Quarterly Report for quarter ended 31 December 1946 – AWM 114/130/1/17.

[8] BCOF Association of Australia/Central NSW Branch Newsletter September/October 1990.

[9] John, *op.cit.*, p.63.

[10] 2/5 RGR War Diary, July-December 1946 – WO 268/546.

[11] Murray to author.

[12] Rajendra Singh, *op.cit.*, p.98.

[13] Hancock to author.

[14] White, *op.cit.*, p.111.

[15] John, passim.

[16] Saxon to author.

[17] Cattle to author.

14. Commonwealth Relations

[1] Horton to author.

[2] These were among a number of perceptive comments by General Hutton, the first commandant of the Australian Military Forces, in 1896. Quoted by Souter, *Lion and Kangaroo*, p.149.

[3] Waddy to author.

[4] Article by Steve Dwyer in the J Force Newsletter of 13 February 1991.

[5] Murray to author.

[6] Saxon to author.

[7] Coles to author.

[8] The full proceedings of the court of enquiry are contained in AWM 114/233/15/1.

[9] *Sun Herald*, Melbourne, 9 July 1989.

[10] Evans, *Thimayya of India*.

15. The British Brigade

[1] White, *op.cit.*, p.350.

[2] Ap Rhys Pryce to author.

[3] *Ibid.*

[4] 2 Dorsets War Diary, January-October 1946 – WO 172/10176.

[5] SMH, 30 September 1946.

[6] *The Scotsman*, 28 October 1946.

[7] COS paper, 23 January 1946 – PREM 8/176.

[8] Cabinet Defence Committee meeting, 22 October 1946 – FO 371/34109.

9 Washington (WDSCA GO) to CINCAFPAC – W 86406/WD 1853, MA.

10 Statement by the Lord President of Council on behalf of the Prime Minister – Hansard, 6 December 1946.

11 McDermot, Foreign Office, London, to Gascoigne, Tokyo, 5 December 1946 – FO 371/54113.

12 FO 371/54113.

13 *Ibid.*

14 *Ibid.*

15 CAB 79,COS(46)296(0), 20 December 1946.

16 Washington (WDGPO) to CINCFE, 7 January 1947 – W 89022/WD 1899,MA.

17 CINCFE to Washington (WDGPO), 7 January 1947 – W 90385/WD 1901,MA.

18 SMH, 14 February 1947.

19 RASC report – WO 268/537.

20 Gascoigne, Tokyo, to McDermot, Foreign Office, London, 9 January 1947 – FO 371/63671.

21 Gascoigne, Tokyo, to Foreign Secretary, London, 28 December 1946 – FO 371/63671.

22 *The Times*, 1 January 1947.

23 *The Times*, 3 January 1947.

24 A 4031 461/46, 19 November 1946, Australian Archives.

25 SMH, 25 February 1947.

26 Reported in *The Times*, 10 February 1947.

27 High Commissioner, Wellington, to Dominions Office, 18 November 1946 – FO 371/54112.

28 COS minute, 21 November 1946 – FO 371/54112.

29 Foreign Office to Cabinet Office, 2 December 1946 – FO 371/54112.

30 White, *op.cit.*, p.361.

31 *Ibid.*

16. The Indian Contingent

1 BRINDIV Fortnightly Intelligence Review, 7 August 1946 – WO 268/768.

2 Evans, *op.cit.*, pp.239–242, is the basic source for this and the subsequent account relating to the Gurkhas, but certain inaccuracies have been corrected following reference to the 2/5 RGR

RGR Quarterly Historical Report for the period and interviews with other officers serving at the time.

3 2/5 RGR Quarterly Historical reports – WO 268/547.
4 PREM 8/587.
5 Quoted by Rajendra Singh, *op.cit.*, p.105.
6 *Ibid.*, p.156.

17. The New Zealand Contingent

1 Recounted in J Force Newsletter, 13 February 1991.
2 Interview on 26 March 1946, reported by Press Association, Dundee, New Zealand.
3 J Force Newsletter, 13 February 1991.
4 Kay, Docs.II, No.636, p.1476.
5 Kay, Docs.II, No.632, p.1470.
6 SMH, 22 May 1949.

18. The British Pull Out

1 AWM 114/130/1/29.
2 SMH, 17 June 1947.
3 *The Times*, 5 February 1947.
4 One such report appeared in the Christian Science Monitor of 1 May 1947.
5 Minute by Dening, 17 June 1947 – FO 371/63803. Montgomery was always ready to pontificate on any matter he thought important, regardless of the consequences. The First Sea Lord noted (ADM 205) that he seemed to have been 'shooting his mouth' in Australia, and although he always made it clear that he was only expressing his personal views, 'as a member of the Chiefs of Staff Committee, some of the things he says are considerably embarrassing'. Several conflicts with the Navy occurred during Montgomery's 1947 tour: arguments over the location of naval headquarters in the Mediterranean and Far East led an infuriated C-in-C East Indies Fleet to complain to the First Sea Lord that the CIGS had not 'the slightest inkling of the responsibilities and functions of a naval C-in-C in peace'.
6 Bevin to CIGs, 23 June 1947 – FO 371/63803.
7 CIGS to COS, 27 August 1947 – FO 371/63687.
8 Joint Planning Staff report on implications of withdrawal, 28 March 1947 – DEFE 4.

[9] COS to Cabinet Defence Committee, 3 September 1947 – FO 371/63687.
[10] Foreign Office brief for Bevin, 17 September 1947 – FO 371/63687.
[11] Foreign Office minute to Bevin of 5 October reported Gascoigne's call on MacArthur in Tokyo – FO 371/63688.
[12] WAR(CSGPO), Washington, to CINCFE, 10 October 1947 – W 87989 DA 47,MA.
[13] CINCFE to WAR(CSGPO), 11 October 1947 – C 56056, DA 51, MA.
[14] AWM 114/130/3/23, October 1947.
[15] Foreign Office note regarding a Parliamentary Question from Teeling – FO 371/69817.
[16] PREM 8/473.
[17] PREM 8/473.

19. Problems for the Australians

[1] C-in-C's Conference regarding reorganisation, 23 December 1947 – AWM 114/213/3/11.
[2] BCOF Order 'Reorganisation of BCOF', 10 April 1948 – AWM 114/130/2/35.
[3] SMH, 25 August 1947.
[4] SMH, 13 October 1947.
[5] SMH, 13 January 1948.
[6] SMH, 2 March 1948.
[7] SMH, 13 January 1948.
[8] SMH, 17 January 1948.
[9] SMH, 20 May 1948.
[10] *Ibid.*
[11] 2 NZEF Quarterly Report for quarter ended 30 June 1948 – AWM 114/130/1/17.
[12] John, *op.cit.*, p.26.
[13] Margetts to author.
[14] SMH, 26 August 1948.
[15] Minute by the Defence Committee, 22 April 1948 – A 2031/68/1948, Australian Archives.
[16] CSGPO, Washington, to SCAP, 26 May 1948 – WAR 82528, DA 518,MA.
[17] SCAP to Department of Army, 3 June 1948 – C 61179, DA 542,MA.

18 CINCFE to Department of Army, 28 May 1948 – C 61072,DA 533, MA.
19 Minute by Dening to Bevin, 12 June 1948 – FO 371/69908.
20 *Ibid*. Robertson finally got his own knighthood in 1950, after what was thought by some to be considerable lobbying in the corridors of power.
21 Bevin to Alexander, 17 June 1948 – FO 371/69908.
22 Gascoigne to Foreign Office, 23 June 1948 – FO 371/69908.
23 Reported by CSGPO, Washington, to CINCFE, 3 December 1948 – W 80501,TD 124,MA.
24 Robertson's message COS 10266, November 1948, reported by SCAP to Department of Army, 23 November 1948 – CX 65659,TD 122,MA.
25 CINCFE to Department of Army, 4 December 1948 – C 66006,TD 127,MA.
26 See Appendix E for details of SCAP's deployment.
27 CINCFE to Department of Army, 4 December 1948 – C 65998,TD 126,MA.
28 *Ibid*.
29 CSGPO to CINCFE, 10 December 1948 – W 80958,TD 130,MA.
30 Margetts to author.
31 Wallace to author.
32 Robertson's submission for reorganisation to JCOSA, 14 July 1948 – AWM 113/3/4/10.
33 PREM 8/1176.
34 SMH, 28 May 1950.
35 Attlee to Menzies, 9 June 1950 – PREM 8/1176.

20. The Commonwealth Air Force
1 The difference in living conditions between ground and air forces has often been a source of some resentment for the Army. They felt that the airmen could retire from the field of battle every night to comfort and a warm bed, leaving the soldiers to carry on in mud and danger. This was less so in the conditions of the war in the Far East, where the fighter squadrons were far more involved in the hazards of ground conflict. The experience of 77 Squadron RAAF (later part of BCAIR), was not untypical: in June 1945 the ground crews landed on Labuan Island to prepare for the pilots and aircraft to follow, at a time when the

Japanese still held part of the island. There were a number of engagements between the Army and the enemy on the Squadron camp perimeter, with numerous bullets passing through the Squadron's tent lines.

2   AIR 27/2400.
3   Winskill to author.
4   AIR 27/2400.
5   Winskill to author.
6   Gunton to author.

21. The Naval Involvement
1   'The British Pacific Fleet 1945', Naval Historical Society of Australia.
2   Report on the British Pacific Fleet, ADM 199/2436.
3   Admiralty War Diary situation report, September 1945 – ADM 199/2323.
4   R J Lupton, article in BCOF Association of Australia Newsletter, March 1988.

22. Korea and the Revival of BCOF
1   Willoughby and Chamberlain, *op.cit.*
2   Current Notes on International Affairs, Canberra, p.420.
3   Stratemeyer quoted by O'Neill, *op.cit.*, p.52.
4   COS Melbourne to C-in-C BCOF, 30 June 1950 – Department of Defence 19/323/12.
5   SMH, 4 July 1950.
6   COS to C-in-C BCOF, 6 July 1950 – Department of Defence 19/323/13.
7   C-in-C BCOF to COS, 23 July 1950 – Department of Defence 19/323/14.
8   C-in-C BCOF to COS, 25 July 1950 – Department of Defence 19/323/14.
9   Cable from Spender to Menzies 17 July 1950 – PM Dept file TS/443/1/81.
10 COS Minute 18/50, 26 July 1950.
11 Current Notes on International Affairs, Canberra,p.511.
12 Australians in both world wars had a marvellous reputation for joining up both over and under age and in spite of medical limitations. Margetts tells of various legendary cases: the soldier who had his 15th birthday in Mersa Matruh; the epileptic who

joined up again under a new name every time detection of his medical condition led to his discharge, and finally made it to Japan, where he became band major of 65 Battalion; and the man who was born with a deformed foot only three inches long, and who went to the Middle East with his boot stuffed with cotton wool ('after bribing some doctor'!) Age limits were difficult to enforce at a time when many children were born at home, and the records, especially in country areas, were poor and inaccurate. If a boy was tall for his age, he could often get in.

13 Horner, *Duty First*, p.65.

14 Farrar-Hockley, *The British Part in the Korean War*, Vol.1, p.180.

15 Foreign Office to Tokyo, 13 July 1950 – PREM 8/1175.

16 Gascoigne to Foreign Office, 14 July 1950 – PREM 8/1175.

17 Private Secretary to Attlee, 20 July 1950 – PREM 8/1175.

18 Minute by Attlee, 21 July 1950 – PREM 8/1175.

19 C-in-C BCOF to COS, 27 August 1950 – CSRA 5954, Box 1661, File 2, Australian Archives.

20 CGS to CIGS, 31 August 1950 – CSRA 5954, Box 1661, File 2, Australian Archives.

21 C-in-C BCOF's Quarterly Report to COS, April-June 1951 – AWM 114/130/1/11.

22 SMH, 29 May 1960.

23 Dingman, MacArthur Foundation Symposium, 21-22 October 1982.

24 O'Neill, *op.cit.*, p.253.

25 *Ibid.*

26 Gascoigne to Foreign Office, 10 February 1947 – FO 371/63673.

27 Meeting between Gascoigne and General Cawthorn of JCOSA, 8 February 1947 – FO 371/63673.

28 Gascoigne to Foreign Office, 27 April 1948 – FO 371/69817.

29 Clutton to Foreign Office, 8 December 1950 – FO 371/83891.

30 SMH, 8 November 1951.

31 This abstruse comment was minuted on a report of MacArthur's speech in Tokyo on the second anniversary of the end of the war (14 August 1947), as it appeared in the US Army newspaper *Stars and Stripes* – FO 371/63687.

32 BCFK Instruction, 14 December 1951 – AWM 114/130/2/43.

33 *Hansard* for 1 July 1952.

34 SMH, 4 July 1952.

35 SMH, 8 July 1952.

36 *Asahi Shimbun*, 3 July 1952.
37 The Japanese Foreign Minister, Okazaki, made a statement to this effect in the Diet on 21 July 1952.
38 SMH, 8 July 1952.

23. Post-Mortem on BCOF

1   Cortazzi, LSE Symposium, 5 July 1991.
2   PWC 111, 13 March 1944 – FRUS,1944,Vol.V,pp.1202-5.
3   It is generally admitted that the success of the various reforms was limited. After the occupation, many of them were repealed or ignored, or redirected along Japanese government lines. The purge of undesirables was abandoned; the police and the bureaucrats recovered their power; and the major corporations which were supposed to have been broken up were resurrected under the camouflage of a network of subsidiaries. The land reforms were partly effective. The most successful and permanent measure was the enfranchisement of women.
4   CAS 80/103,COS(46)270(0).
5   Quoted by Rajendra Singh, *op.cit.*, p.164.
6   Minute of 14 October 1948 – FO 371/69698.
7   Comment made during a discussion at the Institute of Contemporary History, London, in 1991.
8   Passfield to author.
9   Gunton to author.
10 Murray to author.
11 Ap Rhys Pryce to author.
12 Pitcher to author.
13 Gair to author.
14 Seaburn to author.

APPENDIX A
SWNCC Policy Paper 70/5
August 1945

National composition of forces to occupy Japan proper in the post-defeat period

a. This [the US] Government is committed to consult with those of its Allies at war with Japan.

b. This Government is also committed to the principle of united action for the prosecution of the war and acting together in all matters relating to the surrender and disarmament of Japan.

c. The United Kingdom, China and the Soviet Union have a responsibility to participate with the United States in the occupation and military control of Japan and the obligation to assume a share in the burden thereof.

d. While the establishment of policies for the control of Japan is a matter to be entered into by the major Allies in harmony with the United Nations, the United States should insist on the control of the implementation of those policies. The United States should exercise the controlling voice in the occupation authority in Japan proper, should make available its share of occupational forces, should designate the commanders of all occupational forces and principal subordinate commanders, and should keep strategically placed those forces necessary to implement its policies. Furthermore, the occupation authority in Japan should be organised on the principle of centralised administration, avoiding the division of the country into national zones of independent responsibility administered separately.

e. The major Allies should be called upon to make substantial contributions to the occupational force in conformity with their obligations to share in the burden of controlling Japan.

f. Participation in the occupation authority in Japan and in furnishing the forces of occupation may be extended as desired to include those countries, other than the major Allies, which will have made timely request to share in such responsibility and which have actively and substantially participated in the war against Japan.

g. The interests of the United States would be served by the participation of Orientals in the occupation forces and in the occupation authority in Japan.

APPENDIX B
The Northcott – MacArthur Agreement

Occupation force in Japan

SUMMARY OF AGREEMENT BETWEEN THE UNITED STATES AND AUSTRALIA, ACTING ON BEHALF OF THE UNITED KINGDOM, NEW ZEALAND, AND INDIA

January 30, 1946

1. As a result of discussion between members of the British Commonwealth, proposals for a joint British Commonwealth force to participate in the occupation of Japan were agreed upon and conveyed to the United States Government by the Australian Government, acting on behalf of the British Commonwealth Governments concerned.

2. Following recent representations in Washington by the Australian Minister for External Affairs, Dr H V Evatt, the United States Government has now formally accepted the participation of British Commonwealth forces in the occupation of Japan. Arrangements are now well advanced for the force to proceed on the following basis.

3. The force is drawn from the United Kingdom, Australia, New Zealand, and India. The Commander in Chief of the force is Lieutenant General J Northcott, CB, MVO, of the Australian Military Forces. His headquarters are fully integrated with

255

representatives drawn from each service and from each Commonwealth country contributing to the force. Air Commodore R M Bladin, CBE, of the Royal Australian Air Force, has been appointed Chief of Staff to Lieutenant General Northcott.

4. The force comprises:
    (a) force and base troops drawn from each of the contributing countries;
    (b) a land component, organised as a corps, consisting of one British Indian division and two independent brigade groups – one each from Australia and New Zealand;
    (c) an air component comprising squadrons drawn from the Royal Air Force, the Royal Australian Air Force, the Royal New Zealand Air Force, and the Royal Indian Air Force.

5. A squadron of the British Pacific fleet, which includes ships of the Royal Navy, the Royal Australian Navy, and the Royal Indian Navy is stationed in Japanese waters under operational control of the admiral commanding the detachment of the United States fleet.

6. The British Indian division is commanded by Major General D T Cowan, CB, DSO, MC, Indian Army, and includes the 5th Brigade of the 2nd British Division and the 268th Indian Infantry Brigade. The Australian Infantry Brigade group includes the 34th Australian Infantry Brigade commanded by Brigadier R H Nimmo. The commander of the New Zealand Brigade, which is coming from Italy, is Brigadier K L Steward, CBE, DSO.

7. The commander of the air component is Air Vice Marshal C A Bouchier, CB, CBE, DFC, Royal Air Force. His senior staff officer is Air Commodore I D McLaughlan, DFC, Royal Australian Air Force. The air component includes the 81st Australian Fighter Wing of three Mustang Fighter Squadrons; numbers 11 and 17 Spitfire Squadrons, and number 96 Medium Transport Squadron, Royal Air Force; number 4 Spitfire Squadron, Royal Indian Air Force; and number 14 Corsair Squadron, Royal New Zealand Air Force.

8. The British Commonwealth Occupation Force (BCOF) will form part of the occupation forces in Japan under the supreme command of General Douglas MacArthur, Supreme Commander for the Allied Powers (SCAP). He has assigned the land component to the general operational control of the Commanding General, 8th United States Army, who is in military control of the whole area of Japan. The air component has been assigned to the general operational control of the Commanding General, Pacific Air Command, United States Army (PAC USA). Lieutenant General Northcott, as Commander in Chief, BCOF, is entirely responsible for the maintenance and administration of the British Commonwealth Occupation Force as a whole. He has direct access to General MacArthur on matters of major policy affecting operational commitments of the force. On policy and administrative matters affecting the force, the Commander in Chief is responsible to the British Commonwealth Governments concerned through a British Commonwealth organisation set up in Melbourne and known as the Joint Chiefs of Staff in Australia. Their instructions to the Commander in Chief, BCOF will be issued by the Australian Chiefs of Staff. The Joint Chiefs of Staff in Australia (JCOSA) comprise the Australian Chiefs of Staff and representatives of Chiefs of Staff in the United Kingdom and New Zealand and of the Commander in Chief in India. This organisation is fully associated with Australian Joint Service machinery. The Commander in Chief BCOF has the right of direct communication with the Joint Chiefs of Staff in Australia on administrative matters affecting the force. On matters of governmental concern affecting the policy and operations of BCOF, he will communicate through JCOSA to the Australian Government, which acts as the representative of the other Commonwealth Governments concerned.

9. The BCOF will be initially located in the Hiroshima Prefecture including the cities of Kure and Fukuyama. It will be responsible for the demilitarisation and disposal of Japanese installations and armaments. It will exercise military control of the area but will not be responsible for its military government, which remains the responsibility of United States

agencies. The BCOF area will not constitute a national zone. The BCOF may be called upon to conduct military operations outside its normally allocated area. When air support for the land component of the BCOF is required, this will be provided primarily by the BCOF air component. Kure will be the base port for BCOF which will be responsible for the working of the entire port. The Kure Naval Yard will remain under United States naval control.

10. Provision is being made for the BCOF to be represented in the Tokyo Prefecture by a detachment which probably will be of battalion strength. This detachment will be drawn in turn from each national component in the force.

11. The British Commonwealth Occupation Force may be withdrawn wholly or in part by agreement between the United States Government and the Commonwealth Governments concerned or upon six months' notice by either party. It has been agreed also that progressive reduction in the strength of the force will be made from time to time in conformity with progressive reductions which may be made in the strength of United States occupation forces in Japan.

12. The Australian Services Mission, hitherto located in Tokyo, has been transformed into an advanced echelon of Headquarters BCOF with an addition of officers from other Commonwealth components. For the present it remains in the Tokyo area to facilitate liaison with General MacArthur's headquarters.

13. Details of the move to Japan of the various components of BCOF cannot yet be announced but detailed planning is now in progress on the following basis:

(a) naval port parties for the working of Kure port to arrive in the first week of February;

(b) leading elements of the Australian component, including an airfield construction squadron, to arrive in the third week of February;

(c) leading elements of the British Indian Division and the advanced parties of the British Indian air component to arrive about the first of March;

(d) leading elements of the New Zealand Brigade, which is moving from Italy, to arrive about March 23.

APPENDIX C
The Ultimate Objectives of the Occupation

(a)   The ultimate objectives of the occupation forces . . . are

   i.   To ensure that Japan will not again become a menace to the peace and security of the world

   ii. To bring about the eventual establishment of a peaceful and responsible government which will respect the rights of other states and will support the objectives of the United States as reflected in the ideals and principles of the Charter of the United Nations. The Allied nations desire that the government should conform as closely as may be to the principles of democratic government but it is not the responsibility of the Allied Powers to impose upon Japan any form of government not supported by the freely expressed will of the people.

(b)   These objectives will be achieved by the following principal means:

   i.   Japan's sovereignty will be limited to the islands of Japan [defined as the four main islands and the smaller adjacent islands numbering about a thousand, including the Tsushima islands]

   ii. Japan will be completely disarmed and demilitarised. The authority of the militarists and the influence of militarism will be totally eliminated from her political, economic and social life. Institutions expressive of the spirit of militarism and aggression will be vigorously suppressed.

   iii. The Japanese people shall be encouraged to develop a

desire for individual liberties and respect for fundamental
human rights, particularly the freedoms of religion, assembly, speech and the press. They shall also be encouraged to
form democratic and representative organisations.

iv. The Japanese people shall be afforded opportunity to
develop for themselves an economy which will permit the
peacetime requirements of the population to be met.

APPENDIX D
A Mahratta Tale

One of the British officers with the Mahratta battalion at Hamada (Shimane) told the following story:

The officers at the Mahratta camp at Hamada were invited in May 1946 by the Chief of Police and the Mayor to attend a festival in commemoration of Dr Edward Jenner, whose monument (surprisingly) is on a little hill overlooking Hamada. We were escorted there by the Mayor, a little apprehensive as to the form the festivity was going to take.

When we eventually got to the top of the hill we found waiting for us around a stone memorial for Jenner all the officials of Hamada, including the local journalists, who were seated on benches – also a Church of England Japanese padre! After the usual ceremony of bowing we were led to our seats and sat down, still wondering what was about to happen. There then followed a short Christian service intermingled with little speeches in appalling English welcoming us to Hamada and saying how pleased they all were that we were there! During the service all the Japanese stood rigidly to attention with their eyes closed. What amused me most was that I was perfectly certain that we officers and the Japanese padre were the only Christians present and that this was all done for our benefit! Some young schoolgirls from the High School had been brought up for the ceremony to sing hymns which was most pleasant. From what I can gather Japanese music is not unlike Western music at all and the melodies are very attractive.

I think the crowning incident of the whole show was that as

262

soon as this open air service was over, within a few minutes of the last 'Amen', beer was whipped up from somewhere and we pushed all the tables together and proceeded to sit and drink beer, including the Japanese padre, accompanied by seaweed and fish balls to eat! It was all most amusing and very quaint – the Chief of Police had spent most of the service smoking a cigarette, being the only man who was honest enough to show he wasn't acting!

APPENDIX E
Organisation of Occupation Forces by SCAP – 1946

The five divisional areas established by 1946 as an organisational structure for the balanced administration of the occupation following the disbandment of 1st US Army were:

KYUSHU
> Area 16,000 square miles   Population 11 million
> Occupied by 24th US Infantry Division

SOUTHERN HONSHU AND SHIKOKU
> Area 20,000 square miles   Population 10 million
> Occupied by BCOF

SOUTHERN CENTRAL HONSHU
> Area 24,000 square miles   Population 23 million
> Occupied by 25th US Infantry Division

CENTRAL HONSHU
> Area 22,000 square miles   Population 24 million
> Occupied by 1st US Cavalry Division

NORTH HONSHU AND HOKKAIDO
> Area 65,000 square miles   Population 14 million
> Occupied by 11th US Airborne Division

It is worth noting that BCOF had the smallest number of people to look after, and the second lowest density of population, with a strength originally equivalent to two weak divisions.

Index

BRICOSAT (British Commonwealth Sub Area Tokyo) 169, 89, 122, 131, 207
Bridgeford, Lieut-General Sir William 214
Brind, Vice-Admiral E J P, RN 201
BRINDJAP (British & Indian Troops Japan) 127, 28, 29, 41, 42, 44, 47, 65 later BRINDIV
BRINDIV (British & Indian Division) 159, 62, 81, 87, 152, 157,
British Chiefs of Staff: are determined on British participation in invasion of Japan, 3; detailed proposals, 4–5; consider participation in occupation essential, 11; issue directive to Mountbatten, 12; proposals from meet Commonwealth opposition, 12; suggest compromise on command & control arrangements, 15; suggest final appeal to Evatt, 16; indicate occupation proposals to US War Department, 35; assess worldwide manpower needs, 142; recommend withdrawal of British brigade, 142; are pressed by Montgomery for speedy action, 144; put formal proposal to US, 144; are pressed by Montgomery to withdraw remaining British troops, 169; recommend US be approached accordingly, 170; appoint Bouchier as liaison officer to MacArthur, 209–210
British Landing Force xvii
Buchanan, Capt. H J, RAN xvii
Byrnes, James F. 23, 24, 25, 39

Caiger, George 98
Calwell, Arthur A 118–9
Canadian Government 12, 13
Chambers, Cyril 145, 177
Chiang-kai Shek: is prevented by domestic situation from supplying occupation troops, 24; is unlikely ever to provide contingent, 39; supply to armies of through Burma, 83
Chicago Tribune 79
Chifley, J B: asked by Attlee to defuse Evatt situation, 15; unfavourable response to British proposals from, 16; comparison of with Evatt, 16–17; is persuaded by Evatt to accept British proposal, 17; stresses need for early despatch of Force to Japan, 19; releases Northcott for governorship of NSW, 68; is intent on long occupation, 111; asked by Attlee to get US agreement to British withdrawal, 170
Chofu 96, 101, 108
Churchill, Winston S: is determined on British involvement in invasion, 3; agrees Commonwealth participation with Truman, 3; proposes joint Commonwealth force, 4; is replaced by Attlee, 6; lobbies Bevin on joint US/UK control in Japan, 38; influences Allied strategic priorities, 82; calls for Burma campaign brief, 83
Clifton, Allan 98
Clutton, George 214

CORONET, Operation 2
Cortazzi, Sir Hugh 217
Cowan, Major General D T: selected to command BRINDJAP, 27; never meets MacArthur, 86; changes attitude towards Japanese, 100; intervenes in first Gurkha mutiny, 154; asks Thimayya to intervene in Tokyo mutiny, 155; ends command, 157
CSDIC (Combined Services Detailed Interrogation Centre) 187, 188
Curtin, John 80–1

Darwin 110
Dedman, J J 120
Deolali 45
Drain, Dorothy 176

Ebisu 54
Ehime 54
Eichelberger, General Robert L 21, 81, 91, 194
Emperor of Japan 6, 7, 9, 78, 116
Etajima 62, 124, 179
Evatt, Dr. H V: promotes independent Australian role in occupation, 14; criticises UK neglect of Australian interests, 15; is requested by Attlee to change attitude, 15; relationship and comparison with Chifley, 17; persuades Chifley to accept British proposal, 17; reports other Australian achievements in Pacific, 18; recommends integration of BCOF in US forces, 40; persuades US to accept JCOSA, 42; calls for severe settlement with Japan, 111; tries to alter Indian decision to withdraw, 158; assumes occupation role essential for seat at peace conference, 180; mission of to establish Australia as Pacific power accomplished, 222

FANYS 118, 126, 138
Far East Commission 85, 89, 169, 218, 219
Forde, Fran 49
Foreign Office: reacts to modified proposals for invasion, 5; accepts US domination in Japan, 91; opposes withdrawal of British brigade, 143; expresses views on MacArthur's opinion of British brigade, 143; reacts to Montgomery's intervention on complete British withdrawal, 168; supports Chiefs of Staff on withdrawal, 170; is worried by Canberra leak, 170; concedes non-participation in military government, 219; appreciates change of roles with Australia, 222
Francis, Josiah 188
Fraser, Peter expresses concern at long delay, 50; reacts to British withdrawal, 148; repeats doubts about BCOF, 169
Freeman, John 145
Freyberg, General Sir Bernard 161
Fukuyama 62

Gairdner, General Sir Charles: is appointed to MacArthur's HQ by Churchill, 89;